A Note from Coriolis

Thank you for choosing this book from The Coriolis Group. Our graphics team strives to meet the needs of creative professionals such as yourself with our three distinctive series: *Visual Insight*, *f/x & Design*, and *In Depth*. We'd love to hear how we're doing in our quest to provide you with information on the latest and most innovative technologies in graphic design, 3D animation, and Web design. Do our books teach you what you want to know? Are the examples illustrative enough? Are there other topics you'd like to see us address?

Please contact us at the address below with your thoughts on this or any of our other books. Should you have any technical questions or concerns about this book, you can contact the Coriolis support team at techsupport@coriolis.com; be sure to include this book's title and ISBN, as well as your name, email address, or phone number.

Thank you for your interest in Coriolis books. We look forward to hearing from you.

Coriolis Creative Professionals Press
The Coriolis Group
14455 N. Hayden Road, Suite 220
Scottsdale, AZ 85260

Email: cpp@coriolis.com

Phone: (480) 483-0192
Toll free: (800) 410-0192

Visit our Web site at **creative.coriolis.com** *to find the latest information about our current and upcoming graphics books.*

Other Titles for the Creative Professional

Flash™ 5 Cartoons and Games f/x & Design
By Bill Turner, James Robertson, and Richard Bazley

Photoshop® 6 In Depth
By David Xenakis and Benjamin Levisay

3ds max™ 4 In Depth
By Jon McFarland and Rob Polevoi

Game Architecture and Design
By Andrew Rollings and Dave Morris

Flash™ 5 f/x & Design
By Bill Sanders

Fireworks® 4 f/x & Design
By Joyce J. Evans

Dreamweaver® 4 f/x & Design
By Laurie Ulrich

Illustrator® 9 f/x & Design
By Sherry London

To Julie, Ellen, and Cooper.
Always my inspiration, my joy, my life.
—Luke Ahearn

About the Author

Luke Ahearn (Monterey, CA) is the Art Director/Development Consultant on The Army Game Project and a professor of computer science at the Naval Postgraduate School. Before migrating to Monterey, Luke owned and operated Goldtree, a computer game-development shop based in New Orleans, for ten years. There, he designed and developed several game titles. He has also written two full-length novels and several books on the subject of computer-game development.

Acknowledgments

Special thanks to Nick Marks (**www.psychoticepisode.com**) for elevating my ability to burn pixels and jerk the vertex. To my nephew Curtis D. Sorrells, for his constant enthusiasm, ideas, and for understanding what I do.

Thanks to my current teammates on The Army Game Project and Dr. Mike Capps for putting together a game development dream team.

Thanks to the Dead Reckoning Team for staying in the trenches when you were needed, Anthony Thibault, Nicholas Marks, John McCawley, Mike Freimanis, and Josh Eustis. Also thanks to Mike Whalen, Wayne St. Pierre, and T.J. Bordelon. All these guys are the gods of game development and great friends. And thanks to all those who helped Goldtree along the way; Matthew and John Ahearn in particular.

Jennifer Meyer, for her art assistance past and present.

And to all who contributed to this book:

Christian Chang for his images and art in the color studio as well as other areas of the book.

Scott Maclean for his images and level-design expertise.

Cliff Bleszinski, Lead Designer, Epic Games for use of his materials on level design.

Reality Factory (**www.genesis3d.com/~rfactory**/). Ed Averill for starting things and Mike Wuetherick, Ralph Deane, and Terry Morgan for continuing.

Eclipse Entertainment, (**www.genesis3d.com**) for the Genesis3D free game SDK.

Last and most certainly not least; project editor Don Eamon, acquisitions editor Beth Kohler, development editor Catherine E. Oliver, technical reviewer Harry Henderson, copyeditor Mary Swistara, proofreader Chris Sabooni, production coordinator Meg Turecek, designer Carla Schuder, and the many other great folks at Coriolis who helped this book get into your hands.

—*Luke Ahearn*

Contents at a Glance

Part I   2D Interactive Game Art

Chapter 1   Game Art Sources   3

Chapter 2   Game Textures: The Basics   17

Chapter 3   Advanced Texture Creation and Management   57

Chapter 4   Logos: The Essence of Your Project   85

Chapter 5   Menus and Interfaces: The Gateways to the Game World   109

Part II   World Building: Genesis3D and Reality Factory

Chapter 6   Automating Texture Creation   137

Chapter 7   World Building   161

Chapter 8   The Game World Editor   179

Chapter 9   Game World Geometry   197

Chapter 10   Creating a Game World   211

Chapter 11   Adding Models to Your World   239

Chapter 12   Lighting the World   255

Chapter 13   The Reality Factory   273

Appendix   Game Art Resources   351

Table of Contents

Introduction xxi

Part I   **2D Interactive Game Art**

Chapter 1   **Game Art Sources** 3

The Right Image for the Job   4

Working with 2D Images   4

     Texture Creation   4

     Tiling   5

     Color Reduction   5

     Image Compression   6

     Color Balancing   7

     Sizing   7

     Defect and Hot-Spot Removal   7

     Weathering and Aging   8

Scanners   9

     Cleaning Up Scanned Images   9

Digital Cameras   11

Graphic Tablets   14

Online Resources   14

     Texture Sites   14

     Photographic Sites   14

     Fonts   15

Other Game Art Sources   15

     Examining Top Games   15

     Using 3D Applications to Create 2D Assets   15

     Using Other Software to Create Game Assets   15

Chapter 2   **Game Textures: The Basics** 17

Why Do You Need Base Textures?   18

What Are Base Textures?   18

     Determining the Base Textures of a World   18

Tiling Textures   23

     Troublesome Tiles   25

     Testing the Image Tile   27

     Tips for Horizontal and Vertical Tiling   28

Advanced Tiling: Natural Images   30
    Project: Tiling Cobblestones   31
        Changing Lighting   34
Creating Base Textures   35
    Creating a Rust Texture   36
    Creating Brushed Metal   37
    Creating a Star Field   39
    Project: Creating a More Complex Star Field   39
        Creating a Deep-Space Star Nebula   40
    Creating Wood   42
    Creating a Stone Texture   46
    Creating Quick Mud   49
    Creating Parchment   50
    Project: A Space Base Wall   52

Chapter 3   Advanced Texture Creation and Management 57
Planning Your Texture Library   58
    The Texture Library Defined   58
    The Textures You'll Need To Create   61
    Organizing the Texture Library   67
Creating Advanced Textures from Bases   69
    Combining Base Textures: The Importance of Highlights and Shadows   71
    Creating a Floor Tile   73
Putting Your Skills to Work   75
    Project: Making Complex Objects and Dirtying Them Up   75
        Adding Dirt and Scratches   76
    Project: Using a Digital Image to Make a Sign:
       Removing a Flash Burn   78
    Project: Creating Peeling Paint   80
    Project: A Deluxe Castle Door   81

Chapter 4   Logos: The Essence of Your Project 85
Why Create a Logo?   86
The Design Process   87
    Who Is the Audience?   87
    Where Will the Logo Be Used?   87
    What Are the Elements of a Logo?   88
Trademark Your Logo   90
    Register Your Company Name First   90
    Without a Trademark You Are Still Protected   91
    Register Your Logo with Your State   91
    Register Your Logo with the Federal Government   91
Creating Game Logos   91
    Project: Creating the Typical Fantasy Logo   91
        Making the Fantasy Sword   92
        Adding the Shield   96
        Adding the Magic Gold Lettering   98

Project: Creating the Acid-Eaten, Apocalyptic Metal Logo   99
Project: Creating the Basic "Carved from Stone" Logo   100
Project: Creating a Spell-Book Cover Logo   103

Chapter 5   **Menus and Interfaces:
The Gateways to the Game World** **109**
Introduction   110
Ten Usability Principles   110
The 10 Usability Heuristics as They Apply to Games   112
   1. Visibility of System Status   112
   2. Match between [the] System and the Real World   116
   3. User Control and Freedom   118
   4. Consistency and Standards   118
   5. Error Prevention   124
   6. Recognition Rather Than Recall   124
   7. Flexibility and Efficiency of Use   125
   8. Aesthetic and Minimalist Design   126
   9. Error Recognition and Recovery   127
   10. Help and Documentation   127
Creating the Typical 3D Shooter Menu   128
   Color Scheme   129
   Background Art   129
   Menu Choices   130
   Project: Taking the RPG Menu All the Way   132

Chapter 6   **Automating Texture Creation** **137**
Introduction   138
Using Keyboard Shortcuts   138
Working with Unflattened Images   139
   Making Many Targets   139
   Cranking Out Signs   142
   Building Walls with Variations   144
Using Automation Commands   145
   Picture Package   145
   Web Photo Gallery   146
   Batch Processing   148
   Contact Sheet II   150
Creating Custom Brushes   151
Using Action Sets   152
   The Actions Palette   153
   The Actions Menu   154
   Project: Creating an Action to Make That Rusted Metal
      You Always Need   155

Part II   World Building: Genesis3D and Reality Factory

Chapter 7   World Building 161

Understanding Level Construction   162
  Balancing Art and Technology   162
  Knowing the Level's Purpose   163
  Deciding on the World Setting   163
  Planning the Level   164
  Understanding the Level Development Cycle   166
Mistakes to Avoid in Mapping Your Levels   168
  Designer, Evaluate Thyself   169
  Thou Shalt Seek Peer Criticism   169
  Thou Shalt Value Rivalries   169
  Do Thy Homework   169
  Thy Framerate Shall Not Suck   170
  Thou Shalt Deceive   170
The Three Sins of the Beginner   170
  Bad Textures   170
  Blocky Construction   171
  Bad Lighting   173
Texture Planning for the Castle   173
  The Castle Texture Set   175
A Final Note about Organization   178

Chapter 8   The Game World Editor 179

What Is Genesis3D?   180
  Genesis3D and Its Relatives   180
  What Comes with Genesis3D?   181
  What Do I Need to Run Genesis3D?   182
  What Can I Do with Genesis3D?   182
  Genesis3D Features   183
Installing Genesis3D   184
  Troubleshooting Genesis Startup   185
  Backing Up the Default Genesis Files   186
The Texture Packer   186
  Loading the Tutorial Texture Library   187
  Creating Your Own Texture Library   187
The World Editor   189
  The Four View Windows   190
  The Command Panel   191

Chapter 9   Game World Geometry 197

Chapter Overview   198
Basic Brush Shapes   198
  Cube   199
  Sphere   199
  Cylinders   200
  Stairs   201

Arches   201

Cones   203

Brush Types   203

Solid Brush   203

Hollow Brush   204

Cut Brush   205

Sheet Brush   205

Brush Attributes   206

Setting up GEDIT   208

Textures   208

The Grid   209

Chapter 10   Creating a Game World **211**

The World You'll Be Creating   212

Let There Be Cube   213

The Three Main Editing Modes   213

Creating the First Room   214

Accessing and Applying the Castle Textures   214

Texturing Individual Faces   215

Face Attributes and Texture Alignment   217

Testing the Map   225

Placing the Player Start Position   225

Troubleshooting Compile Problems   225

Adding a Courtyard   226

Cloning a Brush to Create a Second Room   226

Placing a Cut Brush to Create a Door
Between Rooms   226

More Face Editing   227

Using Groups   228

Using a Sky Box   229

Seeing the Sky from a Level   230

Putting Up a Grate   230

Adding Magical Light   231

Adding Banners   234

Speed Tips   235

Remember the One-Texel Rule   235

Set the Light Map Scale   235

Use Detail Brushes   236

Avoid Cut Brushes   236

Use Hint Brushes   236

Use Area Brushes   236

Chapter 11   Adding Models to Your World **239**

Making Things Move in Your Level   240

Overview of Models   240

Using the Basic Options on the Models Tab   241

Using the Animation Options on the Models Tab   242

Entities You Can Assign to Your Models   243

Project: Creating and Animating a Windmill   244
  Creating the Blades   245
  Animating the Windmill Blades and Adding a Turning Shaft   248
Animating Doors and Platforms   251

Chapter 12   Lighting the World **255**
An Introduction to Lighting   256
Default Light Level, or Ambient Lighting   256
Basic Lighting Techniques   257
  Setting Mood or Atmosphere   257
  Faking Sunlight in Genesis3D   257
  Accenting Important Game Play Points with Light   257
Genesis Lights and Light Effects Entities   258
  Adding a Light Entity   261
  Understanding Light Entity Properties   262
Lighting the Castle Level   265
  Using the Light Entity   266
  Using Dynamic Lights   269
  Using a Spotlight   270
  Using Fog Lights   270
  Using the Corona Light Entity   270

Chapter 13   The Reality Factory **273**
Introduction to Reality Factory   274
  The Tools That Come with Reality Factory   275
  What You Need to Run Reality Factory   278
  Installing and Troubleshooting Reality Factory   278
  Reality Factory Entity Overview   279
Before Moving On...   279
  Bitmaps Using Alpha Masks   280
  Heads Up Display   281
  Compass   281
  Player Position   283
  Attributes   283
  HUD Element Activation   287
  Weapon and Projectile Definition   287
Modifying the Menu   292
  Defining the Graphics   292
Playing in the Street Level   304
  Environmental Setup   304
  The PlayerStart Entity   304
  The EnvironmentSetup Entity   305
  The PlayerSetup Entity   307
Giving the Player Attributes   311
  Attribute Entity   313
  The EnvAudioSetup Entity   313

Audio Effects   314
    The AudioSource3D Entity   315
    The SoundtrackToggle Entity   316
    The StreamingAudioProxy Entity   317
World Model Helpers   317
    The Door Entity   317
    The MovingPlatform Entity   319
    The Trigger Entity   321
    The ChangeLevel Entity   323
Special Effects   324
    The Teleporter Entity   324
    The TeleportTarget Entity   325
    The MorphingField Entity   325
    The ParticleSystemProxy Entity   326
    Flip Book Entity   328
    The Corona Entity   329
    The DynamicLight Entity   330
    The ElectricBolt Entity   332
    The ElectricBoltTerminus Entity   333
    The FloatingParticles Entity   333
    The EChaos Entity   334
    The Rain Entity   335
    The Spout Entity   336
    The Flame Entity   338
Area Effects in Zones   340
Creating a World in Reality Factory   341
    Project: Creating a City-Street Level   341
        Loading the "street" Texture Library   342
        Face Editing to Create the World Space   342
        Creating the First Building   343
        Cloning to Detail and Create Buildings   344
        EnvironmentSetup   346
        Particle Systems   346
        Rain   347
        Flame   347
        AudioSource3D   349

Appendix   **Game Art Resources** 351

Index 363

Introduction

"I don't know why I did it, I don't know why I enjoyed it, and I don't know why I'll do it again."
—Bart Simpson, *The Simpsons*

Is game development the coolest profession on Earth? Possibly; but although it holds some of the mystique of being a rock star, it also includes much of the tedium of watching paint dry mixed with the stress of an air-traffic controller during a blizzard—while wearing a blindfold.

So, a lot of people are trying to get into the profession, but just as many are trying to get out. I am one of the few, the proud, and the insane who decided to stay in, even when the window of opportunity presents itself for me to bail out. What has all this to do with game art? Well, it is one of the easiest ways into the game industry. Of course, you have to be good at your game-related profession, but if you aren't a crack programmer or a game-development veteran, then your most likely inroad to a game-development career will be as an artist—If, on the other hand, you simply want to make textures for an add-on game level for your favorite game; this book will also be a big help.

In game development, there are generally two types of books on the market. The predominant category is programming books. Of course, programming is important to game development, but we are not all programmers, are we? The secondary category is represented by a scant selection of game-design books that cover various aspects of game design and development. There are no books on game art—sure, you can find many books on high polygon count modeling, texturing, lighting, and animation. You can also find books on specific 2D and 3D applications, but books that approach the task of making game art are not available—which is why I wrote this book.

The steps for creating the artistic material for games are referred to in this book as *game assets*. From the latest version of Quake to Web-site interfaces, what is often referred to as "game assets" can be used in any application from a high-end 3D shooter, a game with a simple 2D interface, or even a Web site with its menu-like setup and functionality. Although most of this book can apply to any project you work on—from a Quake-type shooter to a Quiz show—the difference here is that if you are making a cutting-edge 3D game, you must take several leaps forward in technology and technique, beyond the simple application, to produce assets that works well with the cutting edge application.

So, the notion of the starving artist, while it still holds true to a degree, is beginning to fade as talented computer artists are commanding higher salaries, performing this much sought-after, cutting-edge work. This is partially due to specialization; understanding this alone can help you get a job. Games and interactive art require diverse specializations, even though they tend to be lumped under the "artist" label. You can still be a traditional 2D pen-and-ink artist and do storyboards and conceptual sketches, but more often, artists are required to specialize in some form of art that centers on actually using a computer. A sampling of some computer-related art jobs include interface designer, Web site designer, creative management (art and management combined), 3D modelers (organic, inorganic, high poly, low poly, and so on), animators, level designers, art directors, architectural environment modelers, and a lot more.

The idea of specialization is important; it is rare that one person can do everything well, and even more rare is that they'll have the time to do it. So, by necessity, a designer designs a game, a level designer designs the level, the artist sketches and conceptualizes the look of the level, a level builder constructs and tests the level, a texture artist creates maps for the level as it is rebuilt and detailed by the level builders after testing, and a specialist in lighting goes over the entire map and does her magic.

No matter what your specialization, it's a good idea to start with 2D art and build a firm foundation here as you expand outward to learn the complexities of 3D modeling, animation, and the various technologies and software packages that you will have to learn and master. Also, although being a game artist requires artistic talent, making game textures doesn't. Now, before you send me email about this, please understand what I mean. You can create game textures with no artistic talent, and yes, they will not be as good as those created by a world-class artist, but you can still make a stone floor, a wood plank wall, and a sky full of clouds, for testing purposes or where high-level art talent is not required.

Who this Book Is For

If you are in the middle of a professional game-development effort, if you are the kind of person who wants to try your hand at producing art for computer games, or if you just want to create an innovative logo and Web site, this book can help you get the running start you need. If you are a programmer strapped for a few textures to test your latest graphics engine or application, you can create some decent textures. Eye candy always helps.

The *f/x & Design* easy step-by-step format will help you master some of the coolest tricks and techniques of cutting-edge game art. From logos to interfaces, you will be able to make it all.

The f/x & Design Philosophy

This *f/x & Design* book will help you gain a better understanding of producing art for computer games using both intermediate and advanced techniques. By using key features of the primary 2D and 3D applications, such as Photoshop and 3D Studio MAX, in creative ways, you can create extraordinary art in minutes. This book goes beyond the basic introduction to file formats and applications basics; you are expected to know how to save a file and what RGB means. Instead of the basics, I provide extensive illustrations and real-world projects to help you create usable game art.

What this Book Contains

There is no definitive game-art bible; there can't be, and I won't offend you by pretending this book is the end-all of game art. Computer game art will constantly evolve and change as the technology allows and as the industry continues to bring in new and fresh talent—and even older and more experienced talent, as cash flow allows. This book does present a good stab at game art in its present form, and the techniques shown here will not change for some time.

3D Game Art f/x & Design will quickly take you from the basics of game art to producing commercial-quality game art. Each chapter provides professional-level projects and creative tips. This book's color section, "3D Game Art Studio," displays illustrations of cool techniques and projects; even some samples of game artists' work. The companion CD-ROM is packed with example files, textures, and even a 3D game-level editor and the engine itself.

The following list describes what you will find in each chapter of Part I of this book:

- Chapter 1, "Game Art Sources," gives you an introduction to the various sources and technologies used to create game art; hand-drawn masterpieces, digital images, scanned images, stock images, and from-the-ground-up creation using various computer applications. You will also look at the various techniques for cleaning up and manipulating these images, such as tiling, cleaning, and aging the images.

- In Chapter 2, "Game Textures: The Basics," you actually begin the process of making game textures. You start by learning how to determine which textures, or images, should cover the base geometry of your world. Then this chapter looks at the techniques for the textures look realistic in the world—for example, tiling textures so that no seams show—and you even learn to do this with difficult-to-tile images such as organic or random patterned surfaces. Then I'll guide you through the actual creation of many of the base textures of any world: metal, wood, mud, and more.

- In Chapter 3, "Advanced Texture Creation and Management," you see how the professional game artist and art director use the Art Bible to organize the large amount of textures that are needed for a commercial game, and then you learn about the system used to store these textures. A great deal of time is also spent creating many advanced textures combining bases and using new tools and techniques covered in this chapter.

- Chapter 4, "Logos: The Essence of Your Project." Because artists are often hired for their art skills and then are asked to design logos, this chapter looks at several aspects of logo creation, including the less-than-artistic aspects of making sure that the logo can be used within a business situation. In this chapter, you also make several detailed logos that explore a broad range of styles and techniques.

- Chapter 5, "Menus and Interfaces: The Gateways to the Game World." Interface design is difficult and in this chapter things will hopefully become a bit more crystal for the artist assigned to "design the menu." This chapter takes a look at how to break out the menu assets, how to create them for various game types, and finally it looks at the aspects of a good user interface so your audience won't quit your game before they start playing it.

- Chapter 6, "Automating Texture Creation." Finally, after you know the basics or find yourself doing the same eight commands in a row, you can take several steps to automate your work and speed things up by using actions, shortcut keys, and other Photoshop tools.

In Part Two, you will turn your efforts to actually creating a 3D game world. Actually having done some work in a 3D game editor is critical to not only getting a job with the knowledge, it's the only way you will get screenshots of your awesome work to show off to potential employers. Each tutorial, from Chapter 7 through Chapter 12, builds upon the knowledge you gain from the previous one. Chapter 13 looks deeply into the workings of Reality Factory, a fantastic toolset. The following list describes what you will find in each chapter of Part II:

- Chapter 7, "World Building," looks at the process of designing and developing a game level. It also examines the mistakes most often made by beginners when creating a game level: bad textures, bad lighting, and blocky construction.

- Chapter 8, "The Game World Editor," presents an overview of the Genesis 3D Game World Editor. Here the focus is on getting Genesis to run on your system and setting up the texture tool. Then you look at the editor itself and the major areas of geometry creation: lighting, texture application, and saving the world files properly.

- Chapter 9, "Game World Geometry," covers the basic shapes you can create in your world and the limits you face, but you also are introduced to some cool tricks to help overcome these limits in the editor. This chapter also looks at the various types of geometric shapes, called brushes, and what you can make them do. Effects such as water, transparency, and more can be achieved in your world.

- In Chapter 10, "Creating a Game World," you begin the process of actually creating a level by adding geometry, lighting, and compiling the map. You will be using textures created form part one to create a really cool castle level.

- In Chapter 11, "Adding Models to Your World," we look at the tools that come with Genesis for creating and animating models. In this chapter, you learn how to create a simple door that opens and closes, or an elaborate drawbridge.

- Chapter 12, "Lighting the World," finishes up your level design by lighting it. Genesis has many lighting effects, and this chapter will look at them all. You will learn how to add coronas, make shimmering torchlight, and even add some fog to the level. Lighting makes an immense difference in level quality, as you will see in this chapter.

- Chapter 13, "The Reality Factory." Here, you'll learn about the great tools available in Reality Factory, an add-on to the Genesis3D engine that allows for rapid prototyping of game worlds with many cool effects.

The Appendix lists many game asset resources. Here, you can find books, magazines, Web sites, and other resources to help in your game-art endeavors.

3D Game Art f/x & Design comes complete with a PC-friendly CD-ROM, containing all the images from the tutorials. Also, you'll find two valuable tools that will help you become the best of the 3D game artists: the game development studio Genesis3D and the Reality Factory upgrade.

Keep in Touch

I'm always interested to know what you think of this book. All comments, suggestions for the next edition, and discoveries that you may want to share that will make the paths of other artists easier are welcome. Please email me at **gameart@goldtree.com** with your feedback concerning this book.

Part I

2D Interactive Game Art

Chapter 1

Game Art Sources

*Whether you are re-creating reality or constructing
a vision from a wildly creative mind, you will most likely
use each of the various sources for the creation of
game art to some degree.*

The Right Image for the Job

There are many sources for game art and textures, but you will most likely use one main source, dictated by the look and feel you're trying to achieve in the game and by your own abilities. You will also use numerous sources of game art to supplement your texture library.

For example, if you decide to re-create a real-life location in a game level and plan to use digital photographs of the location, you still must clean up, manipulate, and work with the images in a photo manipulation program such as Photoshop to make them usable in a virtual environment. You will undoubtedly decide that most textures are best if rebuilt, touched up, or augmented in some way. In this chapter, the following sources of game art are discussed:

- Using 2D applications such as Photoshop to create textures

- Using images from a scanner

- Using game art from the games themselves

- Using 3D applications to create 2D images

- Using other software, such as Bryce and Poser, to create game art

Working with 2D Images

Whether you are cleaning up textures, creating them from scratch, or converting formats, you will spend a great deal of time in a 2D-image-manipulation program such as Photoshop. No perfect image comes to the game artist ready to drop into the level editor and be rendered in the game world. In fact, a great deal of texture work is not creating the textures, but cleaning and manipulating the textures to fit into the game world. Consider re-creating the textures that cover every surface in an entire world. Every inch of the ground you walk on must be covered with grass, concrete, metal, or some form of art. Every object must have a piece of art created for it.

The following sections explain different methods of creating surfaces.

Texture Creation

Although you can create almost any surface texture from scratch in Photoshop using filters, effects, and other tools, many game artists don't like this idea. Game art created this way looks bad because artists don't take the time to adjust appropriately the values and settings of the tools being used. Wielding the tools correctly, however, you as an artist can create very good textures that are great as placeholders and sometimes for professional use. Even the worst texture, if it's clear what that texture represents, can be used as a placeholder. In fact, most game development teams maintain a library of placeholder *assets* so they can build the game world quickly and then return later to replace these textures with others of higher quality, images on which they've spent more time and that look much better.

Note: The word *assets* in the game development vocabulary can refer to a sound effect, 3D model, or 2D texture. In the context of this book, it refers to a 2D texture.

Filters, as the kids would say these days, are *the bomb*! You can create many stunning effects for your textures by using only the filters that ship with Photoshop. When used with the other more common tools Photoshop provides (such as cropping, resizing, color balancing, and so on), you can create almost anything you can visualize. While reading this book, you may notice that I often use the Render Clouds filter. I use this particular filter because the natural pattern of a cloud image can be turned into almost any other organic pattern—wood grain, a mountain range, a rock, or water. Later in this chapter, we will discuss how the cloud pattern is used in detail.

> **Note:** The term "organic" does not necessarily mean living or once-living material; here, I use it to describe things "natural, not man-made."

Tiling

Tiling is a popular method in games and virtual environments, mainly because tiling a smaller file over a large area saves system resources and speeds up the computer when drawing the game world. *Tiling*, just as it sounds, is repeating an image and spreading the reproductions out, as you would if you were laying tiles on a floor. Tiling can save time, but the trick is to make the images in a game not *look* tiled. For example, dirt in an outdoor setting should look like a large smooth plane of dirt, not like tiles of a dirt image (see Figure 1.1). In Chapter 2, you will look at how to use a 2D-image application to tile images.

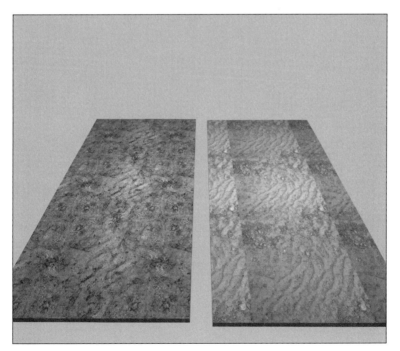

Figure 1.1
Here are two images of dirt on the floor. The image on the right looks like a tiled image of dirt, but the image on the left uses an image that looks more convincing as a dirt floor.

Color Reduction

Because many games require small image sizes, you will need to do all you can to achieve this goal. One method you can employ is to use as low a color depth as possible. Although many newer game engines allow the use of high-resolution, high-color-depth images, use of low-resolution, low-color-depth images is recommended for speed and efficiency. We are still fighting the technology (and we probably always will be), and we all want to include as much code, animation, sound, and so on as possible in a client's games; therefore, another job you will perform in Photoshop is reducing colors in images while trying to keep the images looking as good as possible.

How important is color reduction? Let's take a look: If an image is sized at 640x480 pixels, then you have a total of 307,200 pixels to manage. Because each pixel represents a color dot, you have to store the numerical color information for each pixel. Computers do this by mixing the colors red, green, and blue together to get various colors (RGB color). If you store 256 shades of each color so that you can represent an image as accurately as possible (true color), then 17 million colors (256×256×256) are being stored. This is a lot of color information and a big addition to a file's size.

Adaptive Color Reduction and Color Reduction for the Nonconformist

In games, the artist often uses an adaptive technique when color reducing images. An *adaptive palette* consists of colors selected from the image after the application analyzes the image to decide the best 256 colors to use. Usually, adaptive palettes are fine, but occasionally, you can get an image you don't like because the adaptive process is statistical in nature, and may not select the best colors. I usually use Photoshop's Perceptual option to improve this process when reducing colors. Photoshop determines the best colors for an image by trying to select colors that are closer to the human eye's perception of color.

Image Compression

Although image formats can get complex, there are basically image formats that are designed to store a great deal of information about an image and other formats designed to be as small as possible (for use on the Internet, for example). When working on most images in Photoshop, you will be working from large, high-color, high-resolution, multilayered images for game use, so images can get very large. Although an image in development in Photoshop may reach 10MB or more, the final game-ready image will be a flattened, low-resolution, low-color image.

Some formats in which digitized images can be saved compress the image, and some don't. Compressed images make the file size smaller, but (depending on the image type) with a loss of detail. Graphics compression can be *lossless* or *lossy*. Lossless compression looks for repetitive patterns, but doesn't change the image. Lossy compression looks for repetitive patterns and also averages parts of the image to make it smaller. These parts can never be fully recovered, and they can appear blocky in the image. If possible, try to use the larger lossless image formats. Good choices of formats to use are BMP, TIFF, TARGA, and Photoshop's PSD.

Color Balancing

Color balancing is used a great deal when you're blending textures into a texture library or when blending portions of one image into another. One job of a game artist is not only creating textures, but also making them fit the game world in style, color, and other variables of consistency. For example, maybe you have a world textured in rock with a blue cast, and then create a set of floors from some other stone. If the stone is too red and clashes with the rock, you may have to adjust the color, decreasing the red and increasing the blue in the image. There are many tools in Photoshop that allow the adjustment of color, too many to discuss here, and, in fact, we will touch only on color adjustment as needed in this book.

Sizing

Making an image smaller is known as *sizing*. Sizing is important, especially when starting with digital images from cameras and scanners. Usually in games, the images must be sized to the power of two (128x128 pixels, 256x256 pixels, and so on), and most images are not perfectly square when you get them. The power of two, or *perfectly square*, as we artists say, is more efficient for most game engines. You can draw a perfectly square image faster than an oddly shaped one. A good analogy would be a vending machine with drinks that each cost a quarter. If you give the machine nickels or pennies, it will take you longer to get the money into the machine and longer for the machine to calculate the money before giving you a drink. However, with the enormous amount of mathematical calculations a game engine does to draw the 3D world from various angles, and then to also draw those textures at the right angles, demand that the engine perform these tasks as fast as possible. So, if you had to buy 8,000 drinks from a quarter-based machine, you could do it faster by inserting 8,000 quarters than you could by inserting 40,000 nickels. Therefore, one talent you as a game artist will develop is the technique of fitting images of your world into squares, or figuring out ways to make the world look less square. After acquiring your massive yet perfectly square image, you must make it smaller.

Photoshop offers several ways to size and resize images. The best and most accurate way is to use the Image Size function and simply type the new size values. Photoshop provides the choice of pixels, inches, percentage, and other size values. How to accurately size images is discussed in Chapter 2.

Defect and Hot-Spot Removal

More art than science, cleaning images involves a lot of tools, talent, and patience. A great deal of time is spent removing *flash burns* from shiny surfaces, seams, and objects, especially when using digital images from cameras and scanners. These images often have flash burns, or very hot spots (areas of an image captured by a camera with a simple, direct electronic flash that appear washed out). Removing a flash burn from an image can be easy in some cases and impossible in others. Rebuilding the texture altogether can sometimes be easier and more time-efficient, with a better-looking final version as the result. Figures 1.2 and 1.3 show a sign before-and-after examples of the flash burn removal process.

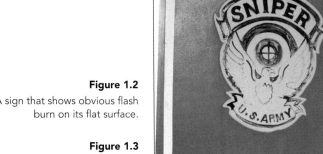 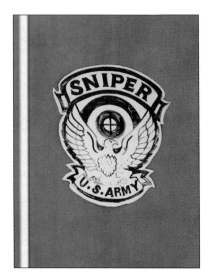

Figure 1.2
A sign that shows obvious flash burn on its flat surface.

Figure 1.3
The same sign, with the flash burn removed from the metal background.

Cleaning also involves straightening images (photographers refer to this process as *perspective correction*) that may not look warped to the human eye, but become skewed when placed in a game level. Borders on doors, lines on signs, and other straight edges can actually be warped by the curvature of the camera lens or by the angle at which the image was captured. If you take a photograph that is even slightly off-angle (any angle other than perpendicular to the subject), it can make a square sign smaller on one side and the top and bottom lines angle toward the smaller end. Figure 1.4 shows a sign that was photographed from a low angle and then reworked to appear straight.

Working with digital images requires a great deal of cleaning, but the result of working from real-life images provides a higher sense of reality for the gamer, and that alone is worth the extra effort.

Weathering and Aging

Photoshop is great for weathering and aging images in a consistent way that allows you as the artist to blend textures into a texture set. Using the various blending modes in Photoshop (such as Hard Light, Multiply, and Color Burn), you can easily "age and weather" images. The Blend modes are located on the Layer palette, and they control how any painting or editing tool affects the pixels in the image. Weathering can be subtle drip stains or blotches of rust or paint. These techniques are discussed in greater detail throughout later sections of this book.

Figure 1.4
The original sign badly skewed (left) and then corrected version (right).

Scanners

A moderately priced scanner is an invaluable tool for the game artist. Photos, other pictures, and numerous small flat objects can be scanned. Just remember that everything I've just discussed—about reducing file size, balancing colors, removing defects, and so on—also applies to scanned images. Additionally, when you're working with scanned images, especially those from printed material such as newspapers and magazines, you will have to deal with (i.e., to eliminate) the patterns resulting from the printing processes of large presses. Fortunately, Photoshop provides a great way to remove these dots, the Despeckle filter.

Cleaning Up Scanned Images

Scanned images almost always look soft and out of focus, especially scanned magazine pictures, because of the process publishers use to print the pages. The printing process for magazines lays down dots of color, and those dots don't scan well. Adjusting contrast and brightness helps, but the best way to remove the fuzziness is to use Photoshop's Unsharp Mask filter (or the equivalent in whatever image-manipulation application you use). The Unsharp Mask filter makes the edges between lines more harsh, or more pronounced, creating the illusion that the image is sharper and, therefore, less fuzzy. The filter does this trick by emphasizing the differences between adjoining areas of significantly different hue or tone. When there is an increase in the degree of contrast at the boundaries of tones, but subtle gradations in tone and hue remain untouched, the result is an illusion of increased sharpness.

Note: The Unsharp Mask is the opposite of anti-aliasing, which makes image edges less sharp.

The Unsharp Mask filter locates the pixels that differ from surrounding pixels by the threshold you specify and increases these pixels' contrast by the amount you specify. In addition, you specify the radius of the region to which each pixel is compared. See Figure 1.5 for an example of unsharp masking.

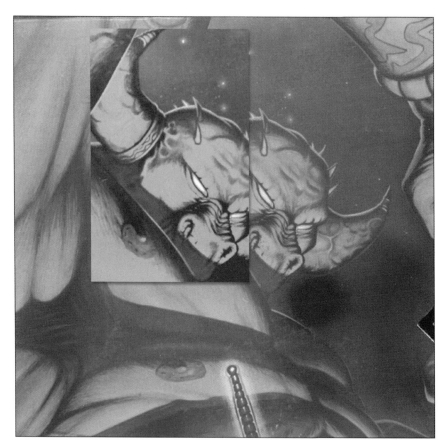

Figure 1.5
Notice the pattern in the original scanned image (the larger image) and then the portion with the Unsharp Mask filter applied to it (the inset image). Notice the increased contrast, especially in highlighted areas, in the inset image.

The Unsharp Mask filter has the following three settings to use:

- *Radius*—Determines the number of pixels surrounding the edge pixels that are affected by the sharpening (or how far out from the edge pixels the mask should go). For game art, stick to the 1 radius setting (because you will be staying in the computer and not working with printable images).

- *Amount*—Refers to the intensity of the Unsharp Mask filter and determines the level of contrast. Experiment on an image-by-image basis to get the preferred results. A lower value sharpens only the edge pixels, whereas a higher value sharpens a wider range of pixels. Be careful: This effect is more noticeable on low-resolution game images than it is on printable images because the pixel radius represents a smaller area on the high-resolution image than it does on the low-resolution game image.

- *Threshold*—Determines how different the sharpened pixels must be from the surrounding area before they are considered edge pixels and are sharpened by the filter.

Saturation Fix

If the Unsharp Mask filter makes bright colors appear overly saturated, convert the image to Lab and apply the filter to the L channel only.

Digital Cameras

Digital cameras, like most computer and photographic technologies, are constantly dropping in price as they increase in power. A digital camera good enough to use for game art is now well within reach of the average budget. Digital cameras can be used to catch images for a variety of uses. Skies, textures of all sorts (grounds, wood grains, signs, and so on), and even faces and body parts to use for game characters can be captured.

The main consideration when taking a photograph for game art is in how the image will see final use. To create a skybox, for example, photograph the sky from five angles: the four points of the compass (north, south, east, and west) as well as straight up. The big job is to make those five images seamless (i.e., a "box" made out of all your sky images). If possible, skyboxes are best made with software applications that can render a sky for you.

> **Note:** Applications such as Bryce, which produce skyboxes quickly and successfully, are discussed later in this chapter.

SkyPaint is a paint tool used to create and edit 3D, seamless, 360-degree panoramic images (such as skies). Using SkyPaint is simple; you start with a backdrop of sky images and use the SkyPaint interface to look around *inside* the backdrop. You can change the backdrop simply by painting on it. Press the Paint This View icon to transfer control to Photoshop (SkyPaint also supports other popular paint programs) and make your changes to that part of the backdrop. To find SkyPaint, just go to this URL: **www.wasabisoft.com**.

There is no limit to the textures you can capture with a digital camera. Although these images will always need to be cleaned up, tiled, etc., starting from the base of a clear digital image can speed your work time and increase the quality of the final texture. Textures can range from base world surfaces to ornaments and special effects. Among the many basic world textures that can be captured easily are grounds such as grass, leaves, cement, gravel, tarmac, and sand.

When taking digital photos, keep in mind that the lens of the camera will likely distort the image, and the lighting will rarely be perfect. Also, the proportions will probably not be perfectly square from the camera, and the image will need to be cropped.

If you look at the example of the images in Figures 1.6 through 1.8, you can see the progression from an original digital image of the MK19 grenade launcher (I got to fire one at a tank! I was on the back of a Humvee… but that's another story) to the texture that was built by the artist and finally the 3D model with the texture applied. This process took approximately a day and is described in the following steps:

1. All of the images and information that pertained to the MK19 were gathered. This information included several high-resolution digital images (originally, 2000×2000 pixels) of a real MK19 and access to the massive Army user's manual (see Figure 1.6).

Figure 1.6

Examples of some of the research materials used in the creation of the MK19 for a game.

2. The package of images to use as reference were then selected and provided to the modeler (Christian Chang).

3. The modeler, Christian, then spent the better part of a day creating the
texture from the original digital images. Every inch of that odd-shaped
weapon needed to be covered by texture, and it all had to be contained
on one square (see Figure 1.7).

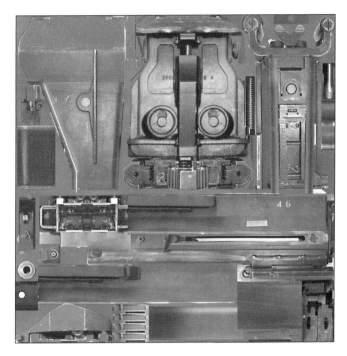

Figure 1.7
The texture developed from the
original images.

4. The texture was also color-adjusted because each piece came from a
different image, and the overall metal and paint had to be blended to
match the others.

5. Finally, the weapon was modeled (see Figure 1.8).

The results, as you can see, were stunning.

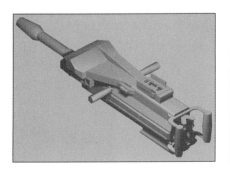
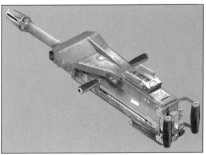

Figure 1.8
The finished model, a perfect
blend between geometry use
and texture detail.

Graphic Tablets

Graphic, or drawing, tablets are, like most technology, constantly dropping in price and increasing in quality and capability. These tablets are really useful if you're a talented artist and you can draw directly onto the tablet and get stunning results. These tablets are useful for hand-sketching and coloring images; drawing free-hand lines or graffiti; and adding organic, or hand drawn, details such as smudges, drips, and spatters to images, but are not necessary for most game art. Many artists use graphics tablet to hand sketch and color everything from character skins to elaborate paintings.

Graphic tablets offer artists more control by emulating natural writing or drawing processes. Personally, if I need to sketch a few lines or draw some graffiti, I reach for the graphic tablet. Newer tablets offer a greater degree of sensitivity and pressure, and with them you can achieve subtle and natural effects. Using the pressure-sensitive capability of the pen, you can vary the size and/or amount of the effect. By allowing computer artists to draw with natural freedom and creativity, as if they are using their traditional pens and pencils, tablets ease stress both physically and mentally. Some graphics tablets can even detect tilt and other input as well as pressure. Some tablets come with plug-in software that allows you to apply filters (such as blur, noise, and despeckle) in controlled areas. Using the pressure sensitive ability of the pen, you can vary the size and amount of the effect, helping to reduce the loss of image quality while allowing the application of filters—such as blur, noise, and Despeckle—to specific areas.

Online Resources

There are many online resources for game textures that you can access. Some sites offer the game textures ready to go, but others are a resource of digital images, fonts, clip art, and so on.

To find game texture links and resources, use a search engine such as Google (**www.google.com**), and type "game textures" as the keyword search. This kind of search will net you a large set of links to game textures and resources. Some of the most useful types of online sources are described next.

Texture Sites

Some Web sites specialize in game-ready art. Some are directed toward architects; others, primarily hosted by game fans, are typically geared toward a certain game engine, and have many packages of game-ready art. Quake, Unreal, and Half-Life all have game fans who have created texture packs for their games and engines. A list of these sites is provided in this book's Appendix.

Photographic Sites

Many sites have large photographic images that can be used in game art. Many sites offer images for purchase, but many more sites offer free images. NASA is an excellent example of a site with free images to use.

Fonts

Several Web sites are dedicated to fonts, which are a collection of characters with a unique look to them. The typeface contains the features by which a character's design is recognized. The great thing about fonts is that they are available in many styles, and many are free. These sites are also listed at the end of the book in the Appendix.

If you need graffiti, mock-Chinese, elfin script, or a font with a certain look, chances are good that you can find it at no cost on the Internet. Fonts can be embossed on a leather texture for a spell-book cover, colored with a metal texture and embossed in wood, or even used as a logo.

Other Game Art Sources

This chapter has generally discussed using Photoshop to create and manipulate images and textures, but there are many other tools that you can use and other sources of art and inspiration.

Examining Top Games

Examining assets from top games is the best way to learn and is a great source of game art if you are not going to use the art to make money. If you are making a MOD (modify an existing game to make a new game) or an add-on level for a game and you use the game's base textures set, proper credit must be given.

Typically, top games come with the tools to edit and create the levels for that game. You can usually import and export the textures, add and create your own, and customize the textures to your liking. Using established tools and professional levels is a great way to learn texture creation, level editing, and more.

Using 3D Applications to Create 2D Assets

Using professional 3D packages such as Max, Maya, Softimage, Lightwave, and Rhino, you can create almost anything and render one frame for a texture. Usually, a 3D package is used to generate *animation* (multiple 2D images that can be played in sequence like a film to simulate movement). Game artists quickly realized that they could model, texture, and light complex objects; render only one of those frames; and then use the resulting image in a game. Figure 1.9 presents an illustration of this process using a complex item such as a blast door on a spaceship. Although using a 3D application can be more expensive and more complex, if you use this kind of application, you can create any object you can imagine, texture it, and then light it.

Using Other Software to Create Game Assets

Programs such as Bryce allow you to create stunning outdoor scenes (skies, water, mountains, and so on) for breathtaking natural worlds very successfully. Bryce is a perfect application for both beginners (who need the ease of use) and advanced users (who want the level of quality and detail Bryce offers). Bryce's

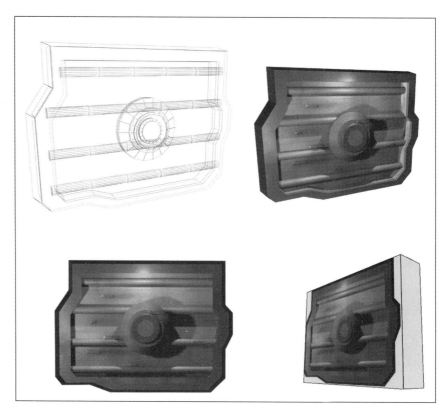

Figure 1.9
A blast door that was modeled in
3D Studio Max, rendered as an
image, and applied to a simple
game object.

flexibility is due in part to the fact that it ships from the manufacturer loaded with libraries that allow you to start creating immediately. Basic objects such as mountains, seas, and rocks are available; all you have to do is assign textures to the objects, place lights in the scene, and then render it. As you become more proficient at the process, Bryce allows you to customize and create almost any aspect of the world and to import and export formats—even use the USGS (United States Geological Survey) data, which is free, in your 3D models.

Moving On

This chapter explored the different sources of game art, including creating textures in 2D applications, and using scanned images, digital cameras, graphics tablets, and online resources. This chapter also examined the possibility of finding inspiration in sources such as current best-selling games. (Just be careful not to use copyrighted material without permission!)

Chapter 2 focuses on how to use Photoshop to make your own game textures. You may be surprised at what you can create using Photoshop—anything you can imagine, and then some!

Chapter 2

Game Textures:
The Basics

*No matter how detailed or complex your texture set and
your world get, you will always go back to basics, so you
will need to have a good grasp of quickly creating the basic
surfaces in most worlds: wood, stone, metal, and more.*

Why Do You Need Base Textures?

Although your typical commercially released computer game can contain several hundred textures in each level, you will see that only a few base textures cover the common surfaces of any given game world: floors, walls, ceilings, and large redundant surfaces. This is done for various reasons, and the two biggest reasons are as follows:

- *World consistency*—Most worlds have a consistent wall, floor, and ceiling texture. A castle, for instance, may have walls of rough-cut stone, floors of polished stone, and ceilings of wooden planks.

- *System requirements*—Most computer game developers work under an ever-present set of limitations. Using a base texture reduces the number of textures loaded for the game.

So, although a game world may contain hundreds, or even thousands, of textures, they are all composed of base elements and materials such as wood, stone, or metal. That is what we will be looking at in this chapter.

What Are Base Textures?

Base textures are the set of textures that will cover most of your game world. In an exterior scene, this may be the ground and sky, even a base tileable tree bark for the trees. In an interior scene, this is usually the floor, walls, and ceiling. Although as mentioned previously, base textures generally refer to common surfaces such as wood, ground, stone, and so on, they can also be surfaces that are common in your game world, but not in the real world, such as lava, poisonous slime, solid gold bricks, and more. A base texture is the common denominator of surfaces in your world. In general, base textures are plain, tileable, and representative of the game's world, story, and other elements.

Determining the Base Textures of a World

As a game artist, you need to be able to look at a scene, whether real world or fantasy, and extract the base texture set needed to cover that world. You must develop the ability to look past the lighting, ornamentation, special effects, and even bullet marks, bloodstains, and dirt to see what base elements the world is created from. In real life, you can think of it this way: If you were to empty your room, you would more easily see the simplicity of the surfaces of the floor, walls, and ceiling. Look at the wall in even lighting after a fresh coat of paint, and that is the base texture for that wall, probably a subtle texture at best. Maybe the floor is composed of wooden boards, tiles, or a carpet. Remove the stains, dents, and other wear and tear from the furniture, and evenly light the room, and that is the base texture for the floor. Figure 2.1 shows a typical realistic scene from a real castle. Notice the walls of stone, the roof, the water, and the sky.

Note: Please note that the final game-ready file size will be relatively small, but the working versions of the textures as unflattened, high-resolution Adobe Photoshop files can be large.

Note: Throughout this book, you will find the term *level* often used. Level is typically used in a computer game to denote a division in the world. This is how the term is employed throughout the book. In a racing game, for example, the level may be called a track; in a sports game, it might be called an arena, and so on.

Figure 2.1

This is a real-world scene of a castle. Notice the base textures, the large areas that make up the world.

In Figure 2.2, you see the raw images used to create the stone for the walls and other base textures. The stains, seams, foliage, and other distinguishing features of the surfaces have been removed.

If you look closely at Figure 2.3 and compare it to Figure 2.2, you may be able to see the differences between the images. All the images shown in Figure 2.3 are now square and have been cleaned up. Look at the dirt, for example; the same dirt base and final image are used in Figure 1.1 (in the previous chapter) to illustrate good and bad tiling of base images. You can see that this texture set is a completed game-ready set of textures that will be used in the level editor to create this real-world scene in a game engine, and that the textures fall into categories; there are base textures for the walls, the ground, the roof, and even the water in the moat.

Now, you are ready to build a scene using basic shapes and the base textures. In Figure 2.4, you can see that the scene in the game world looks like a Hollywood set of the real-world scene. You haven't yet added details, such as lighting or ornamentation. When you do add lighting and some ornamentation to the scene, it will make a difference (see Figure 2.5).

Although the textures used are base textures, they do not have to be plain in the sense that they are flat and lack punch, or depth, but they do have to tile well. Figure 2.6 shows examples of both well done (on the right) and poorly done (the left) base floor textures from a game. The poorly done texture does not tile as well, even though it is actually a texture that is simply plain concrete, as does the texture with grass and cracked dirt—the image with more depth.

Figure 2.2
The set of base textures and images we will use to re-create the real-world castle scene.

Figure 2.3
The texture set of game-ready images we will use to create this scene in a game.

Figure 2.4
A screenshot of the real-world scene built using only basic shapes and base textures.

Figure 2.5
Here is the castle scene with lighting, ornamentation, and other details added.

Base textures are generally *tileable*, or laid out like the tiles on a floor. There-fore, much of the texture artist's initial job is to create textures that are a balance between tileable and deep. A *deep texture* is one that contains a feeling of depth, but the challenge is that any outstanding aspect of the texture will show up as a recognized pattern in the tiling when the texture is placed on a large game-world surface. Notice how the leaf in the grass texture of Figure 2.7 pops out when placed in a ground scene in Figure 2.8.

Figure 2.6
Base tiling textures do not have to be plain and ugly. The plain and ugly texture to the left actually does not tile as well as the richer texture on the right.

Figure 2.7
This is a great-looking patch of grass.

Figure 2.8

But a great-looking patch of grass may not be a great base texture; see how the leaf draws attention to the tiling of the texture as well as to that dark corner of the original image that now stands out.

Of course, you can clone out the leaf in the grass texture. Cloning is a tool that you will use a great deal in creating textures, but you also have to be careful that the overall texture doesn't appear too tiled. Only so much detail and depth can be handled in the texture itself. You will learn later how to use ornamentation, detail, lighting, and other tools to make a rich and complex level efficiently. To create basic textures, you'll often use the Photoshop tools of filters, motion blur, noise, and other effects.

Tiling Textures

In the following exercise, you'll use Photoshop to tile an image and then to smooth the edges of the tiles where they meet:

1. Start with a new Photoshop file and make it 400×400 pixels. For this exercise you can use an image of your own you would like to tile or simply take one from this book's companion CD-ROM.

2. Now choose Filter|Other|Offset (see Figure 2.9), and enter the following values: Horizontal 200 and Vertical 200. The Horizontal and Vertical values are the number of pixels needed to offset the image, so our 400-pixel image offset at a value of 200 pixels will move the image halfway across the canvas. Make sure that you have the Wrap Around option checked, and Preview if you would like to see the texture updated as

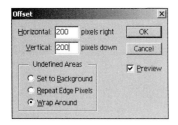

Figure 2.9

This is the Offset dialog box; you will see a great deal of it as a game artist using Photoshop.

you work. The Wrap Around option tells Photoshop to repeat the image and not simply move it over by the pixel value you enter.

You will notice that what happens to the image is that the lower-right quadrant is put onto the top-left quadrant, and so on. In effect, it looks as if four copies of the image are placed together and then the center of the four images is placed on the edges of the new image. Figures 2.10 and 2.11 illustrate this concept.

Figure 2.10

This is the original image before we tiled by using the Offset filter.

Figure 2.11

This is the image after the Offset filter was used on it. Notice the rearrangement of the image.

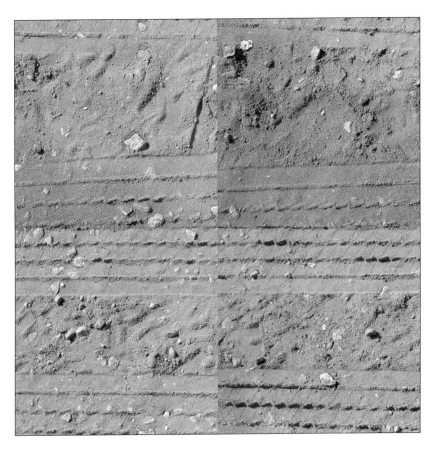

Figure 2.12
Notice the clearly visible seams where the offset images meet.

3. Now you should see some harsh edges or seams (see Figure 2.12). This is where the Clone tool comes into play. Using it, you can blend the edges of the image where the clouds meet. Usually, you will want to use a larger, softer brush and clone near the area you are cleaning up.

Troublesome Tiles

Sometimes, you may be trying to tile an image that is unevenly lit or is in some other way troublesome when you're trying to use the Offset filter method of tiling. In these instances, you can do the following, or some variation, depending on the parts of the image that are problematic:

1. Open the window.psd file from the companion CD-ROM. Use the Square Selection tool, and select and copy the half (or even quarter, in some cases) of the image that looks best (see Figure 2.13).

2. Paste the copied portion onto its own layer.

3. Depending on the orientation and problem area of the image, you will now flip the copied portion of the image. Using the window image you are working on, copy the bottom half of the image and then vertically flip it so the center lines up perfectly, and the top and bottom edges are actually the same (see Figure 2.14).

Note: Do not rotate the image; flip it. If you rotate it, the image will not line up properly.

Figure 2.13
The bottom half of the window in this image is lit by the sun and the top half is in shadow.

Figure 2.14
See how the bottom half flipped up creates a perfect copy of the bottom—only now it's on the top—for good tiling (also notice the hard seam between the two halves).

Figure 2.15
Erasing the seam with a soft brush creates a seamless transition between images.

4. There may be a seam where the layer with the copied portion of the image lies over the old version. If so, you can erase the hard seam with a soft brush. This usually works surprisingly well (see Figure 2.15).

Testing the Image Tile

When you finish cloning the image and smoothing it out, you can easily test how it tiles. You can offset the image again to get a general idea of how well it tiles (pressing Ctrl+F will reapply the last filter you used). For a better idea of how well the image tiles when applied repeatedly over a large surface, you can do the following:

1. *Flatten* the image (a command in Photoshop that combines all layers in the image into a single layer). Select the entire image by choosing Select|All or pressing Ctrl+A. Then choose Edit|Define Pattern. This saves a copy of the selected pattern in RAM.

2. Open a new image. If your system can handle it, make the image exactly twice the size of the original, or more in multiples of two from your original image size. In this case, an 800×800 image will work.

3. Now choose Edit|Fill and select Pattern. You will see the image tiled across the new canvas; and any seams or hot spots should draw your eye (see Figure 2.16).

Figure 2.16
To see if an image tiles well, we're testing it by repeating it over a large canvas.

Tips for Horizontal and Vertical Tiling

Sometimes, textures are supposed to tile in only one direction, either vertically or horizontally. You'll tile vertically in the case of square support columns, for example, where there are seams on the top and the bottom of the image that need to meet up. You'll tile horizontally in the case of a wall texture where there are seams on the left and the right of the image to tile. See Figures 2.17 and 2.18 for examples of horizontal and vertical tiling.

These one-way tiling textures are usually a bit easier to create because you are blending only one seam as opposed to four. You may notice that when you're trying to blend a seamless tile that tiles in both the horizontal and vertical directions, you also have to deal with the place where the four corners meet as well as the seams. This middle spot is usually more difficult to clone and blend than a straight seam is. Not only is the blending easier on one-way tiles, but you can also cut and paste to make flawless tiling easier. For example, see Figure 2.19.

Of course, when you're tiling a texture that already has seams in the image—items from the real world such as paneled walls, floor tiles, or repeating patterns (see Figures 2.20 through 2.23)—it is always best to use those seams to your advantage when tiling the texture.

Figure 2.17
See the vertical tiling on this column. If this tile were tiled horizontally, it would not look quite right.

Figure 2.18
This tiled wall looks good horizontally, but if it were tiled vertically, the dark bottom and bright top would clash.

Figure 2.19
As in the previous example, copying and flipping half the window makes the tiling flawless.

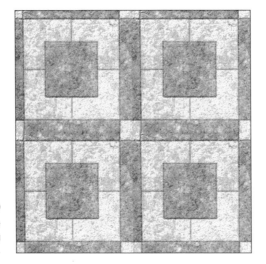

Figure 2.20
A floor tile that is supposed to be a tile is a prime example of using seams to your advantage.

Advanced Tiling: Natural Images

Tiling some images is easy, while others may present quite a challenge. Some of the hardest to tile are the natural images from digital photographs. As an example, we will use an image of some cobblestones in the next exercise. Achieving a smooth and continuous tile with an organic pattern such as these cobblestones, as opposed to cinder blocks or some symmetrical pattern, is a challenge.

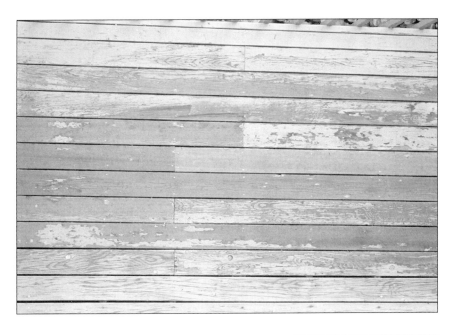

Figure 2.21

This tiling plank wall has many seams and gaps that can be used to aid the texture artist in creating a cleanly tiling image.

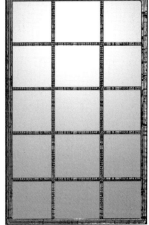

Figure 2.22

(Left) Even stones have many seams and spaces that allow for easy tiling.

Figure 2.23

(Right) Windows are among the easiest things to tile. They can be tiled by the pane as well and used to cover small and large holes with the same texture.

 ## Tiling Cobblestones

This exercise involves tiling an image of cobblestones in Photoshop:

1. This exercise is much easier with the grid on, so go into the Preferences and set the grid size to any number as long as there are at least 8 to 10 grid squares over your image. For the image in this exercise, set the gridlines to every 32 pixels.

2. Now open the stone.psd image file from the folder for this chapter on the companion CD-ROM (see Figure 2.24).

3. You will notice that the image is 640×480 pixels, but you eventually want a 256×256-sized (square) image. So, start by making the image square. You first must determine how to do this without stretching or

Figure 2.24
This is the raw cobblestone image we will be tiling. Tiling organic patterns such as this can be very challenging.

distorting the image. Choose the portion that you will crop out. In this example, I chose the middle of the image where it looks the cleanest. Now, if you use the Crop tool to outline an 8×8 square area, you will have your 256×256 image, but you'll want to outline a 10×10 square area, so that you have the border needed to make the tile work right (see Figure 2.25).

Figure 2.25
Notice how the image has been cropped to make it square. Keep in mind that you will need to remove any elements that may make tiling difficult.

4. Select the bottom two grid rows of the image. Copy this selection by pressing Ctrl+C, and then paste the copy by pressing Ctrl+V; this will create a new layer. Hold the Ctrl key and click-and-drag the selection to the top (see Figure 2.26). (Having the grid lines visible and the Snap option turned on will make this step easier.) Use the Eraser tool to re-move the area from the small selection at the top and make the seams seamless. Use a medium-sized, very soft brush, and work carefully.

Note: Try clicking the Eraser tool off and on as you work as opposed to holding it down continuously; if you make a mistake while erasing and you use the Undo function (Ctrl+Z), it will undo all the work done while the tool was active.

Figure 2.26
Here we copied the bottom two grid rows of the image and pasted them on the top of the image.

The reason we use this small selection—rather than copying half the image, flipping it, and then erasing the middle of the image—is that this helps reduce the tiling you might see if a larger portion of the im-age were repeated using the previous method. The previous method works well where you have smoother surfaces with lighting you want to normalize.

5. Now you can use the Crop tool. Select everything but the bottom rows you copied, and crop them from the image, and you will have an im-age that seamlessly tiles, at least vertically. Now, you can tackle the horizontal tiling. Start by flattening the image and repeating the pro-cess from above. Take the two grid rows from one side and drag them over to the other. Clean, crop, and you are in business.

Note: Remember, when you're tiling a texture in both the vertical and horizontal direc-tions, you have to be careful that the corners are clean. To achieve this, work on the middle 85 to 90 percent of the seam and leave the corners for another step. When you have most of the middle section of the texture cleaned up, dupli-cate the layer and use the Offset filter on the top layer. Do your cleanup on the top layer where the corners meet.

Changing Lighting

Now that you have mastered tiling textures, here are some final tips for making your textures their best. This stone image we used looks great on a cobblestone street during the day, but if you were to use this in the streets of a game world when it is supposed to be night, it would look funny—washed out and too bright. Instead of simply dragging the Contrast and Brightness settings up and down, we can make the stone look the way it would at night on a street in some dark and scary fantasy city.

In Photoshop, follow these steps:

1. Load the tiled stone image you've just created.

2. Select the entire image (Ctrl A), copy it (Ctrl C), and then paste it (Ctrl V). You now have a new layer with the duplicate image.

3. Run the Gaussian Blur filter on this new layer (choose Filter|Blur|Gaussian Blur) and make it fairly blurry, as shown in Figure 2.27.

Figure 2.27
The copied layer with the Gaussian Blur filter applied.

4. Now invert the image (Ctrl+I) and desaturate it (by selecting Shift+Ctrl+U).

5. Set the layer mode to Overlay.

6. Now it is a simple matter of adjusting this layer's brightness and contrast (choose Image|Adjust|Brightness/Contrast) to make the image look the way you'd like. Figure 2.28 shows the original version and the finished version. Figure 2.29 shows each of them used in a game scene—day and night.

Figure 2.28
Here are the first (original, left) and the relit (right) versions of the cobblestone images side by side.

Figure 2.29
Here both cobblestone images are used in the same scene in a game world: day (left) and night (right).

Creating Base Textures

Now you will look at various ways of creating textures. Which is the best way? There really is no one best way. You will use all the tips and tricks presented here, depending on your needs, and as you develop more textures and games, you will undoubtedly learn many more. Whether you start with scanned-in art or digital stills or are creating all your textures in Photoshop, you will always use a bit of each technique to get your textures just right.

The easiest and quickest way to create base textures is to use an image manipulation program such as Photoshop or something similar. Photoshop allows you to create game textures completely within the package, or by using other assets as a base. To start with, we will look at creating textures from the ground up, using Photoshop. Knowing how to do this will allow you to quickly generate placeholder assets for your project, so the programmers and level editors have assets to work with as you perfect your textures, and you will never be stuck looking for a good patch of stone to photograph or waiting for the programmer to bring the digital camera back to the office.

In the following exercises, you'll use Photoshop to create a few commonly needed assets in games. These assets can then be used to create more detailed and complex textures with techniques you will learn a little later.

Creating a Rust Texture

Most computer games have a need for rusty metal, whether you are creating a space port with rusty walls and control panels, or a medieval fantasy world with rusty metal hinges and weapons. Rust is the game artist's best friend.

To create a rust texture in Photoshop, follow these steps:

1. Create a new image document and make it 600×600. At times, I deviate from the larger 800×800 size because the filters in Photoshop are affected by the size of the image.

2. Fill the background with a very light brown. I used RGB 158, 139, 117.

3. Add noise to this layer with the Noise filter: Choose Noise|Add Noise. Set the amount to 40, Gaussian, and make it Monochromatic.

4. Blur this layer by choosing Filter|Blur|Motion Blur. Set the angle to 45 and the Distance to 45. After you complete this step, your image should resemble Figure 2.30.

Figure 2.30
Here we see the beginning of a rust texture.

5. Distort the layer by choosing Distort|Ocean Ripple. Make the Ripple Size 9 and the Magnitude 9.

6. Make a new layer, then select a darker shade of the brown we used earlier for the background color (I used RGB 104, 66, 24).

7. Now use your Paintbrush, and with a really soft brush, paint some random lines back and forth (see Figure 2.31). You may want to use some Motion Blur on this layer if you don't like how it looks when you are done.

Figure 2.31
A paintbrush, some random lines, and the Motion Blur filter will spice up this image.

8. Change this layer's mode to Color Burn and set the opacity down a little.

9. Create yet another layer, and set the background color to black. Render some difference clouds (choose Filter|Render|Difference Clouds), change the mode to Color Burn, and turn down the layer opacity to about half. Difference Clouds generates a cloud pattern similar to Render Clouds, but instead of filling the image layer with the clouds, it blends the generated Clouds with the existing image.

10. Create another layer. Fill the layer with the brown color again and add some noise. Change the layer mode to Soft Light.

Now you have a really nice base rust texture (see Figure 2.32). We will be using this texture later, in several exercises, to make walls and other metal objects.

Creating Brushed Metal

Brushed metal is easy to create in Photoshop and is very useful as a base. As always, you work from large to small, so let's start by creating a new image:

1. Start with an 800×800-pixel image. Set the background color to black and the foreground color to white.

Figure 2.32
A really nice base texture for rust that took only minutes to create.

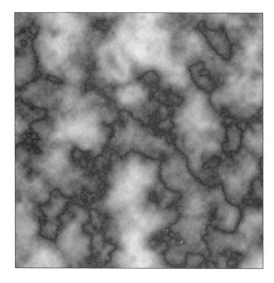

Figure 2.33
The start of metal, created by rendering clouds and difference clouds a few times.

2. Render some Clouds (choose Filter|Render|Clouds). Now render Difference Clouds by selecting Filter|Render|Difference Clouds twice. You should have an image that looks like the one in Figure 2.33.

3. Bump the contrast down a little, and then choose Image|Adjust|Brightness/Contrast. Set the contrast to –10.

4. Add noise by selecting Filter|Noise|Add Noise. Use the following settings: Gaussian, 20; Monochromatic.

5. Now add some blur. Choose Filter|Blur|Motion Blur. Settings: Angle 0 and Distance 15.

6. Then choose Filter|Sharpen|Unsharp Mask. Settings: Amount 50, Radius 5, Threshold 0.

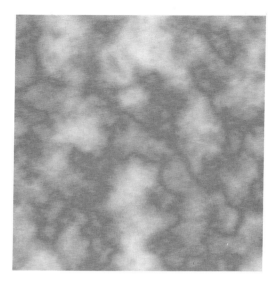

Figure 2.34
Base brushed metal—not much
now, but you will build on it later.

Like most base textures, this does not look like much now (see Figure 2.34), but
look at a real piece of brushed metal under even lighting and this is what you
see. After you apply some effects to these bases in the next chapter and begin
to build up a texture, you will see what can be done with a few simple base
textures and some creativity.

Creating a Star Field

Our next base is a very useful one—a star field. With a few easy steps, you can
create some really nice stars for your sky. Start with an 800×800 image.

1. Create a new layer and fill it with black. Now add some noise; this
    change will be the stars. Choose Noise|Add Noise. Settings: Amount 40,
    Gaussian, and Monochromatic.

2. Now choose Image|Adjust|Brightness/Contrast. Settings: Brightness -55,
    Contrast +40.

3. Again, choose Image|Adjust|Brightness/Contrast. Settings: Contrast
    +50. You should see the stars pop out as in Figure 2.35.

4. You can repeat Step 3 if you would like fewer, bigger, or brighter stars.

 Creating a More Complex Star Field

Now we'll build on the basic star field and make it a little more
complex:

1. Copy the star layer from above and increase the contrast dramatically.
    Choose Image|Adjust|Brightness/Contrast. Set the Contrast to +50.

2. Enlarge the layer by choosing Menu|Edit|Free Transform (Ctrl+T).
    Shift+hold to make the transform uniform, and drag the layer out a
    good bit beyond the edges of the canvas. Using this method you can

Figure 2.35
The stars at night are big and bright in your computer.

make larger stars that are further apart and brighter. This adds greater depth and more realism to your sky. After you are satisfied with your work, press Enter. Photoshop will make the changes permanent.

3. Use the Magic Wand tool to select the black from this layer and delete it.

You now have a star field with more depth and variety (see Figure 2.36). Remember that you can move the larger upper layer about for randomness to the star pattern, and you can flip the layer vertically or horizontally.

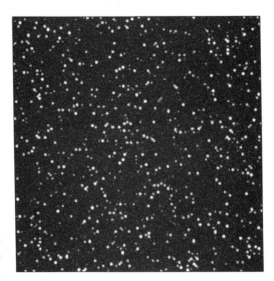

Figure 2.36
The deluxe star field; notice the larger, more random stars.

Creating a Deep-Space Star Nebula

Often the space scene in a game must be broken with some detail or feature, and a cloud nebula is a good one to use. With this effect, you can also create a cold, deep space look where our sun is but a distant light in a cloud-like galaxy.

1. Using your deluxe star field created above, create a new layer and set its mode to Screen.

2. Make your foreground color a bright blue and the background color black.

3. Use the Round Selection tool (The Elliptical Marquee) and set the feather to 25. Select an oval shape in the middle of the image.

4. Now render some clouds; choose Filter|Render|Clouds, and then Filter|Render|Difference Clouds. If you run the Difference Clouds filter a few times, you will get several variations that begin to look very nebula-like.

5. Now choose Filter|Distort|Twirl. Settings: 700. Your image should look like Figure 2.37.

Figure 2.37
The beginnings of a universe.

6. Duplicate the nebula-cloud layer.

7. Do a Free Transform (Control "T") and turn the layer about half a turn. Choose Image|Adjust|Brightness/Contrast. Settings: Contrast -40. You need to move your cursor over the squares at the ends of the selected area until the cursor changes to the bent arrows. Then hold down the left mouse button and rotate the image, letting up on the button when you are ready to stop rotating. When you are ready to make the change permanent, press Enter.

8. The final step is to put the distant sun in the center of your swirling galaxy. Create a new layer and fill it with black. Set this layer on Mode|Screen.

9. To make the sun, choose Filter|Render|Lens Flare. Settings: 82%, 105 mm prime. By having the sun on its own layer, you can move it about easily and not have the lens flare rendered right over your galaxy image.

10. Now you can zoom into the rendered sun and use the Smudge tool to pull out a few solar flares (see Figure 2.38).

Figure 2.38

Deep space, with our sun small and far away.

Creating Wood

To create a passable wood texture, you can do the following in Photoshop:

1. Create a new image that is 256×256 pixels. Choose a light brown as the foreground color and a dark brown for the background color.

2. Run the Clouds filter (choose Filter|Render|Clouds), and then run the Difference Clouds filter several times until you have a good balance of pattern.

3. If you like, you can add some noise here (choose Filter|Noise|Add Noise). Make sure that you use a low amount and choose the Uniform and Monochromatic options.

4. Now add curves by choosing Filter|Distort|Shear.

With some tiling, you can make this a nice piece of wood. However, although it is wood grained, it isn't very realistic (see Figure 2.39). This is where you can depart Photoshop and go grab a digital image of some wood. I've included several images on this book's accompanying CD-ROM, and depending on the surface that you want to cover, you can choose old wood, weathered wood, pine, or one of the other files. Employ some of the tiling tricks you learned to make a tiling wood image that can be used later as a base for almost anything made of wood, such as tables, beams, telephone poles, and floors.

Figure 2.39
A passable wood grain, but not very realistic.

To create a base tileable wood for general purposes, start with the image named cedfence.jpg and do the following:

1. Make a duplicate of the image before altering it. Always keep your original images intact for future use.

   You may notice that this image is not perfectly square. Being *perfectly* square is almost always demanded by today's game technology. The reasons are basically mathematical; the computer can process a square image faster. This is referred to as the order of two, generally 32×32, 64×64, 128×128, 256×256, etc. So, first make the image square.

2. Fit the image in your window by selecting the Magnifying Glass tool and right-clicking on the image. Select Fit In Window from the context menu. Now right-click again and select Zoom Out. This rather large image should now fit on your monitor with some room left over for you to work (Figure 2.40).

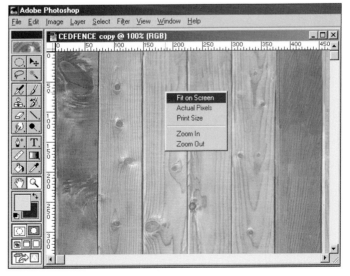

Figure 2.40
Even large images can be quickly sized to fit on your monitor so you can easily work on them.

3. Select the Crop tool from the toolbar.

4. Hold down Shift and drag out a crop area that covers as much of the image as possible without going off the canvas. Position the crop area on at least one seam of the boards and in an area you think will be easy to tile (see Figure 2.41). As you can see, the seams of the boards do not line up correctly; some boards are much darker than others, and you have some work ahead of you.

Figure 2.41

Cropping an image to find seams to help you with your tiling job.

5. Now that you have cropped the image, right-click on the header bar of the image and select Image Size. It does not really matter what size the image is, but it should have exactly the same pixel height and width. If the image size is off by one or two pixels, deselect the Constrain Proportions box (Figure 2.42) and type in the right number. For example, if the image is 512×513, change the 512 to 513. This one-pixel stretch of the image won't do any damage to the image, but if your measurements are off by more than a pixel or two, go back to Step 5 and make sure you are holding down Shift when you define the crop area.

6. Duplicate the layer and make sure the new layer is selected.

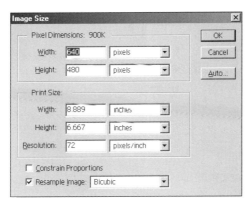

Figure 2.42
The Constrain Proportions box
unchecked so you can size an
image to exact pixel sizes.

7. You can use this particular texture as floorboards, and although the texture will have to tile in two directions, the seam of the tile can be matched to the seam in the image and eliminate a lot of work. In effect, you only have to worry about tiling in one direction because the seams will help with the other direction. However, you still have to examine the seams and make sure that they meet cleanly. To make the seams of the board meet cleanly without changing the size of the image, perform a Free Transform (holding down Shift so it is uniform) and drag out the layer a bit larger than the image. Do this until the seams meet up at the edges perfectly, as in Figures 2.43 and 2.44.

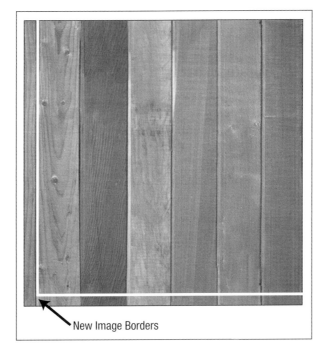

New Image Borders

Figure 2.43
The seams of the board do not
naturally meet the edge of the
image so you must use Free
Transform to match the seams
that you want to use with the
edge of the image.

Figure 2.44
The image Free Transformed to make the seams of the boards meet the edge of the image. The image size is the same, but the portion of the image you want to use was made larger to fill the image (note the loss of the leftmost board).

8. Crop the image again and check that it is perfectly square.

9. Referring to "Tips for Horizontal and Vertical Tiling" previously in this chapter, tile this image. First, copy the top of the image and flip it and drag it down. Then, erase the seam and flatten the image and repeat the process for the sides. Finally, use the Clone tool and a larger, very soft brush and clone out the knots in the wood. Test the image by using the Define Pattern and Fill|Pattern method, as described in the preceding section.

10. Finally: If you are making this base texture for a certain type of game or setting, keep this in mind and adjust the color balance, contrast, and other settings to reflect your world.

Creating a Stone Texture

In this exercise, you will use Photoshop to create a stone texture. To do so, take the following steps:

1. Start with a new image that's 800×800. Select a dark gray for your foreground and a light blue for the background.

2. Choose Filter|Render|Clouds.

3. Choose Filter|Noise|Add Noise. Set the amount to 3, Gaussian, Monochromatic.

4. In the Channels window, create a new channel and select it.

5. Choose Filter|Render|Difference Clouds.

6. Choose Filter|Noise|Add Noise and keep the same settings.

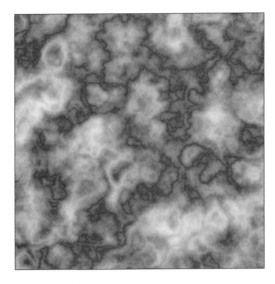

Figure 2.45
The image is ready to make stone as it is—a balance of patterns.

7. Choose Filter|Render|Difference Clouds, and press Ctrl+F to repeat the action until the channel is balanced with black and white as shown in Figure 2.45.

8. In the Layers window, select the layer you were working on before. Choose Filter|Render|Lighting Effects. Settings: Intensity 59, Focus 69, Properties: Gloss 100, (Shiny) Material 48 (Metallic) Exposure 6, Ambiance 4. Set the Texture Channel to the new channel you created in Step 4, and the height to 100.

9. Adjust the direction of the light to your liking.

10. Adjust the contrast and brightness by choosing Image|Adjust|Brightness/Contrast. It will most likely look best with the Brightness and Contrast up.

Experimenting with these sets of effects, you can make all sorts of stone and even surfaces like dinosaur or troll skin (see Figures 2.46 through 2.48).

Figure 2.46
The finished stone texture with burned-in red streak to simulate dinosaur skin.

Figure 2.47
A wet cave wall with light from below.

Figure 2.48
A mossy cave wall or more dinosaur skin? It all depends on how you use it.

Wetting the Stone

Now let's go one step further and make the stone look wet:

1. First, copy the texture layer.

2. Apply Lighting Effects to the bottom layer and keep it matte or nonglossy.

3. Then apply the same Lighting Effects to the top layer but turn up the glossiness. Now, while you are on the top layer, choose Layer|Add Layer Mask|Reveal All.

4. You should use the Difference Clouds filter on the layer mask a few times and then adjust the Contrast and Brightness.

Creating Quick Mud

To make a gooey wet mud texture quickly, do the following in Photoshop:

1. Create a new 600×600 image. Press the D key to set your foreground and background colors to the default.

2. Apply the Clouds filter to the layer by choosing Render|Clouds, and then apply the Difference Clouds filter to the layer. Keep applying this filter (Ctrl+F) until you have a very organic image, veined with black.

3. Apply the Emboss filter by selecting Stylize|Emboss. Here, I set the Height to 6 and the Amount to 220%.

4. (This is the step that makes the texture look like wet mud.) Create a duplicate of the layer and use Gaussian Blur on it, use 3 pixels. Invert the colors and set the layer mode to Overlay.

5. Adjust the hue and saturation by selecting Image|Adjust|Hue/Saturation, and make sure that the Colorize box is checked. Bring the hue and saturation down a bit. You can also adjust the Brightness and Contrast of this layer and get different ground effects. I was able to create a nice dusty rock, similar to what you might find in a desert (see Figure 2.49).

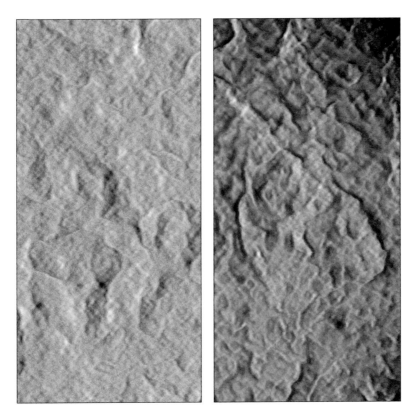

Figure 2.49

The dusty desert (left) and wet mud (right) textures.

Creating Parchment

In this exercise, you will create a paper parchment texture, complete with ripped edges. This texture will be used primarily in a game. To create a parchment texture for high polygon/high-resolution 3D work, you would want to have a more subtle texture, maybe even by scanning real parchment. For game purposes, you are usually creating images that will be color-reduced and shrunk dramatically, so you have to try to compensate for the loss of quality. Therefore, you will create a parchment texture that is rather rough to the eye, but will look great in a game.

To create parchment texture, follow these steps in Photoshop:

1. Create a new image, 600×600, and make the background white.

2. Create a new blank layer. Fill this new layer with a golden yellow (I used RGB 164,143,0).

3. Run the Texturizer filter by selecting Texture|Texturizer, and select the Sandstone texture. Set the Scaling at 100% and the Relief at 10. Leave the light coming from the top.

4. Choose Filter Brushstrokes|Crosshatch. Set the Stroke Length to 9, the Sharpness to 2, and the Strength to 1. Your image should look like the one shown in Figure 2.50.

Figure 2.50
The paper texture shaping up.

5. Create a new layer. Here, you will define the outline of the paper. Use a hard and narrow brush, and sketch the jagged outline of your page using pure black.

6. Fill the area outside the page area with black. You may notice a small outline or halo effect of the yellowish color around the fill area. To fix this, hit the paint bucket one or two times, and it will fill over this defect. You will now have an image that resembles the final parchment page in outline, as shown in Figure 2.51.

Figure 2.51
The black area around the parchment page is actually a layer over it defining the edge of the page.

7. Use the Magic Wand tool to select the black area, go to the paper layer, and cut away the outer edge of the paper. You can now hide or even delete the black outline layer.

8. Run the Spatter filter (choose Brush Strokes|Spatter). This will make the paper look rough on the edges and finish the texture of the paper itself. Set the Spray Radius to 10 and the Smoothness to 5. See Figure 2.52 for an example of the completed texture.

Figure 2.52
The completed page of parchment.

If you need to use this parchment in a game as a sheet of paper, that involves different steps than using this paper as a basis for a Web site, where you can go in and age the paper, write on it, and add a drop shadow. We'll look at these aspects of taking our textures further in the coming chapters.

PROJECT A Space Base Wall

Let's use the base textures we made to create an actual game texture. We will start with the standard space base wall.

1. First, open the rust texture from the previous exercise. As always, duplicate the original so you always have it to work from.

2. Flatten the image. Go to Layer and choose Flatten Image.

3. Duplicate the background layer and name it "Trim." Apply the Drop Shadow effect (leave the settings at their defaults), and apply the Bevel and Emboss filters. Set the Style to Emboss and the Depth to 3 and the Blur to 2.

4. Select a huge portion of the middle of the image, leaving the bottom area a little larger than the top. Delete this area from the image and you will already have a cool rusted panel wall (Figure 2.53).

Figure 2.53
A cool rusted panel.

5. Turn on the grid. Because this is a 600×600 image, set the grid spacing to every 60 pixels. This will divide the image evenly and make your work easier. Also, because one of our goals is clean tiling, you should always work this way.

6. Now use the grid to select a square from the middle of the panel on the background layer. Paste the square into its own layer and name it "panel." It should appear centered in the new layer. Copy your effects from the previous layer, and paste them here by right-mouse–clicking on the layer and choosing Copy Effects from the context menu. You paste effects in the same way by right-clicking on the layer and choosing Paste Effects from the context menu. Your image should look like Figure 2.54.

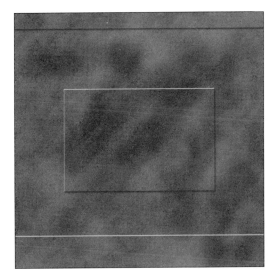

Figure 2.54
Notice how the grid evenly divides the image and how the new panel just created sits neatly in the center.

7. To add bolts to metal, create a new layer and name it "bolts." Paste the same effects from the previous layers into it. (For speed's sake, you can simply duplicate a layer that has the effects you want to use and simply Select All and Cut.) You will want to zoom in a bit here as you work. Set your grid lines to appear every 20 pixels, and turn the grid on if you had turned it off.

8. Select a color similar to the wall color, maybe a bit lighter. Select a small hard brush and simply paint in a circle (which magically appears to be a bolt due to the effects) every few grid spaces, as in Figure 2.55.

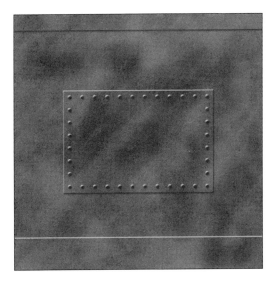

Figure 2.55
Bolts are made easy with layer effects in Photoshop.

9. Go back to the "panel" layer, drag out two guides, and make sure they snap to the center of the panel. Make a roughly square, or horizontally rectangular, selection inside the panel. Use the guides to make sure the selection is snapped to center, and copy the selection. Paste the selection into a new layer and name it "vent cover."

10. Create a new layer under the "vent cover" layer, but over all the previous layers. Set this layer's mode to Color Burn and take it down to about a setting of 23%. Airbrush some black lines coming from the vent and going in all directions. You can also apply a Radial Blur to this layer to help make the burns look better. You can see in Figure 2.56, and in the image included with this book's companion CD-ROM (CH2_057.tif), that I also added some drips to the wall.

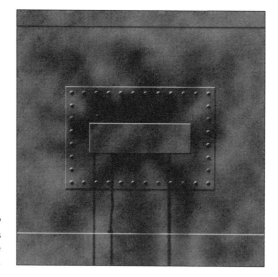

Figure 2.56
Notice how the blast marks coming from the vent and the drips add to the texture.

11. Create another layer and name it "decoration." You can do anything you want here; for example, select a few areas, fill them with red, lower the Opacity to around 50%, and apply the Spatter filter by selecting Brush Strokes|Spatter.

12. For a final, menacing touch, add a skull. Simply set your foreground color to black, add a text layer, and then paste in the effects you copied previously. The effects will still be in RAM so you don't need to recopy them. Take the Opacity down to about 50%, and type a capital "N," using the Wingdings font. You can see the results of this 12-step texture exercise in Figure 2.57.

Figure 2.57
Here is the completed Space Base Wall texture with an ornament (the skull) and stains.

If you keep this image in layers, you can add or delete items like the vent cover and the burns. You can interchange the skull font with other fonts, so the walls will indicate whether a player in your game world is in a good place or a bad place. Working from a layered image like this also helps keep the appearance of the game world consistent.

Moving On

In this chapter, you learned the fundamentals of texture creation. You learned how to decipher what a base texture set is, and how to create one. You looked at the challenge of tiling textures and even how to do advanced tiling with natural patterns.

In Chapter 3, you will look at how you create more advanced textures and texture sets, using even more cool effects and techniques. You will also look at how massive texture sets are managed by game-development teams.

Chapter 3

Advanced Texture Creation and Management

After you have a set of base textures, you can begin creating detailed textures. Two things happen: You will create more textures than you dreamed possible, and you will have to organize them so they'll be of use to you and to the development team.

Planning Your Texture Library

When you get your texture skills to an advanced stage, you will also need to raise your organizational skills to the same level, or you will have a hard time finding those great textures you created. Before looking at how to create advanced textures, you will look at the process of breaking out the texture library into a structure that will allow you to quickly create, save, and retrieve those images. Taking the time to properly break out and organize your texture library will also help you in the process of creating textures during development. The heads and subheads of a well-organized texture library can be used as a worksheet during development to determine the textures needed in any given area of your game. As you will see later in this chapter, a complex game world can be broken down into sets and subsets of materials, and this structure allows you to quickly go through the directory structure and use it as a checklist to review the textures needed in the world.

After we look at texture library organization, we will look at some advanced techniques for texture creation. You can go much farther than simply creating base surfaces like wood or stone. In this chapter, you will learn how to combine bases to make a floor tile that may be part wood and part stone, or a door that may be wood and various types of metal. You will learn about weathering, aging, and dirtying up your images so they not only look good, but also blend together and appear to have been subject to the same environment. Weathering and aging also help fulfill the designer's vision in the "setting and atmosphere" department. For example, if you are creating textures for a game that features an "old and abandoned" warehouse level, than you can develop the texture sets for the warehouse—crates, cinder block walls, and all the other surfaces you will need to cover your warehouse with—and then apply some weathering and aging that will make those surfaces look dirty, old, and even abused.

First, take a look at how to determine the textures you may need in your texture library. Then you will learn how best to organize your textures.

The Texture Library Defined

A texture library is exactly what it sounds like—a library of complete, game-ready textures. As with any project that involves a great deal of information, you will have to develop ways to organize and maintain that information. Also like books in a library, you will organize your textures in groups and subgroups, going down to any level of complexity that you require to keep track of the images in your library. This structure doesn't have to be terribly complex, but it does have to be usable. A simple system of headings, subheads, and a naming convention can fill your needs.

In addition to creating texture libraries, you will also be managing libraries containing many other resources, such as raw digital images, scans, 3D models, research, font collections, and so on. For example, the following list describes the libraries that I must maintain for my current project:

- *Raw Digital Imagery*—Because the project I am currently working on is tasked with re-creating reality, we (the other developers and I) have a massive library that contains thousands of digital shots of real-world locations. We have long shots of places, medium shots, and hundreds of close-ups of surfaces and objects for texture creation, such as grass, stones, concrete, wood, tree bark, and signs, to name a few. We also have a huge library of high-resolution digital images of almost every weapon, vehicle, and object found on an army base. We are constantly adding to this library, and all these images must be named and stored in a series of folders and subfolders. We may have the following folder structure, for example:

  C:\Raw_Images\Weapons\MK_19

  In the MK_19 folder, you will find all the images for this weapon, usually 6 to 14 close-up views, depending on the weapon size. There are also images of the weapon being used, carried, and fired—whatever we can get. As another example, we have the C:\Raw_Images\Signs folder, where there are Traffic Signs, Warning Signs, Official Signs, and so on.

- *Textures, Working*—These are textures that are in various states of completion ranging from just started to almost complete. This library will almost certainly be the largest in both number of files and file size. As an example, in the Raw Images Library, I may have one high-resolution 2MB image of a wooden fence, but in the working directory I will have multiple versions of that wooden fence texture. In the game, the fence may need to cover a large area, but there will be areas where the fence may look different; it may be broken, faded, or burnt. While in the process of creating the fence texture, I will be working on unflattened Photoshop files in high resolution, so these images will grow as large as 50MB, possibly larger.

  Usually, I will create a clean and fairly plain initial version that tiles well, and I'll save it (that's one 50MB file, with more to come). If I ever need that base tiling wood texture, it is there. I don't have to go through the steps of re-creating that texture in the future. Then I make a copy, and, with the copy as a base, I will create many other versions of the fence, versions that blend seamlessly as they are all created from the same base texture of the fence. As I create those other versions, they will each be stored as a high-resolution, unflattened Photoshop file.

  It is a good idea to store many such versions of your images, in as many stages as you possibly can, provided that you have the storage capacity. It will be common to revisit textures—and even entire texture sets—to make changes, adjustments, and new versions. The better your assets are organized, the quicker you will be able to fill texture needs.

> **Note:** The raw images are *never* deleted or overwritten. Instead, make copies to work on, so you can always go back to the original, in case you make an irreparable mistake or the file becomes corrupt.

> **Note:** Photoshop saves images in layers; you can edit one layer without affecting the others. These multiple-layer images are known as *unflattened* images. Working in layers is like having many clear palettes to draw on. On the bottom layer, you might draw a grassy field; on the next, a tree; on the next, a cow—you can create as many layers as needed. If you don't like the cow, you can remove or replace it without affecting the other layers. The downside: Each layer makes the file size larger.

- *Textures, Complete*—When a texture is finally looking its best and you are ready to put it in the game, make a copy of it so the original large, unflattened file will remain as it is. Take the copy and flatten it, reduce it in size and color depth, and perform whatever other operations are needed to make it ready for use by the game editor. Remember, we are working large (I usually work at 2000×2000 pixels) and then reducing down to 256×256 or 512×512, either of which represents a significant reduction in size. Then store all these completed game-ready textures as they are *before* they are imported or converted into the game editor. When a texture file is used in a game editor, it can sometimes become corrupted, or the texture library may need to be rebuilt quickly or reorganized for some reason. You will be ready to make those changes quickly if the images are all stored in this way. Having the textures stored this way also is handy if you want to print contact sheets or show the textures in the game by using Photoshop's Contact Sheet function.

- *Texture Libraries, Game Formatted*—Finally, you will most likely end up with texture files that are in some unique form to be used by the particular game engine you are working with. In some cases, the game engine may read textures from directories in their native format, reading common file types such as bitmaps directly off the hard drive instead of dealing with a special format, but most of the time you must import textures into a special file format for the game engine to read. Most world editors require that you import textures into a library that their software maintains because there are special variables that can be assigned to textures and special effects. Also the texture import process can validate files by checking that they are the right size, dimension, and color depth, and meet any other requirements. After you import the image, remember that you can't get to it by using Photoshop; you now need to access it via the editor for use in the game world.

Texture libraries should all follow the same organizational structure as closely as possible. If you have a raw image stored in C:\ground\grass\dead_grass.jpg, then you should also find, in the Textures, working library, a folder called Ground and a subfolder named Grass. The Grass subfolder will contain many versions of dead grass. The same structure should also appear in the texture libraries used by the world editor. This is important because having a different structure or naming convention for each step of the process would quickly become overwhelmingly confusing, if not paralyzing.

A consistent naming convention and organizational structure also makes it much easier to generate a status report on texture progress based on what library the texture is in. You may have a simple worksheet, something like this, for a texture artist to maintain.

Texture Status Report

Level: The Old Warehouse

Artist: (Artist Name)

W = Working, R = Raw Image, C = Complete

Texture name:	Currently in:	% complete	Filename
Ground, Gravel	W	75	gravel001
Ground, Gravel w/grass	R	0	gravel002
Ground, Grass, dead	C	100	grass004

These are the libraries of assets I can call upon on this particular project, but if you were making a game that used no digital imagery and you were not trying to re-create the real world, then you might not need the Raw Image Library. In fact, you may have only the working and the complete stages. Some games may rely on 3D art and will therefore have 3D models, their textures, and final renders of the 3D scenes.

So, now you know the basics of how to organize a great many game textures and assets into libraries, but before you even begin to create those textures, you must know what textures you are creating. To determine this, there are a few questions you must answer.

The Textures You'll Need To Create

You have learned what a texture library is, next, you need to figure out what textures to create to fill those libraries. And you probably won't be doing this by yourself. Often it is not solely the texture artists' job to help break out the texture needs of a game; rather, there's a meeting of the minds involving all the individuals on the team who are trained and experienced with the game-type being designed and the technology being used in development. The more people who are involved, the more factors you might have to consider.

When the designers, producers, level designers, and programmers see what you have initially broken out as a list of textures needed for the game, they will most certainly have feedback for you. You may have broken out a texture list that contains sky boxes, or a set of six images that seamlessly fit together to fill the inside of a cube that will form the inside of your world's sky. The programmer may come to you and explain that a new process for the sky is being used that does not require the tedious sky box technique, but involves flat images that will appear to go off into the horizon as a real sky does. The level designers may come to you and explain that they are using a new approach to building sand and they need more variations on the base building materials than you have listed — and on and on. You'll need to keep track of all these requirements, and then some. So, here are some questions that need to be answered as you prepare to break out your game's texture needs.

What View of the World Does the Game Offer?

The first consideration when building a texture library is the view of the world the player will have. The player's POV (point of view) will definitely have some bearing on your texture needs, helping to determine how much detail you need to put into the textures and even what your approach will be in creating the textures. A door seen from a car driving by at 200 miles an hour (when you are the driver) doesn't need to be at the same level of detail as a door that is seen from the player's eyes when that player is able to walk right up to the door and inspect it. The "200 MPH drive-by" can be a small brown square, whereas the face-to-face version of the door will require more detail and will also need to be a larger image. Building textures for a first-person shooter will require a very different library than that of a third-person game, a god game, or a racing game; the genre will influence, or may even determine, the POV.

The type, or *genre*, of a game is the first, and most fundamental, bit of information you must gather. Here are some of the types of games on the shelves and the texture needs for those types of games:

- *First-Person View*—Usually this is a close-up view that shows the player highly detailed doors, walls, and interior spaces. If you are able, open the texture library of a typical 3D shooter, and you will see many walls, floors, and ceilings, similar to those shown in Figure 3.1.

Figure 3.1
This is the first-person view of a game world. The level of detail for this view must be higher than that for some other views.

- *Third-Person View*—Similar to first-person, but the camera has a broader range of movement. Often, as texture artist, you must be concerned with the first-person view as well as with the broader picture, because the camera will often give the player visual access to portions of the game not seen in first-person, as shown in Figure 3.2. The character also becomes fully visible in this view.

Figure 3.2
This is the third-person view. This view often lets the players see parts of the world that the first-person view may not let them see.

- *Vehicle-Based View*—This view can be similar to the first-person view, if the vehicle is in a building. Many vehicle-based games, however, take place in airplanes, tanks, race cars, and starships.

  The texture needs of a racing game will be different from those of a tank game. Tanks are generally allowed to slowly roam a large piece of terrain (grass, trees, and sky), whereas a race car generally streaks along a predetermined course (road, past banners and the stands, hills, bridges, and sky). As you can see in Figure 3.3, a helicopter offers an even larger view area.

- *Orthographic View*—This view looks down on the game world and usually offers a broader view where up-close detail is not nearly as important as seeing the layout of the surrounding streets or hallways of the world, as you can see in Figure 3.4.

As you can imagine, combining any two or more of these game views will at the least add to your work load, if not multiply it exponentially. Imagine a game that allowed a player to go from a first-person walkabout to flying a helicopter. There are games that allow this, but the tradeoff is that the world is large and not very detailed. And the artists, programmers, and all involved had to do additional work in every area to create this functionality. New code had to be written, design had to accommodate the expanded player world, more art had to be created (or used more repeatedly), and more sounds needed to be generated, models created, and so on.

Figure 3.3
This is the vehicle-based view. Of course, flying a helicopter lets you see more of the world.

: You are at the edge of the world!

Figure 3.4
This is the orthographic view, a broader view than the third-person view, but not quite as big as a helicopter.

Where and When Does the Game Take Place?

Game setting and atmosphere are very important in the equation of generating game assets. If you are building a game that is set in a city of an ancient civilization as opposed to one set in a vast, open terrain setting where there are only a few simple buildings, then your texture needs and focus will be very different. For the ancient city, you may be creating hundreds of textures for buildings, statues, ornamentation, and more. For the modern-world game, chances are you will be focusing on creating many ground textures and spending a great deal of time tiling and tweaking them because they are visually prevalent in the game.

Game setting also affects the organization of the texture library. In the case of the ancient city, with all of its marble textures and ornamental pieces, you may have several libraries just for the marble textures. In contrast, a game that has only a few marble textures show up anywhere in the game world may have that texture labeled under another library of materials, or even as "miscellaneous."

Finally, game setting will also determine how you make your textures. For example, in one game development project, we had to make every single texture in a 3D application because the game was set in outer space on alien worlds, where literally nothing we were creating existed anywhere in the real world. We spent hours planning and experimenting with 3D modeling, lighting, and rendering. We were indoors most of the time during development—in high creative mode; we were always brainstorming new worlds to create. On the other hand, I am currently involved in a game project that is quite the opposite. Every single object and surface exists in the real world and, therefore, must be represented accurately. So, we've spent a great deal of time literally "in the field" with digital video and still cameras capturing every detail possible. We've also spent a large amount of time learning reality (not making it up) and trying to get that into the game. We rarely use a 3D program (for textures), and we often use Photoshop to touch up, clean, and manipulate digital images. Thus, for different game settings, you might be working indoors or out, being freely inventive or painstakingly realistic, creating new images or scanning and fixing existing ones.

How Is the Game World Divided?

What are the common game world divisions? This information partially comes from game type. If you are developing a driving game, an indoor shooter, or a massive outdoor level, your game world divisions may be floors, ceilings, and walls; or tracks and banners; or—in the case of a large outdoor level—forest, desert, and polar ice.

How the world is divided obviously determines what the focus of the game will be. A shooter that is mostly indoors will focus on making the up-close details of floor, walls, and indoor ornament look good, while the massive outdoor game will want the grounds to look their best; grounds should tile well and look as realistic as possible as they are the main focus. There may be more sky textures to deal with: trees and plant life and even weather effects. How the world is divided may break out texture libraries, as shown in the following outline:

3D Shooter (primarily indoors)
> Walls
>> Brick
>>
>> Concrete
>>
>> Wood
>
> Floor
>> Tile
>>
>> Metal plate
>>
>> Wood
>
> Windows
>> Panes
>>
>> Sills
>>
>> Glass

Outdoors Game
> Grounds
>> Dirt
>>
>> Grass
>>
>> Grass, dead
>>
>> Mud
>
> Trees
>> Leaves
>>
>> Bark
>>
>> Branches
>
> Water
>> Blue
>>
>> Dark
>>
>> Dirty

What Technology Will Be Used to Develop the Game?

How the game world is divided from a texturing and assets point of view is derived to a great extent from the game technology being used. If you are using all your computing power to render large and ornate rooms, then chances are you can't also have vast and impressive terrain. And likewise, a game with vast and impressive landscapes will have small and simple buildings. Even when we have games with both, we will still be trading off, meaning that a game with both a large terrain and detailed buildings could lose the buildings and have even larger terrain, and vice versa. Just as there are many game types, there are many game engine types, and each has a type of game it processes best. For a good article explaining all this more fully, go to **www.3dactionplanet.com/features/articles/gameengines**.

Technology also determines organization. In the Unreal game editor, you are able to create texture libraries and subgroups in those libraries. This makes organization easier and makes communication between artists and level designers easier. With Genesis3D, which you will learn about in Part II of this book, most of your organization must be done outside the editor and the texture library built before you open the editor. With Unreal, you can import images as you work and organize them in the editor.

Organizing the Texture Library

After you work out the texture requirements for the game, you organize them into a library that will be easy for you—and for any other artist working on the textures—to access and update. You will also have level builders using your textures, and they, too, need to know where to find what they want. Here I am strictly addressing the organization of assets by groups and names. Another method employed when many people are using and working on the same assets is file management, where special software—like that the software programmers use for version control—is used to make sure that no file is deleted, corrupted, or overwritten. File management will not be discussed at length here, but it is a topic you will eventually address in game development.

There are more than world textures in a game (floors, walls, and ceilings). There are also textures for the *HUD* (the Heads-Up Display, as shown in Figure 3.5), splash screens, menus, and many other places where art is used. The asset list shown in Table 3.1 is for a typical 3D shooter, and as usual, your needs may add, subtract, or break out any of the headings in Table 3.1. A game that is strictly indoors, or has few trees, may not have an entire library devoted to trees. A game with a few trees may have those trees stored under "organic," "miscellaneous," or even as a subgroup of "wood."

When you're planning the texture needs, organization, and methods of texture and asset creation, keep in mind the player view, location and setting, world divisions, and game technology. Any of these can drastically alter the sample texture list shown in Table 3.1. For example, an indoor game may not have a terrain library. Also, many games have few or no signs and therefore will not require a sign library.

Now that you can organize textures with the best of them, it's time for you to create more textures. You can start by learning to combine the bases you made in Chapter 2 to create all new, more complex textures.

Figure 3.5

The HUD, or heads-up display, is the (usually transparent) interface overlying the game where the players can see their health, armor, ammunition, and other vital information.

Table 3.1   Texture list for a typical 3D shooter.

Asset	Description
Buildings	Building textures usually tile in one direction when they are walls with a notion of top and bottom. Some games need walls to contain details such as pipes and windows, whereas other games will model the pipes and windows separately and require only a tiling texture of a brick or stone. Building textures are images such as roof tiles, trim, wall surfaces, windows, floors, and doors.
Decal	Decal textures are small textures with an alpha channel (an invisible area of the image) used for stains and marks on the game world. Decals are also used for small posters, signs, and even light switches on walls.
F/x	These are textures created for use during the game and not put in the level by a level editor; they are usually handled by the programmers and called by the code during game play. These are the textures used when a dynamic lightning bolt strikes, when a weapon is fired and you see the muzzle blast, or when a bullet hits the wall and you see the small bits fly. These textures are also used for in-game effects such as smoke, explosions, fire, sparks, and other particle-type systems.
Masonry	Masonry includes tiling bricks, cinder blocks, concrete, stone, and similar heavy surfaces.
Metal	Metals can be tiling sheets of aluminum, corrugated tin, beams, pipes, and more.
Missions	Sometimes, you may have images that fit no real category, but if an image appears in a level, it needs a home. Usually, you will reserve this library and, when you find that you are sticking images in it, examine the images. Often, you will want to create a new library for them.
Organic	Organic textures are different from terrain textures (below) because organic textures don't have to cover large patches of terrain. They are designed to cover smaller areas and objects such as rocks, plants, and dirt patches in the terrain.
Signs	In any real-life situation, in places inhabited by civilization, you will encounter signs—traffic signs, warning signs, official signs, business signs, and the many other signs people see every day.
Terrain	These are maps that are to be used on large terrain areas, typically grass, rock, and dirt.
Trees	Trees can include bark, branches, leaves, and billboards of trees.
Wood	Wood includes beams, crate sides, paneling, plywood, and generally man-made wooden items.

Creating Advanced Textures from Bases

If you look closely at the world around you, no matter where you are, you will see that it is composed of some basic surfaces. In my office there is carpet, white sheet rock walls, ceiling tiles, and the weird stuff our desks are made of—compressed meat loaf, I think. These are all plain, easily created and easily tiled textures; see Figure 3.6. Figure 3.7 shows a scene using these four basic textures.

Figure 3.6
The four basic textures used in a modern office scene. These base textures are easy to create and tile.

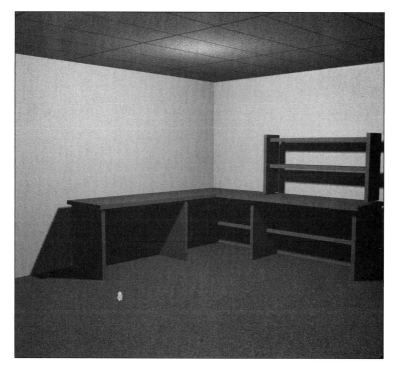

Figure 3.7
The office scene with textures applied, plain but pretty.

Other worlds are created in the same way as the real world, with basic surfaces underneath as well. Consider a castle, for example. You may have walls made of a base stone that is a bit more complex to come by and to get to tile just right. Then, you have wooden beams that hold the tiled slate roof up and the ornate wooden door with banded iron hinges and really cool metal studs, all dripping with rust and slime. Suddenly, you will have hit the point where a few tiling base textures no longer fill the bill. Figure 3.8 shows the basic castle scene, using only the base textures to cover the geometry.

Figure 3.8

Here is a castle with brand-spanking-new stone and a door made with wood, but where are the hinges, the knob, and all the rest? Well, frankly, where is the believability in this scene?

While the office scene looks pretty good and believable (because it is an office and it is acceptable that the office may be smooth and have clean surfaces), the castle scene is lacking in atmosphere and believability because it is too clean. (Not to mention the castle door, which is simply several wooden slats at this point.) With the addition of weathering and aging, and by combining textures, we can really make this castle scene come to life, as in Figure 3.9.

If you are tasked with having to create the entire texture set for that castle scene—including the door, complete with brass pull ring and ax chop marks—how do you begin to create that complex texture set? Simple, you break that texture down in the same way that you broke down the world space, as illustrated in Chapter 2. The castle door in Figure 3.10 is composed of a base wooden board, a base metal texture, and that cool glowing rune. If you look closer,

Figure 3.9
Here is the castle scene with
the door texture. The glowing
hand is a magical symbol of
protection, added for effect.
You will learn to make the door
texture at the end of this chapter.

you will also notice that the door is not just those base materials laid on top of
each other; there are also highlights, shadows, aging (weathering), and some
wear and tear in the form of nicks, dents, stains, and so on. In this section, you
will learn how to apply all these effects quickly and easily to your materials to
create stunning textures.

First, break down your texture needs as you did in Chapter 2. In that chapter,
you learned how to examine a scene and break out the base textures, or common tiling images, that cover the common areas of your world. Now you will
learn how to look more deeply, and how to break out detailed objects and
surfaces so that you can re-create them in Photoshop.

Combining Base Textures: The Importance of Highlights and Shadows

One of the easiest and more impressive textures you can make from combining bases is a texture that simulates ornate floor tiles. And as simple as a floor
tile may be, it requires some attention to detail if it is to look good. Two of the
most important of these details, and ones that you should always pay attention to in your textures, are *highlights* and *shadows*.

To give some depth to a 2D image, you can use Photoshop to add highlights
and shadows by using the Bevel And Emboss layer effects. The trick to making
a 2D image have depth and also appear to be three-dimensional is to know

Figure 3.10
This intricate castle door can be broken down and re-created in minutes once you know how to pull out the base texture and then apply the basic lighting, aging, and other details to the texture.

just how far you can go with the effect. Some highlights and shadows are necessary for an image to have depth, but if you push the effect too far, it will actually have the opposite effect and make the image appear to be flat. Look at Figure 3.11 and you will see that the combined base textures in this object look flat, but with some highlights and shadows it has some nice depth (see Figure 3.12).

Figure 3.11
Combined base textures with no highlights or shadows are very flat.

Figure 3.12
Add highlights and shadows to
the base textures and you have a
nice image.

Creating a Floor Tile

As you did in Chapter 2, you're going to work in Photoshop here. Start this exercise by opening the file "marble texture" from the companion CD-ROM.

If you examine the image of the completed tile, you will see that it is composed of no more than a copy of the initial marble texture layer, which has been repositioned and colored to fit the tile pattern. To perform this same kind of finishing, take the following steps:

1. With the open "marble texture" file in Photoshop, copy the layer twice. You will not be using the very bottom (or background) layer, but because you can't apply effects to the background layer, you need to copy it for this exercise.

2. Color the topmost layer using Image|Adjust|Hue/Saturation. Here, I simply clicked on the Colorize option, and it gave me the color I preferred; you can, however, play with the Hue, Saturation, and Lightness sliders to get any color that you desire.

3. Use the guides to divide the image in half horizontally and vertically. If you like, you can use the grid tool, but I find it easier when dividing an image in half to go to the background layer and drag out the guides until they snap in place.

4. Make a square selection on the top layer you colorized (holding down Shift so the selection will be perfectly square), and center the selection by snapping it to the guides. Right-mouse click on the selection and Invert the selection by choosing Select Inverse from the context menu.

5. Delete the selected area of the image. You should now have a small square of colored marble in the exact center of your image. Press Ctrl+T to Free Transform this layer, and hold down Shift as you do so you can rotate the square of marble exactly. Your image should now look like Figure 3.11.

Now, to make the floor tile more closely resemble the one shown in Figure 3.12, follow these steps:

1. Start on the first layer above the background layer and apply the Layer|Effects Bevel And Emboss. Use Inner Bevel and leave the default settings.

2. Copy the effects by right-clicking on the layer and choosing the Copy Effects option (Layer| Effects|Copy Effects). Then paste the effects into the top layer where the smaller marble square is.

3. You may notice that Figure 3.12 also has the lines that come from the corners of the small marble square. To accomplish that effect, simply create another layer between the two marble layers, paste the effects into it, and then draw some 3-pixel-wide lines in. Holding Shift will make the lines straight, and using the guidelines will make them straight.

This floor tile image went together pretty quickly, and it looks good. Here, the tile texture is in use in Figure 3.13.

Figure 3.13
The floor tile, created in minutes, in use in a scene.

Putting Your Skills to Work

This is the tale of how, one day, I had to build army-issue ammo boxes from nothing. Yep, we needed an ammo box texture and there was little time to make it, so I went to our photo archives, and all they had was this very low-resolution image. I would have to build the texture from scratch.

I simply started with an army green layer, made it dirty, cut out the areas that needed depth, and I was done. If you need an image that you don't currently have on hand, you may want to search the Internet; you might find some royalty-free images that will suit your purpose. In the following project, you will learn to build a more complex object from the ground up.

PROJECT Making Complex Objects and Dirtying Them Up

Building a complex object is that simple, but—just for the exercise—I will walk you through the steps here. Building complex objects is easy because when you break them down, they are never as complex as they seem. The ammo box is a great example. In Figure 3.14, you see the actual photo reference with which I started.

Figure 3.14
The small image of the ammo box was enough for me to build a high-resolution texture from the ground up.

1. Start with a new Photoshop file; make its dimensions 400×400 pixels, and its file type RGB.

2. Fill the background layer with a green (I used RGB 96, 107, 86), and divide it in half horizontally and vertically using the guides.

3. Create a new layer and name it "Handle". Apply the layer effect Emboss and change the Depth to 2 and the Blur to 4.

4. Now draw out the handle shape from the front of the ammo box. A trick I used to make the handle symmetrical was to draw out half the handle and then copy the layer and flip it Horizontally. You can also draw a selection, fill it with color, and then draw a smaller selection and delete the inside of the rectangular handle. If you use the guides, you can line up the selections to make the cutout perfect.

5. Create a new layer with the same layer effects and name it "Thing 1". Use the same technique to draw the things on the top of the ammo box. I deviated from the exact ammo box design and created three layers like this (I actually copied Thing 1 twice and resized it).

6. Finally, there is a latch type object that covers the top part of the handle and the bottom of the lowest Thing layer. I made this with a filled selection (same layer effects as all the other layers) and used selections to chop out square and round parts of the object until I had the latch object. Your image should look like the one in Figure 3.15.

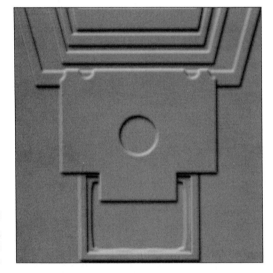

Figure 3.15
The front of the ammo box before the war, clean and freshly painted.

Adding Dirt and Scratches

The ammo box is too clean, so you will have to dirty it up. The techniques for doing this can be broken down by three types of dirt: atmospheric, usage wear and tear, and random stuff.

- *Atmospheric dirt* is subtle and evenly collected dirt and dust on surfaces. Dust that settles on objects in a room is a good example of atmospheric dirt.

- *Wear and tear* from normal to heavy usage consists of darker stains where dirty hands have been and other such contact. Also, for machinery, wear and tear might be shown with bright metal patches or areas where parts may rub against otherwise grubby hardware.

- *Random stuff* is the stuff that always happens, but with no real pattern involved; for example, the object was dropped, splattered by mud, or left in the rain.

To make this ammo box look really worn out, do the following:

1. Make a copy of the ammo box file you just created, and merge all the layers except the background.

2. You should now have two layers, background and the merged layer (I named the merged layer "Stuff"). Apply the Noise filter to each of these layers (Gaussian, Monochromatic, and Amount 5) and this will be your atmospheric layer of collected dirt.

3. On the background layer, airbrush a dark circle behind the hole in the latch of the ammo box.

4. On the "Stuff" layer, apply the Outer Glow Layer Effect (Blur 20 and Intensity 9) to add more depth and help with the dirtying process.

5. Create a new layer on top of these and name it "Worn Edges". Set its mode to color burn and take the Opacity down to 30%. Now, use the airbrush and brush some dirt all around the edges of the box and the latch. Use a smaller brush size to get around the smaller parts, if you like. This is the wear-and-tear staining.

6. Finally for the random stuff dirt, I created two new layers, one named "Rust" and one named "Dirt". I set each layer in the Color Burn mode and set their Opacity to 15%. In each layer, I pasted images of spattered food and dirt. The final ammo box image can be seen in Figure 3.16.

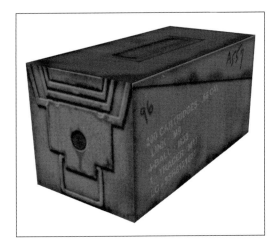

Figure 3.16
The final ammo box image on a 3D model. The top and sides were created in the exact same way as the front. For the side, I simply used the mouse to do some hand lettering and the text tool to put some official looking text in as well. The dirt and worn areas were also done in Photoshop.

PROJECT Using a Digital Image to Make a Sign: Removing a Flash Burn

Using digital imagery for textures is great, but the hardest thing can be to remove the flash burns you often get when the flash goes off as you take the picture. Figure 3.17 shows a sign that's 1,500 miles away from where I work, so I couldn't go and retake the photo; I had to remove the flash burn by hand and rebuild the sign. This is not as hard as it sounds.

Figure 3.17
The original digital image with the flash burn in the center.

Here's how you can handle this situation:

1. I started with this image. Notice the flash of white in the middle of the sign. Also notice that the sign was photographed crookedly (see Figure 3.18).

2. I cropped the image to the edges of the sign. You can see how crooked the borders of the sign are.

3. To rebuild the sign, you must first make the background. Start by duplicating the layer and using your Color Picker to select a color off the sign that is about the mid-range of the colors on the sign. Now fill the background with this color. Add noise to this layer (Filter|Noise|Add Noise; Gaussian, Monochromatic, 17).

   This background looks plain and even, but that is how the sign looked when it was first made, even before the letters were applied. This sign is being reproduced the same way it was built—step by step. You'll even apply the weathering as the last step.

Figure 3.18
The sign cropped. You can see how crookedly it was photographed.

4. Now create a new layer named "White Lines" and apply the Bevel And Emboss layer effects to it (Inner Bevel; Depth 3 and Blur 2).

5. Make a selection approximating the outer borders of the white lines in the original sign and fill this selection with white. Apply the same amount of noise as you did to the background (Ctrl+F will apply the last-used filter). Make another selection to cut out the inside of the white area and use the guides to line it up perfectly in the center.

6. Now you'll redo the letters. Fortunately, the U.S. Army often uses a font on its signs that is similar to Arial Black. Simply create three text layers in white, one for each line of words in the sign. You can use the Free Transform option on text to get the letters sized perfectly to the sign.

7. Render the text layers and apply the noise filter to them as well. You can also copy the effects from the "White Lines" layer and apply that to the text layers.

8. And for the grand finale, add the image "splat" on the top layer and set the Mode to Color Burn and the Opacity to 30% (see Figure 3.19).

What you just did was build the sign as it was built in real life, starting from scratch. You used a base material, painted on the letters, and then weathered it. Rebuilding the sign from the ground up was actually quicker than trying to remove the flash burn with the clone tool, or other such tedium. And not only was this quicker, the results are much better, especially for use in games. If you look at the original cropped image in Photoshop, you will see how the camera lens distorted all the letters and white lines. Trying to straighten those would be impossible. Our image has lines and letters that are lined up perfectly.

Figure 3.19
The rebuilt sign.

PROJECT Creating Peeling Paint

This quick and easy effect is not only a great effect; it can make several good textures out of one base. Here's how to create the effect of peeling paint:

1. Open the image "planks", create a new layer, and then name it "Paint".

2. Use the Magic Wand tool on the planks layer to select an area where the peeling paint will go; you will have to play with the Tolerance Level of the Magic Wand (I used 8 to 10) and with whatever color you select. This effect looks best if you don't have more than a third of the image selected.

3. After you have the image selection in place, switch to the Paint layer and select a large soft brush and the color of paint you want—I used white because lighter colors tend to work better and look more realistic for this effect. Now, airbrush most of your selection.

4. Already it looks great—like peeling, worn-off paint—but for the final touch, simply add the Craquelure Filter (Filter|Texture|Craquelure). You can play with the settings and get effects ranging from rough paint to paint coming off in chips. Figure 3.20 shows the original plank image and the painted version.

Now you are ready to tackle a really complex texture, but even this cool castle door isn't much more difficult to create than the textures you made in the preceding exercises. Once again, study this image; you will see that the door is made of bases: a rough-hewn wood, a metal, and a glowing rune (or symbol). All these textures are simple base textures, and you will again build this door the way you built the sign: step by step, as you would in real life.

Figure 3.20
This is the original plank image with no paint (left), one version of the paint (center), and the more rough version of paint (right).

PROJECT A Deluxe Castle Door

To build the door, start with the fresh wood and add the metal hinges and then the aging and weathering effects. Most objects' textures can be built by using this three-step process: create the base materials, construct the object, and add the effects.

To make the door, take the following steps:

1. Open the image "woodplank.jpg" and notice that this is a tiled wood from the previous chapter that I simply fit to my door dimensions and cropped. (I even created a black background here, so I could add line variation by erasing some of the seams between planks.)

2. Now, apply the bevel and emboss effects to the planks. The Bevel And Emboss filter also affects the edges of the planks (where you erased the seams), and they look better.

3. Copy one of the planks, paste it into its own layer, and copy the layer effects from the planks as well. Rotate this plank 90 degrees and copy the layer to make the second (lower) door timber. Leave the plank a little bit too long so you can move it down and use the other side of it for the lower timber; this way the timbers won't look the same. Then, cut off the excess of both timbers. Your image should resemble Figure 3.21.

4. Now that you have the base of the door, you need to add the hinges. To create the fancy hinge, I used nothing more than a lowercase "a" in the Wingdings 2 font. I then applied the brushed metal effects from Chapter 2 onto the "hinge," to complete the font-to-hinge transformation.

    If you want to corrode the hinges a bit, run the Filter|Brush Strokes| Splatter on them and experiment with the foreground and background colors. I also added a small amount of a black outer glow to make the hinges look surrounded by some dirt as if they had been there awhile.

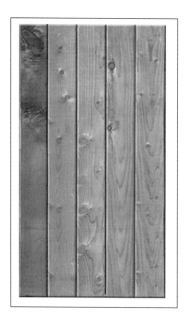

Figure 3.21
The base wood plank used to make the base of the door.

5. Create a new layer named "Hinge Bolts" and copy and paste the layer effects from the hinges to the bolts. If you are using the metal effects from Chapter 2, you should also have the Bevel And Emboss settings right for this layer. Make some small bolt heads for the hinges and the cross beams of the door (see Figure 3.22).

Figure 3.22
The door is shaping up with hinges and bolts.

6. To make the brass pull ring for the doorknob, create a new layer called "Pull Ring", and line up two guidelines where you want the center of the ring to be. Make a circular selection, line it up to snap in the center of the two guides, and fill it with a darkish yellow. Make a smaller circular

selection and center it as well and use it to cut out the center of the pull ring. Apply the noise filter to the layer (Noise|Add Noise; Gaussian, Monochromatic—play with the amount) and then apply the Brushstrokes|Spatter filter to the layer. Paste the Layer effects in and you have your pull ring. Follow the same process on a new layer to create the little pull ring hinge.

7. Now you can start the weathering. As with the ammo box, you simply create a layer called "Weathering" and set the mode to Color Burn and Opacity to 25%. Paint in black around the bottom of the door and the pull ring.

8. To add some mold, create a new layer named "Mold" and set the mode to Hue and the Opacity to 32%. Select a medium green and set your airbrush to Dissolve. Paint some mold down the length of your door.

9. For random stains and drips, add a layer called "Stains" and set the mode to color burn and the Opacity to 40%. You can use black and red here to make some splats, streaks, and drips from the top of the door to the bottom. Use the Smudge tool to make some of the stains look smeared.

10. To add that "barbarian wants in your castle" look, add some gouges. Create a new layer named "Ax Gouges" and leave it in normal mode. Set the Opacity to 44% and select your airbrush. Set the airbrush's Fade to random steps between 12 and 55 for this exercise. Set the layer effects to Bevel And Emboss|Inner Bevel. Settings should be Depth 6, Blur 5, and the direction needs to be down. Now make some varying length and thickness marks; they will appear to be gouged into the door. Figure 3.23 shows the progress thus far with the gouges.

Figure 3.23
Weathered, molded and stained, this door is looking good.

11. Now, add the final layer of stains and junk. Create a new layer named "Stains" and paste in the same texture from the ammo box and set the mode to Multiply and the Opacity to 79%.

12. You are ready for the final touch, the magic rune, which is simply the uppercase "H" in the magical Wingdings 2 font. Make the letter white and add the Outer Glow Layer Effect. Make the color of the glow yellow and the settings as follows: Mode Hard Light, Opacity 83%, Blur 16, and Intensity 363.

The end result of this project is your deluxe, magical castle door—a door that you created, which you can see in Figure 3.24.

Figure 3.24
The final version of the deluxe castle door.

Moving On

In this chapter, you learned how to organize textures and how to determine which textures you need to create, and you also learned how to create those textures. Understanding how to break scenes, objects, and anything you see down into their base components of materials, lights and shadow, and other effects will help you create anything from the ground up.

In the next chapter, I will take you through the process of logo design. The logo is possibly your most important piece of art because it represents your game, company, or project.

Chapter 4

Logos: The Essence of Your Project

A game logo represents the game in look, feel, setting, genre, and in many other ways. Often, an artist is called on to create a logo before much of the game is in place.

Why Create a Logo?

Often, especially in smaller development studios and companies, an artist may be hired for one job (such as creating textures for a 3D space) and then be assigned other tasks (for example, creating a logo for the project). Although the two tasks may seem related in that they both require art skills, creating a logo actually takes a bit more of an understanding of the project, the company, and the audience of the product.

You may wonder, "Why do I need a logo?" Alternatively, you may already assume that you need a logo, but in either case, it helps in your artistic design of a logo to understand why you are creating one. The logo is like the cover of a book, and many people still buy books by their covers (I am the first to admit that I am occasionally one of those people). A logo is often the first and strongest indicator to investors, publishers, developers, and customers of what to expect from you and your project. A well-done logo can convey the message that a team has ability and is serious about their project. A poorly done logo only speaks poorly of all the members on the team. Even though your logo will initially interest potential talent and investors; eventually, the logo you design may appear everywhere, in large and small versions, in black and white or in color, on boxes and in magazines. A quickly done, unprofessionally realized logo will only repeatedly send the message, "Quickly done and unprofessional." Of course, you want the logo you design to convey everything it is related to (such as your game and/or your company) in the most positive light. A logo can convey game genre, setting, and more. A game about race cars may have the text slanted and blurred to indicate speed; a fantasy game will usually have elements of magic, dragons, swords and more in the logo, and a game marketed to guys may have an alluring-yet-tough female (Tomb Raider is a good example of this) in the logo.

Your logo will have a lot to do with the impression a customer takes away after looking at it. Coca-Cola is an excellent example of a great logo, with a script type that enables you to identify the logo even if the name is written in a foreign language. Nike's "swoosh" symbol, McDonald's golden arches, FTD's figure of Mercury, the winged messenger, are all logos that are instantly recognizable. There is a great site with all this information at **www.mclane.com/ publications/publications.htm**, and look under the Reports section, which is a law firm's newsletter about intellectual property issues. This issue is complete with examples of recognizable logos (and what they cost to be designed—which may surprise you).

The logo that you design may be the decisive factor between a potential customer noticing your game on the shelf or passing it by. Of course, you want more than just a "potential customer!"

The Design Process

The process of designing a logo involves some research and conceptualizing. When developing your logo, whether you are the artist or are directing the artist, you need to ask yourself a few questions, including the following:

- Who is the logo's intended audience (or audiences), and what do you wish to convey to them with your logo? The answers to these questions will go a long way toward determining the logo's overall style.

- Where will the logo be used? The answer to this question can help you determine the logo design's constraints and production values.

Who Is the Audience?

Along with what your logo represents (such as a game genre), your logo's intended audience helps to determine the content and style of the logo. A logo for a fantasy game is going to have a different feel from the logo for, say, a god game or a racing game. And a logo for a children's game is going to be different from the logo for a game aimed at, say, teenagers.

Where Will the Logo Be Used?

Where the logo will be used will affect your design and production decisions. Logos used on corporate stationery have different requirements, for example, than do logos to be used in the game's packaging and advertisements.

Letterhead, Envelopes, and Business Cards

If you are designing a corporate logo, stationery will be more of a concern. For a full-blown game logo that is supposed to be a piece of art gracing the cover of a box, you may not need to worry about how well it translates into a small, one- or two-color logo for letterheads and envelopes. For corporate or company logos, however, your design should be simple and recognizable because it will grace your letterhead prominently.

Like your letterhead, your business card should feature your logo prominently (and also contain all the same contact information). There are many types of business cards—horizontal, vertical, and even odd-shaped ones.

Packages, Magazine Ads, In-Store Displays, and More!

When you start to design product logos, you should be more concerned with the advertising venues where large, full-color versions of your logo will be printed. These displays are an excellent reason for creating high-color, high-resolution versions of your logo. It is common for game logos to be printed in full color on the box and in print advertisements (of course) but also on large banners for trade shows. Finally, if you are fortunate enough to develop the next Doom or Tomb Raider, you need to consider the billboard and movie screen venues as well.

> **Remember to Check the Basics**
>
> Experience says, "Before spending all the money on printing, make sure that you include all necessary contact information." This information includes company name, address, phone number, fax number, email address, and web address (and spell check it!). Also, contact the United States Postal Service to make sure that your layout will work in their automated systems (**www.usps.gov**).

What Are the Elements of a Logo?

A good corporate logo doesn't need to be fancy or complex. In fact, it should not be, for the production reasons given in the preceding section as well as the fact that you probably want the company to appear as an efficient, no-nonsense entity.

For the game, however, you will want the logo to convey whatever will appeal to the target audience. Although most companies, even game companies, usually want to appear as serious and businesslike, the logo for a product can be silly or adventurous, or any other message you want to convey about the product that may or may not be the same message you want to convey about your company.

Simplicity

If you are designing for a straightforward, no-nonsense type of company, then a simple logo may be what's right for the job. If the job calls for corporate elegance, a font or simple symbol (even if you are an incredible artist and a huge H. R. Giger fan—go to **www.hrgiger.com** for the details) may be what is needed. If appeal to children or some style other than a huge black-metal, pipe-laden, woman warrior is needed, then you may be off-course. A good company logo is usually simple in design, appealing in color, and clearly understandable as to what it represents.

Art and Marketing

A logo (or logotype) can be initials, a name, a symbol, or some combination of those elements. For computer games, logos are often much more—even works of art. In this chapter, you will learn how to create some of those fancy logos. However, before getting into that, look further at what goes into a logo. Along with basing your design on game genre, target audience, intended usage, and artistic considerations, you may want to think about designing with additional marketing factors in mind.

Laws of Design

The best book I have found on logo design is *The 22 Immutable Laws of Branding*, by Al Ries and Laura Ries (Harper Collins, 1998; ISBN: 0887309372). In it, the authors discuss many aspects of logo design as it applies to marketing, and among the most applicable here are what the authors call the laws of shape and color. These aren't laws of physics or anything like that; these are guidelines that the authors have found to be effective in strengthening the brand—the identity and market presence—of a company or product. Having a strong brand helps to distinguish your product from your competitors' products. Remember that standing out from your competitors is one step on the way to trouncing them!

The Law of Shape states that a logo should be designed to fit the eyes, meaning that because the human eyes are binocular and side-by-side, the ideal shape for a logotype is horizontal. This translates into proportions of roughly two units wide and one unit high. A two-by-one horizontal shape will provide the maximum impact for your logotype. These proportions will translate well wherever the logo is used—on billboards, brochures, letterheads, advertisements, home pages, or business cards. Remember that readability is still more important than a fancy typeface that expresses the attribute of a product or company more than it allows the consumer to read it, especially when you are designing a new, never-before-seen logo.

The Law of Color states that a logo should use a color that is the opposite of the company's or the product's major competitor. This will make the logo distinctive, but care should still be taken when choosing a color because different colors mean various things to people. For example, the following list shows some of the psychological and cultural implications of some colors:

- Red is the color of energy and excitement. In the West, red is an in-your-face color. In China, however, the color red connotes joy and happiness.

- Blue is the opposite. Blue is peaceful and tranquil. Blue is a laid-back color.

- In the world of brands, red is a retail color used to attract attention. Blue is a corporate color used to communicate stability. For example, Coca-Cola red and IBM blue.

- The other primary colors are in-between. Orange is more like red than blue. Green is more like blue than red.

- Yellow is a neutral color. But it is also the brightest color. (Its brightness is the reason yellow is often used to communicate "caution," as in yellow traffic and construction lights.)

According to *The 22 Immutable Laws of Branding*, the largest companies have the first choice of colors and will usually select the best color that is most symbolic of the category they are in. John Deere is the leading brand of farm tractor, and they picked green—the color of grass, trees, and agriculture—as their logo's signature color. Color consistency over the long term is important. Some colors are burned into our minds; think of Coca-Cola red, Caterpillar yellow, United Parcel Service brown, and IBM blue. What Big Blue did for IBM, a big, bold color might do for your logo.

Color

Because colors often have a profound impact on viewers, consider that psychologists agree that the colors red and orange produce excitation, dark blue induces comfort and relaxation, and so on. To choose appropriate colors, think about the personality you want to convey for your business. Primary colors are wrong for most high-priced professionals, while silver and black wouldn't fit the fun image you want for a kids' gym.

Additionally, consider how you might extend the color scheme of the logo beyond the original context (usually, at first, stationery and business cards). Do you think that you will use the logo on clothing, stenciled on a van, or stamped onto calculators or clocks? A lot of people don't wear certain colors (yellow, pink) well, while other colors (light blue, gray) don't stand out well from a distance. Bright neon hues might not match the black/silver/beige of technology objects. Consider all these aspects whether you are designing a corporate or a game logo.

Just as people's personalities are continually evolving, the colors they prefer also vary. The colors you enjoy the most could possibly change as a result of your age, sex, or a myriad of other environmental and social factors. Today, there are many theories that link an individual's color preference to personality type. It may be worth your time to study not only your audience, but also what their color preferences may be.

Costs

Finally, you may need to consider the costs involved in the printing process. Selecting common colors the printer has on hand and limiting the number of colors (including black as one color) will keep costs down wherever you use the logo in production.

Trademark Your Logo

After the logo is designed, it is a good idea to consider legally protecting it. I mention this here for three reasons: First, a lot can be done fairly simply on this matter, and there is no reason that you shouldn't understand the basics (it may make you look good, too!). Second, in my experience, people are always asking the artist about this topic. Third, chances are you will find yourself involved with a small and/or inexperienced group that may not think to take care of this little detail. And it's important to take care of; I have seen some small and talented groups blackmailed by predators that do nothing but look for properties that are unprotected that they can trademark, copyright, and purchase the domain name for and then try to sell these properties back to the creators.

The following information is designed to be general advice about trademarks. For definitive information, contact a trademark attorney.

Register Your Company Name First

The law does not always require it, but make sure that no one else is already using a selected name before you design your logo and print a thousand tee shirts. It's a good idea to register your desired business name in the states you plan to do business in.

Without a Trademark You Are Still Protected

Just by using your logo on your letterhead, business cards, and in other places, you automatically have some trademark protection, even if you don't officially register your logo with a state or federal entity. So you don't need to panic if you haven't registered your trademark yet. Still, registering it will make it easier to protect, so don't wait too long.

Register Your Logo with Your State

Usually, you can obtain a trademark for your logo at your state's Department of Commerce (call your local office to learn the details). To trademark a logo is the best way to document that you are officially using the logo. Then, if another business tries to use your logo (or a similar one), you will have proof that you had first rights to the logo.

Register Your Logo with the Federal Government

Most businesses register trademarks only within the states in which they do most of their business, but that trend is changing rapidly with the advent of the Internet and the globalization of commerce. Whether you are planning to do business in one state, a number of states, or worldwide, federal registration is a good idea. Contact the U.S. Department of Commerce for more information or go to their Web site at **www.doc.gov**.

After you have an idea of the audience and the product for which you are developing a logo, you are ready to start creating that logo. Here, you will concentrate on the game-type logos that are more like works of art and are not the simple fonts and one-color logos often developed for corporations.

Creating Game Logos

Game logos are fun to make because they are like works of art. You usually don't need to limit yourself to a range of colors or to be constrained in your design to a simple symbol that captures the essence of the product. If you are making a logo for a fantasy game, you can have a large metal sword and glowing magical runes. If you are making a logo for a futuristic game, you can have corroded metal and weird lighting. It is a chance to be creative—and what artist wouldn't jump at the chance to really create something?

Start by going through a project to make a logo for a fantasy game.

PROJECT Creating the Typical Fantasy Logo

Here, you will create a typical fantasy logo. I say "typical" because there are elements that are typically found in a fantasy game: swords, shields, magical effects, and golden stuff. So, you will make a logo featuring all of these elements. You first need to make the sword, then the shield, and finally the lettering.

> **Note:** Registering your logo as a trademark is only the first step in protecting it. You also have to monitor its use and make sure that no one is infringing upon it. If you fail to police your logo's use (if you repeatedly let people use it without your permission), you can lose the rights to it. There have been cases of such trademarks as Kleenex and Trampoline being lost since their use was not protected.

> **Note:** Many of the following exercises may produce very large files. You may want to copy and flatten your images at different stages to make them more workable on your system. All of these exercises are done in Photoshop.

Making the Fantasy Sword

Breaking down the logo into its elements, you will create a sword, a shield, and then some gold lettering. First, you will make the sword. To do so, take these steps:

1. Open a new Photoshop file and make it 800×800 pixels. Make the background white. Start by dividing the canvas in half, horizontally and then vertically, using the guides.

2. Use the Polygonal Lasso to drag out a shape of half the sword blade and fill it with a light gray. Figure 4.1 shows the half-sword blade I created, but you can get creative with your version of a sword blade. The trick is to keep the sword blade in a pleasing shape, which takes some experimenting. Because you are creating half the sword first (later, you'll mirror it), it is a bit harder to visualize the final blade. Some experimenting may be in order. Make sure that the center of the blade is straight and snapped to the center guideline.

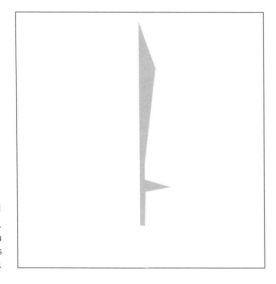

Figure 4.1
Here is half a sword blade. Mine looks like this, but you can experiment with shapes and complexity.

3. Now, add the metal look to the sword. Because metal is most easily recognized by the reflections it creates, we will simulate a diffuse reflection of light by rendering lighting effects. Run the Render Lighting filter (Render|Lighting Effects), and try to get it close to Figure 4.2.

Don't worry about getting your image to look exactly like mine. The trick here is to learn to get the effect you are going for. You may want to make a darker, more sinister sword or a brighter sword with more light on the blade. Play with the effects of the light. The Render Lighting filter allows for a great deal of variation. You can adjust light type, brightness, shininess, color, and more.

Figure 4.2
The Render lighting filter makes
the metal look shiny, but you may
want to make it look darker.

4. Now you need to copy the layer containing the blade half, and flip it horizontally (Edit|Transform|Flip Horizontal). Use the guides to line the blade halves up exactly. Make sure there is no gap between the blade halves. You may have to turn off your guides (by using the Ctrl+; short-cut key combination) to do this and then zoom in with the Magnify tool to be sure.

5. To give more depth to the blade, apply the Render Lighting filter to this half of the sword as well. Doing this on both halves of the blade separately makes the lighting look like it is hitting two distinct surfaces and strengthens the illusion of a sword with a thinner blade. Keep your settings from the previous Render Lighting, but play with the position of the light. So instead of simply reapplying the filter as is, go back through the menu selections Filter|Render|Lighting Effects and move the light around for a better lighting effect on the blade. I found moving it lower on the blade makes for a better effect.

   When you are pleased with the lighting on the blade, merge the layers with the blade halves together.

6. To make the blades look a bit more realistic, like they have been used on a battlefield, start by applying the filter Brush Strokes|Spatter and the filter Distort|Ocean Ripple with their default settings. When you have finished, it more closely resembles a worn and hand-hammered blade. You can also apply the Bevel and Emboss layer effect with the Inner Bevel option checked to give the blade a deeper edge if you plan to use the sword in larger format.

7. At this point, add some decorative detail to the blade. Create a new layer named "Sword Detail"; set the Mode to Color Burn and the Opacity to 60%. What I did here was to start by simply drawing a black line down the middle of the blade. Next go to the Blade layer; select the area around the blades and invert the selection. You will have everything inside the blade shape selected. Now go back to the Sword Detail layer, contract the selection (Select|Modify|Contract; 8 pixels), and stroke the selection (Edit|Stroke; 3 pixels). After doing this, you will wind up with a really cool blade edge decoration. Repeat the above process a time or two more to make multiple lines on the blade.

8. Next, you need to make the hilt of the sword. Create a new layer called "Hilt" and load the metal texture created in Chapter 2 (metal.psd) in this layer. Use the Circular Selection tool and draw a flat, wide oval. Use the Selection tool and the hard-edged eraser to create your hilt design. The thing to keep in mind here is symmetry and balance. Keep your hilt design balanced.

9. You can detail the hilt as you did the blade. Simply copy the "Sword Detail" layer, so the effects settings are already there just as you need them, and name the layer "Hilt Detail". Select everything on this layer and then delete the selection to get rid of the pixels from the other layer. Now repeat the process in Step 7. Do this only to the hilt, and when you contract your selection, do it only six pixels because the hilt is thinner than the blade. You can see what I did to the hilt in Figure 4.3.

Figure 4.3
The hilt on the sword.

10. Now to create the handle or grip, make a new layer named "Grip". Turn your guides on, if they are not on already, and make a small oval-shaped selection. Center it on the guide and it put right under the hilt. Fill the selection with a light brown, and you should have an image like Figure 4.4.

Figure 4.4
Here is the shape of the first part of the grip.

11. Now use the layer effects Bevel and Emboss. Select Inner Bevel, and turn both the Blur and the Depth up to 20.

12. Use a hard-edged eraser and erase the curve from the top and bottom portions of the grip piece. Hold the Shift key to make the deletion straight. Then, duplicate the layer six to eight times, depending on the thickness you made the grip piece. Line up all the layers, and then merge them.

13. To make the grip taper downward as it does on real swords, use the Edit|Transform|Skew option. Finally I added a bit of noise to the grip (Add Filter|Noise|Noise; Monochromatic, Gaussian, Amount: 12). Your sword should look like Figure 4.5.

14. Save this file. You will need to open it again later in the exercise.

Figure 4.5
The finished sword.

Adding the Shield

But what's a sword without a shield to go with it? To create the shield, take the following steps:

1. Open a new file and make its size 800×800 pixels. Make the background white. Start by dividing the canvas in half horizontally and vertically so we can center our shield.

2. Use the round selection tool and drag out a circular selection that fills the middle of the canvas. After you have done this exercise all the way through, you can make the selection almost any shape you want for the shield, but to begin, make it a small round shape. After you have mastered the techniques, you will be better able to use odd shapes. Since we will be fitting the swords around this shield later in this exercise, you also need to not make the shield too large. Finally, use the metal texture from Chapter 2 to fill this area.

3. Open the file "Door.psd" from Chapter 3 and copy the wood layer into this image. Cut out a plank from the door and center it in the image. Duplicate the layer and rotate the second plank 90 degrees so you have a cross, as shown in Figure 4.6.

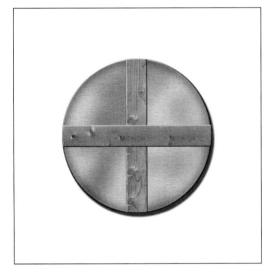

Figure 4.6
Here is the shield with crossed wooden beams.

4. Go to the "shield" layer and select the area around the shield. Go back to each of the wooden planks layers, and delete the portions of wood extending beyond the shield. The wooden cross should now end precisely at the edge of the shield.

5. Copy the original metal layer. Place it on top of all the others, name it "cap", and change the Depth and the Blur in the Bevel and Emboss effects both to 20. Make a small round selection (holding the Shift key to make it perfectly round) and center it in the middle of the shield by using the guides. Invert the selection (right-click and choose Invert Selection from the context menu), and delete the outer portion of the metal. You should now have a round cap in the middle of the shield.

6. Duplicate the original shield layer again and name it "Outer Ring". Place this layer on top of all the others. Use the circular selection tool to chop out the middle of the shield. Once again use the Shift key to make the selection perfectly round, and use the guides to line it up in the center of the shield. This will form an outer ring on the shield. I dropped the Drop Shadow from the original layer effects and added an Inner Glow for effect.

7. Add some metal studs, as you did on the door in Chapter 3. Create a new layer and name it "Studs". Apply the Bevel and Emboss effects (Depth 20 and Blur at 6). You can use the grip or some guidelines to paint in the studs in exact places on the shield. Use a hard paintbrush with a light gray for the studs.

8. Now age the shield a bit. Merge all the layers, open the file "dirt pan" from the companion CD-ROM, and put it in a layer above the shield. Set the layer to Color Burn and the Opacity to about 60. Remove the area of drippy material from around the shield by selecting the area around the shield and then going to the dirt layer and deleting it.

9. Finally, open the sword image and paste the sword over the shield. If you think the sword you created was too squat or not proportional, use the Free Transform tool (Control+T) and stretch it a bit. Center the sword over the shield and use Free Transform to rotate it to a dramatic angle.

   Copy the layer, flip it horizontally (Edit|Transform|Flip Horizontally), and apply a Drop Shadow to the swords. See Figure 4.7 for the final shield image.

That is the shield with crossed swords. Next, you will learn how to add the magical lettering to the logo.

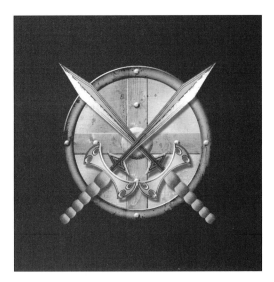

Figure 4.7
Here is the final shield image with crossed swords.

Installing New Fonts

If you need to install the font, first close Photoshop. In Windows 2000, for example, Select Start|Settings|Control Panel. Now, right-click on the Fonts selection and, from the context menu that appears, click on Open. Now, select File|Install New Font. Browse for the location in which you stored the font file and select it. You will need to restart Photoshop so it will load your new fonts.

Adding the Magic Gold Lettering

Adding the magical lettering is made easier because you can go on the Internet and download hundreds of free fonts for use in your logos. One of my favorite sites is Fonts & Things (**www.fontsnthings.com**); here you can find hundreds of fonts that are free to use. For this logo, I chose the Barbecue font, a freeware font by Harold Lohner. Always check the font's accompanying readme file, however, to make sure that the font is truly free, for both personal and commercial use.

To add the magical letters, take the following steps:

1. Install the Barbecue font on your computer (see the note on installing fonts). Then select the font in Photoshop (with the Text tool active), and type your text. Make the text white.

2. Then add the Outer Glow effect, and make the glow yellow (Normal Mode, Blur 36, and Intensity 300). You can use any font you wish here if you are unable to get the Barbecue font, or you want a different look for your logo.

3. After experimenting with font and glow colors, change the background of the image to black (see Figure 4.8).

Figure 4.8
The final logo with magical letters.

Creating the Acid-Eaten, Apocalyptic Metal Logo

This logo is actually an easy one to create. It's similar to those found on futuristic, post-nuclear holocaust games.

1. Create a new 800×800-pixel image and make the background black. Divide the image in half with the guides.

2. Load up the "brushed metal" texture from Chapter 2 on a new layer. Use the Image|Adjust|Brightness/Contrast to darken it a bit.

3. Select the Text tool and type your text. Make the text color black. I used the Crass font available from Fonts & Things, but you can use any font you want—the thicker the font, the better, for effects such as this. Select a letter of text with the Magic Wand and then right–mouse-click and choose Similar from the context menu. Invert the selection, then go to the metal layer and delete the metal from around the letters.

4. Copy the original text layer and render it using the Layer|Type|Render Layer option. Select the text; then right-click and choose Similar so that all the text is selected. Now render clouds (Filter|Render|Clouds). This procedure will fill the letters with the cloud pattern. Apply the filter Brush Strokes|Spatter to this layer to make the clouds look a bit more like beaten metal.

5. To make the metal look acid-eaten, use the Magic Wand and select a portion of color, any color, from the layer of text we just created in Step 4. Right-click in the selection and choose Similar. Here, you want to get a selection that randomly covers the text. Not too much and not too little, and you do not want a selection that covers one half the text but not the other.

If you are having trouble making a good selection, an alternate way is to make the first selection using the Magic Wand and then hold down Shift and make selections at random spots on the image. Delete the selected portion of the clouds. Copy your layer effects from the metal layer to this layer to see the full effect.

6. Now copy the upper layer of eaten metal and apply the Mezzotint filter to it (Pixelate|Mezzotint; long lines). Set the layer mode to Color Burn and the Opacity to 50%. You can run the Filter Spatter (Brush Strokes|Spatter) to chew up the top layer of metal more, and you can also colorize the metal using the Image|Adjust|Hue Saturation options.

   For a last touch, I added a green outer glow to the top layer (Mode Normal, Blur 16 and Intensity 104). This added the eerie nuclear effect that made the logo jump.

After you complete the preceding steps, you have the basic acid-eaten metal logo, as shown in Figure 4.9.

Figure 4.9
This is the acid-eaten metal effect on text.

PROJECT Creating the Basic "Carved from Stone" Logo

Making the carved-from-stone logo is fairly easy. The stone effect you will be creating here will look more like the Flintstones, but by simply altering the font, the stone shape, and the color, and by applying other filters, you can make variations that will have drastically different looks and feels.

To create the basic carved-from-stone logo, follow these steps:

1. Open a new image 800×800 pixels and make the background black. Drag out two guidelines for vertical and horizontal centering.

2. Load the stone texture from Chapter 2, and place it in the second layer and name it "Stone".

3. Now duplicate the Stone layer and name it "Stone Text". You should have applied to this layer the Bevel and Emboss effects (Depth 5 and Blur 5).

4. Use a thick font like Arial Black and type in your text. Center it in the image. Select the text by using the Magic Wand, and Invert the selection.

5. Go to the Stone Text layer, and delete the stone from around the letter selection.

6. Apply to the Stone Text layer the Inner Glow effect (Blur 24, Intensity 317). Also apply the Bevel and Emboss effects (Inner Bevel; Depth 20, Blur 5, and change the direction to Down). The stone is looking pretty nice as is, but to give the stone a rough carved look, you can do some more. See Figure 4.10 for the current version of the stone logo.

Figure 4.10

The beginnings of the stone logo as carved by a modern machine.

7. To make your stone look really carved on and a bit old, first burn some stains into it. Now, create a new layer and name it "Stains". Place this layer under the Stone Text layer, but above the Stone layer. Set the mode to Color Burn and the Opacity to 29%. Use a thick, soft brush, and Airbrush some black wear patterns on the stone.

8. Now you can go back to the Stone Text layer and make that stone look more like it was carved out by cavemen than by a modern machine. Start by applying the Ripple filter (Filter|Distort|Ripple; Amount 150, Medium). This makes the edges all uneven with a rough-hewn appearance. Now apply the Craquelure Filter (Texture|Craquelure|Crack Spacing 11, Crack Depth 2, Crack Brightness 5) to make the inner stone look chipped away; see Figure 4.11.

Figure 4.11

The final stone log, rough-hewn and hand carved.

You can also make a variation of the stone logo by using a different font and adding some glowing effects.

1. Start by duplicating the stone logo file from the previous exercise.

2. Go to the Stone layer, and use a hard eraser to make the lines a bit straighter. Don't use the selection tool, as that will make the stone look machine carved. Use your own hand and get a slightly uneven edge to the stone.

3. Now choose Image|Adjust|Hue/Saturation and check the Colorize checkbox. Adjust the stone so it looks a bit reddish.

4. For the font, I used the Cartouche font (freeware font by pearlygates, available on Fonts & Things). Make the font color black and type in your text.

5. Select the text by using the Magic Wand, and Invert the selection. Go to the Stone Text layer, and delete the stone from around the letter selection.

6. Apply to the Stone Text layer the Inner Glow effect (Blur 24, Intensity 317). Also apply the Bevel and Emboss effects (Inner Bevel; Depth 20, Blur 5, and change the direction to Down).

7. To make this lettering different, you can make it look more like gold leaf than like rough-hewn stone. Start by colorizing the stone yellow (Image|Adjust|Hue/Saturation; check the Colorize box; and use Hue 61, Saturation 47, Lightness +14).

8. To make the surface look like gold leaf, use Spatter (Brush Strokes|Spatter; Spray Radius 10 and Smoothness 5). Make sure you press the D key to set your colors to the default (Foreground black and Background white). Adjust the Brightness and Contrast of this layer both up by 20.

9. For a final and magical effect, you can duplicate the Stone Text layer and name it "Stone Text Copy". Clear the effects from this layer by right-clicking and choosing Clear Effects from the context menu.

10. Remove the color from this layer by using Desaturate (Image|Adjust|Desaturate). Run the filter Radial Blur (Blur|Radial Blur; Amount 60, Blur Method Zoom).

11. Set the layer mode to Hard Light. Use the Free Transform function (Ctrl+T) to make this image fill the frame, but do not go out of the image frame.

12. Use a large soft eraser to erase the middlemost and brightest portion of this layer, right in front of the letters, but leave a little of this effect overlapping the edges. You can see the final stone logo variation in Figure 4.12.

Figure 4.12

A variation on the stone logo that has a drastically different look and feel.

PROJECT Creating a Spell-Book Cover Logo

For the final project, you will create the front of a spell book, an old leather tome with metal end caps, odd symbols, and other cool details.

1. Open a new file and make it 800×800 pixels. Set up your horizontal and vertical guides.

2. First, you will create the leather cover. Create a new layer and name it "Leather Cover". Drag out a selection that's about the proportion of a book cover, and have it use up most of the image space. Center the selection by using the guides.

3. Fill this selection with black, and then add noise to it (Noise|Add Noise; Monochromatic, Gaussian; Amount 30).

4. To create the leather texture, we have to emboss it (Filter|Stylize|Emboss; Height 2, Amount 160). Also render some Difference Clouds (Render|Difference Clouds). I had to run them a few times to get the effect I liked.

5. You can also colorize the cover (Image|Adjust|Hue/Saturation: select the Colorize checkbox, Hue 27, Saturation 35, and Lightness +6). Play with these settings if you like. I chose to produce a brownish hue for my cover.

6. Apply the Bevel and Emboss effects to this layer (Bevel and Emboss; Inner Bevel, Depth 15, Blur 5). These selections will give the book an edge and some depth.

7. You can also create some quick-and-easy decorations that will add a lot to the cover. First, create a new layer named "Cover Decorations" right above the cover, and set the mode to Color Burn. Drag out a rectangular selection that lines up with the inner edges of the book, and center this selection by using the guides. Now stroke the line (Edit|Stroke; 8 pixels) and apply the Bevel Emboss effect to it (Emboss: direction Down, use the defaults otherwise).

8. One last touch: Create a text layer, type the uppercase letters "ABCDEFGHI", and choose the Wingdings font. You will see a large number of hands. Set Layer Mode to Hard Light and take the Opacity down to about 65. Position these hands across the top of the cover. Duplicate the layer and drag it down to the bottom of the cover.

That is our basic mottled leather cover, as you can see in Figure 4.13.

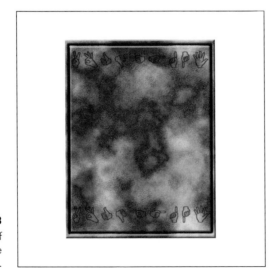

Figure 4.13

The basic leather cover of the Spell Book with some decoration applied.

9. Now you will create some decorative metal caps for the corners of the book. Open the metal image "metal.psd" from Chapter 2 and paste it into a new layer named "Caps". Make a copy of this layer, as you will be using the metal material a lot in the following steps. To make life easier both on you and your machine, hide the layer when it's not in use.

10. Start the cap by cutting out a small piece of metal about the size you want the cap to be. Then use the hard-edged eraser, the selection tool, or both to sculpt a cap you like. You can see what I did in Figure 4.14. I actually used two layers and sculpted two pieces to fit together to form the cap.

11. When you have a cap you like, copy the layer and flip the cap horizontally and move it to the other corner of the book. Repeat the process until you have four caps on each corner of the book.

12. If you used more than one layer, as I did, to create your corner caps, then it is best if you do not merge the cap layers. Duplicate each of them and flip them and move them separately. The reason is that the light and shadow effects of the Layer Effects will change with the positioning of the layer. If you flatten a layer and move it, the effects will not respond and adjust, and it will be noticeable. For example, if you merge the layers, and the highlights and shadows are frozen in place, then they will be at odds with the original version when you copy and flip it.

13. After all of the cap pieces are in place, you can link the layers and merge them.

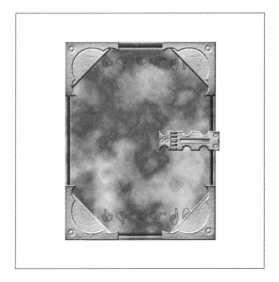

Figure 4.14
The spell book's corner caps, made from a metal texture and some digital sculpting.

14. Use the same method as defined in Step 9 to create a latch for the book. Make a copy of the metal layer, and use the erasers and selection tools to sculpt the layer. One trick I used was to zoom in and use a 1-pixel eraser to erase small lines that give the impression of a hinge in the latch. I also used a lot of guides to help me get the erasers and selections perfectly lined up as I sculpted.

15. When you are finished with the metal caps and the latch, merge the layers together. Apply the Craquelure filter to the metal (Texture|Craquelure; Spacing 34, Depth 1, Brightness 1) for a rough, beaten metal look.

16. One more touch to the metal—bolts. Create a layer named "Bolts" and simply paint round bolts in the corners of the caps and on the latch. Apply the Bevel and Emboss filter (Pillow Emboss; Depth 11, Blur 8).

17. Now would be a good time to make a copy of the unflattened file. In the copy, merge all the layers except the background. Turn off the background and use the Merge Visible command.

18. To dirty up the book, open the "dirty pan.jpg" file and put it on its own layer above the book. Set the layer mode to Overlay and the Opacity to 50%. Position it as you like. Go to the book layer and select the area around the book. Return to the Dirty Pan layer and delete the area around the book.

19. Create another new layer right above the book and name it "Darken". Set the mode to Color Burn and the Opacity to about 30%. Use a large, soft airbrush and the color black to burn the edges of the book.

20. The text here is simply a text layer with the Times New Roman font in boldface. Make the text yellow. Duplicate the layer. On the bottom layer, apply the Pillow Emboss effect (Depth and Blur both 10), and on the top layer, apply the Inner Bevel effect (Depth 12 and Blur 4). This is a way around the limitations of the layer effects in Photoshop. If you want a hard-edged text set in a soft pillow emboss, this is the way to do it since Photoshop doesn't allow that combination of effects.

21. Optionally, if you made the fantasy logo previously in this chapter, you can paste it into its own layer above the cover and emboss it in, and you can add a Wingdings font symbol. A black font that is embossed into the cover can look really ominous. And here is your spell book logo in Figure 4.15.

Figure 4.15
The final spell book logo.

Moving On

In this chapter , you learned about making logos, a task often asked of a game art specialist. If you as the artist are also expected to know how to legally protect the logo and know the audience, you are well on your way. If, however, you are the lucky artist who has landed the fun job of creating a game logo, I offer my congratulations—you've arrived.

In Chapter 5, you will look at the menu and interface portion of the game. It is not just creating new icons or picking a font, as many treat this process. Understanding menu and interface issues is important to the success of a game.

Chapter 5

Menus and Interfaces: The Gateways to the Game World

Sure, you can make a menu look good; make a few buttons, choose a cool font, stick that cool logo you created somewhere on the screen, and you're set. Designing a menu that works well, however, is a bit more involved.

Introduction

In this chapter, I will discuss the rules of menu and interface design as well as the process of breaking out and creating game menus. Just as you had to draw a distinction between the game logo and the corporate logo, you also must draw a distinction between the conventional GUI (graphical user interface) and the game interface. The traditional graphical user interface for applications or operating systems—such as Windows or the Macintosh OS—is different from the interface for such games as Diablo, Doom, or Civilization. However, an understanding of proper interface design is not only helpful, but also imperative for a good game. The title of this chapter calls the menu "the gateway to a world," but it is a gateway only if it is a good menu that is well designed and implemented; otherwise, it is a locked gate.

And now, the "Heuristics and Evaluation" sidebar presents a new word—and the definition of that word—for your vocabulary.

Ten Usability Principles

Basically, what game artists need to know can be summed up in 10 easy rules. Nielsen and Molich did just that in their paper, "Heuristic Analysis," which was developed in 1990 (Molich and Nielsen, 1990). Their 10 objectives for user interface design are as follows.

1. *Visibility of system status*—The system should always keep its users informed about what is going on, through appropriate feedback and within reasonable time.

2. *Match between [the] system and the real world*—The system should speak the users' language, with words, phrases and concepts familiar to the users, rather than system-oriented terms. Follow real-world conventions, making information appear in a natural and logical order.

   Here's an example of violating this rule: In early versions of a modem application, you could have looked everywhere for instructions on dialing a phone number so that you could download files from someone. Nowhere in the text, contents, or index was there a mention of "dialing." The terminology the developers used—"Connect to a session"—was the culprit. You didn't dial a number; you "connected to a session." Now, that's not exactly intuitive.

3. *User control and freedom*—Users often choose system functions by mistake and will need a clearly marked "emergency exit" to leave the unwanted state without having to go through an extended *dialogue* (informational text that may or may not be found in the classic "Windows" dialog boxes). The system should support Undo and Redo commands.

Heuristics and Evaluation

Heuristics—The informal, judgmental knowledge of an application area that constitutes the "rules of good operational design judgment" in the field. Heuristics also encompass the knowledge of how to solve problems efficiently and effectively, how to plan steps in solving a complex problem, how to improve performance, and so forth. From the Greek—"*Heuriskein*, to discover." *The Decision Support Systems Glossary*, which you can find at **www.dssresources.com/glossary**.

Yeah, even I have a hard time digesting that one. So what's a "heuristic"? According to Perkins—Perkins, DN (1981) *The Mind's Best Work: A New Psychology of Creative Thinking*. Cambridge, MA: Harvard University Press—heuristics is a rule of thumb that often helps in solving a certain class of problems but makes no guarantees. In other words, there are no guarantees in interface design, only principles and guidelines. In computer science a "heuristic" is often contrasted with an "algorithm"—the latter is a precise set of steps that is guaranteed to work under the specified conditions. Many problems can be adequately addressed with heuristics even though there is no verifiable algorithm for nontrivial cases.

For evaluation, there's yet another way of looking at heuristics: "Heuristic evaluation (Nielsen and Molich, 1990; Nielsen 1994) is a usability engineering method for finding the usability problems in a user interface design so that they can be attended to as part of an iterative design process. Heuristic evaluation involves having a small set of evaluators examine the interface and judge its compliance with recognized usability principles (the "heuristics")." — from "How to Conduct a Heuristic Evaluation" at **www.useit.com/papers/heuristic/heuristic_evaluation.html**.

4. *Consistency and standards*—Users should not have to wonder whether different words, situations, or actions mean the same thing. Follow platform and game genre conventions.

5. *Error prevention*—Even better than good error messages is a careful design that prevents a problem from occurring in the first place.

6. *Recognition rather than recall*—Make objects, actions, and options visible. The user should not have to remember information from one part of the dialogue to another. Instructions for use of the system should be visible or easily retrievable whenever appropriate.

7. *Flexibility and efficiency of use*—Accelerators (or things such as hot keys and other less than obvious commands unseen by the novice user) can speed the interaction for the expert user so that the system can cater to both inexperienced and experienced users. Always allow users to tailor frequent actions.

8. *Aesthetic and minimalist design*—Dialogues (and dialog boxes) should not contain information that is irrelevant or rarely needed. Every extra unit of information in a dialogue competes with the relevant units of information and diminishes their relative visibility.

9. *Error recognition and recovery*—Help users recognize, diagnose, and recover from errors. Error messages should be expressed in plain language (no codes), precisely indicate the problem, and constructively suggest a solution.

10. *Help and documentation*—Even though it is better if the system can be used without documentation, it may be necessary to provide help and documentation. This kind of information should be easy to search, focused on the user's task, list concrete steps to be carried out, and not be too large.

Now these "Ten Usability Heuristics" are the basic rules that apply to not only the interfaces and menus you may devise in a game, but also to game design. Several of these usability heuristics touch on areas that are meant to guide the application designer. In traditional software development, there is no hard line between the application and the interface. In Word and more traditional applications, for example, you tend to think of the application as a collective package. In games, however, the pervasive feeling is that you must go through the menu to get to the game "world," and the interface is always in the way. This should never be the case. Later in this chapter, you will look at some principles of menu and interface design that you as an artist should know, because (as with logos) you will most likely be expected to know this stuff or at least contribute—and you will appear as though you know what you are talking about in meetings when you spit out the word "heuristics."

Does all this mean you must be less creative? No. In fact, it's the creative solution that is often the best in fulfilling these objectives.

The 10 Usability Heuristics as They Apply to Games

A game is supposed to be fun, and needlessly navigating interfaces is not fun. I'm not discussing navigating an elaborate inventory system or a complex mission system, complete with maps and character biographies—that might be part of the game play and a fun aspect of the game as well. By "not fun," I mean being forced to navigate an elaborate inventory system that is poorly organized and that detracts from the game, especially when that inventory system may not be needed. Or worse, not having an inventory system when one is desperately needed. The sad truth is that the interface is almost never treated as an area that needs careful design and that is integral to the product; the interface is usually an afterthought and is considered something that you can patch together after the game has been developed.

> **Note:** I chose the game Unreal Tournament to use as a consistent example throughout this chapter. It follows all of the 10 principles.

In this section, you will look at the 10 usability heuristics as they apply to game design. Keep in mind that some of these usability heuristics apply to the game artist more than others do, so some are discussed at length and some are not.

1. Visibility of System Status

The system should always keep users informed about what is going on, through appropriate feedback, and within reasonable time.

In game terms, a lack of status information will cause game players to have such reactions as, "I just cast a spell and nothing seemed to happen. It was a spell of invisibility, but I don't know if I'm invisible," "How many rockets do I have left?" or "Where is that darn magic elf foot I just clicked on, where did it go?"

During the game play, the interface should be as minimal (non-intrusive) as possible but readily available to the players when they need it. Your users should feel in control, but not responsible for everything; neither should they feel out of touch with the character and the goings-on in the world. So, the old days of the HUD (heads-up display) or in-game menu taking up half the screen are gone. Now it is expected more and more that a specific portion of the interface will be available when it's needed—and only when it's needed. For example, suppose that a character jumps into water and swims; only then does the "holding breath" status bar pop up, letting the player know that they have a limited amount of time to be under water before "drowning." When the player is under water, the bar reduces in size, indicating they are running out of air. If they stay too long, they drown; if they come up for air, the bar disappears. If they dive back in the water, the bar reappears with a full air supply. Now, if that status bar was always there, even though the player was under water maybe 10 percent of the time in the game (and, for example, trudging through a desert the other 90 percent), the "drowning bar" would clutter the screen needlessly and make a system status update hard for the player to interpret. Figures 5.1 to 5.3 show some good examples of the HUD, an in-game menu and an "as-needed" status message.

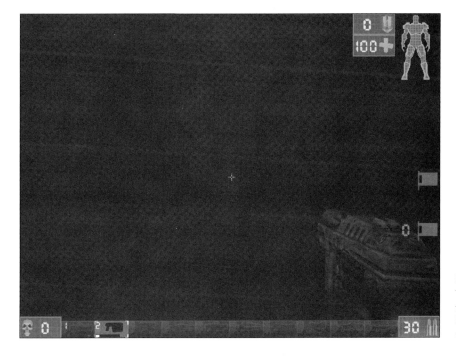

Figure 5.1

The HUD (heads-up display) in the game Unreal Tournament. Notice that the HUD takes up a minimal amount of screen space.

Figure 5.2
The in-game pull-down menu for Unreal Tournament. The menu takes you out of the game, but is fast in loading and in making changes.

Figure 5.3
An "as needed" status message. This particular message lets you know that you picked up a particular item.

I'm not saying that players never see any information in the game. I do mean that they should never have to strain to find important status information. Certain bits of important information can—and should—be designed as part of the interface that may show in the game up to 100 percent of the time. Windows 95, 98, 2000, and so on have the Task Bar, visible practically all the time so you can access any open file, choose menu commands, and tell what time it is. In games, you have certain common information—such as Health, Armor, and Ammo for shooter games, or other information (the amount of magic or a hand of cards for other types of games). Players should be able to glance at the game screen and gather the most urgently needed information immediately. The decisions for what needs to be shown, how often, and to what degree of prominence are design decisions that should be made before the artistic menus and interfaces are laid out. See Figure 5.4 for a good example of the results of good design choices for a HUD.

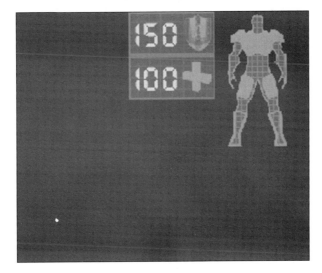

Figure 5.4

Looking at the Unreal Tournament HUD again, you'll notice that they have common information displayed in an easy to understand format—Health, Armor, Score, and so on.

You should also make sure that the system, or computer, status is always clear to the user. When a button is clicked, the user should know immediately what is happening as a result. The button should appear to be pressed, a sound should be played, and the desired result should happen. If the player must wait, make it clear that the system is working for them; use an hourglass, a spinning sword, or some other indicator that the player's request is being processed. Animate this cursor as well. The movement will let the user know that your game hasn't crashed, it is only thinking. If an event may take longer than a few seconds, display a message for the user (see Figure 5.5 for a good example of this kind of message). If possible, let the users know how long they may have to wait. As an example, if a player casts a spell of protection and the computer adds a bonus to their armor score, but the player has no indication that it happened, they will assume it did not. That is why games will play a sound, show a cursor indicating that a spell is active, change the player model in the game with one that looks like a spell has been cast on it, put a glowing light or special effect around the player—or numerous other indicators that the player indeed has some magic about him.

Figure 5.5
The "PRECACHING" (otherwise known as the Loading message) is displayed every time the game is paused to load the assets of a level into RAM. This lets the users know their system is not locked up, but rather that it is working and currently busy.

If you are unable to indicate an amount of time in which a process will take place, use progress bars as many installation programs do. Installation programs often use bars to communicate the overall progress of the installation and the progress of individual files being copied. In a game, you can use such a device as well; only your bars can be framed by stone, metal, or in some other way that matches the style of your game. Even a simple text message is useful if it informs users while they are waiting for a long process to take place.

After any long process, give the user plenty of notification that the process is complete, in case they have walked away from the computer or turned their attention elsewhere. Play a sound effect (beep, whistle, roar, music), display a dialog box telling them what was just completed (in case they forgot), and thank them for waiting.

Visibility of system status is important for many reasons, but what's most important is the "I'm coming" you shout to players who are knocking on the door to your world.

2. Match between [the] System and the Real World

The system should speak the users' language, with words, phrases and concepts familiar to the users, rather than system-oriented terms. Follow real-world conventions, making information appear in a natural and logical order.

In game terms, clicking the backpack opens an inventory system, clicking the spell book opens a list of spells, and clicking the words "Enter the Arena" in a fighting game means "start the application."

Sometimes called *human interface objects*, these objects include the folders, documents, and Recycle Bin in Windows. In games, these objects would be the swords, shields, magic books, and other items. These items serve the following functions in a menu:

- They are objects that are very familiar to humans in the real world or that adhere to a set of understood standards in game worlds.

- They can be interacted with—seen, heard, and even the perception of touch given.

- They are standardized in the application in terms of look, feel, and behavior.

- They should always speed up the user's work, not slow it down.

In game design, artists use these human interface objects, or metaphors, in their menu and interface designs all the time. An icon of a backpack in a fantasy game generally tells the player that they can carry stuff, and if they click on it, they can add or subtract items from inventory. Metaphors in design are great for orienting a player quickly to the interface. These design metaphors also pertain to sound. When a player clicks a sword and drags it over to the ground to drop it from his backpack, a metallic clang as it hits the ground can be very satisfying and can make the player feel immersed in the game world.

Metaphors are usually based on familiar concepts in the real world or on concepts that are based on conventions of a fantasy world. For example, a crystal ball, a sword, and a dagger in fantasy metaphors usually mean magic, battle, and thievery. A red cross on a HUD will mean health. A magnifying glass means zoom in, and of course, when an hourglass appears, the game developer is telling you to wait. In the case of Unreal Tournament (see Figure 5.6), there are the typical first-person shooter icons for health, armor, and ammo, but there are also the body icon (what armor is worn) and the red and blue flags to help the player keep track of the game status during a game of "Capture the Flag."

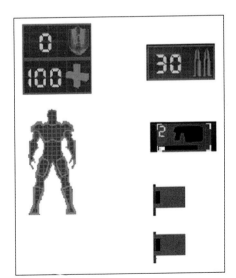

Figure 5.6

Although you see very artistic items from the Unreal Tournament HUD here, they are clearly referring to familiar concepts; Health and Armor, Ammunition, the player's body, weapons selected, and the red and blue flags.

3. User Control and Freedom

Users often choose system functions by mistake and will need a clearly marked "emergency exit" to leave the unwanted state without having to go through an extended dialogue. The system should support Undo and Redo commands.

Most games do not support Undo features, and whether the game you are working on supports an Undo feature has more to do with the programmers and game designer than with the artists. Many games do have features that allow players to save their games at certain points, but that is not an interface issue; here you are getting into the area of game balance and design, and that is not the focus of this book. As it relates to menus, the Undo option pertains mostly to backing out of the menu system.

This principle applies mainly to in-game play; as players explore the world and die, they can reload the game. If they can too easily reload the game every two feet, then there is no challenge and the game becomes boring. Players can do absolutely the most deadly actions to explore the world—wade through lava, jump in spinning gears, fight the head demon with a rock—all to see what would happen in each case. Then they can reload the game and do it right. On the other hand, when a player has to start the game or level over every time they die, that is no fun. There are games that make you replay significant portions of the game when you die—and they are usually panned for that in reviews.

What does this mean to the game artists? Not much in terms of actual menu layout, but this is a concept that you should be aware of for one good reason—knowing more than the minimum it takes to do your job helps you advance beyond where you are at the present.

4. Consistency and Standards

Users should not have to wonder whether different words, situations, or actions mean the same thing. Follow platform [and game genré] conventions.

This applies to the Windows or Macintosh interface, and it applies to games as well. Because of the dynamic and creative nature of games, artists always think that they can deviate from this heuristic, but they cannot. The nature of the game (pun intended) is that game artists are always pushing the boundaries of technology, the genre, and creativity and therefore introducing new conventions to keep up with. So, while the personal computer has gotten more powerful, there is still not a major difference between using Word 2000 and Word 95; they are actually a lot more similar to each other than an early version of the Ultima series of games and the latest version.

One example of a standard in applications using the Windows platform would be the Open and Save commands in the File menu, and the Cut, Copy, and Paste commands in the Edit menu. Many of the formatting options and shortcut keys that work in Word also work in Photoshop. Even if you are new to Photoshop, you can navigate the interfaces in a basic way because you know where to look for things.

In a game (especially if you are an experienced gamer), there is also a set of standards, but there are also often standards that are displayed in nonstandard ways. While you're in the menus, you can load a game, save a game, create a new player, and even look at the credits as standard game options; in these areas, games are fairly consistent, so much so that Unreal Tournament actually went to a Windows type navigational standard for their menus (see Figure 5.7). When you get into game interfaces and actions, however, things get a bit more deviant. For example, consider the act of picking up an item in different 3D games.

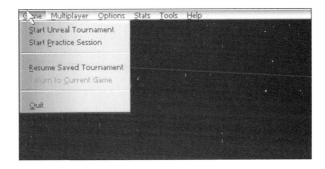

Figure 5.7
The Unreal Tournament
Windows-type menu system.

In games like Unreal, Unreal Tournament, Quake, Quake 2, Doom, and other fast-paced 3D games where shooting is the prime goal, you automatically pick up an item if you walk over it. This is easy on the player and, I would argue, fairly realistic. If, in real life, I was running away from a gun-toting maniac or a screeching raptor and I needed to snatch the medical kit off the table I was dashing past, you bet your sweet life that this motion is going to be automatic. I won't give much more thought than I do to breathing to picking up that object as I run past it. During the intense action of Unreal Tournament, you can pick up items by "running" over them (see Figure 5.8).

In some slower-paced games, such as hybrid genres of the first-person shooters and role-playing games, you must walk over to an item and hit a "Use" key. The game Hit Man had this type of function, but also took it a bit further. You could click on the item with your mouse and decide whether to pick up the item. While this function provides more control, it is still easy and doesn't slow the game down more than it should, given the type of game it is.

Now, in the game EverQuest, if you want to pick something up, you have to open your backpack and make sure you have room for the item. You have to click on the object and then place it in the backpack. You have to manage your inventory to some degree, deciding what you'll carry, what you'll wear, what is worth keeping. EverQuest allows for the use of headgear, rings, armor, clothing, weapons, and a pouch in which you can put stuff and then put in your backpack, and more. This is quite involved, but it's a fun and needed part of the game. It is a balanced game-play element because, in EverQuest, you can find a safe place to manage inventory, whereas in a fast-

Figure 5.8

In Unreal Tournament you don't stop to smell the roses—you step on them and keep running. Here, you see two weapons (you've already picked up and are now carrying the third weapon at the lower right) that require only that you walk over them to pick them up.

paced first-person shooter, you would die before the backpack was half open. This aspect of inventory management is also part of the game play on another level. Players can find or make unique items and sell and trade items.

The worst-case example of breaking the convention of easily picking up an item was in a game I actually liked a lot—Trespasser. In Trespasser, in order to pick up an item on the ground, you had to be almost on top of the item, crouch down (in most cases), use the mouse to extend the arm of the character and maneuver it over the item, and press another button to grab the item, and then chances are, you would hit it against a tree and drop it. You could also rotate the wrist and other actions, but I never got past that level. Some called this game an arm simulator. I thought the whole arm thing was totally unneeded and simply hindered the game play. No one wants to stop and make that mundane action in slow motion.

Even with all the advancements and deviations those in the game development industry can muster up, there are still standards and conventions, and you need to question your reasons for breaking them if you try. The expectation of consistency is there, even in computer games. And as I said, you do have tremendous freedom in the design of the interfaces and menus without breaking any of the rules. Most important is that the user is happy. You needn't be so strict in your design, depending on the experience level of the user, but you still need to pay attention to the following aspects of interface design, listed in order of importance.

Keep Hidden Functions to a Minimum

All functions should be available through a menu, a toolbar, or some other logical navigation technique. Shortcut key combinations are simply that, shortcuts, not the only route. Any function that can be performed only if the user happens to know the secret key combination is considered invisible and is poor design.

Keep Navigational Functions Standard

All the conventions that are used to navigate the menus and interfaces of your game (icons, window borders, scroll arrows, cursors, button states, and so on) need to have the same appearance, do the same thing, and be documented and controlled. If they are not documented and controlled, havoc ensues. You know us artists; we will design a different cursor for every function and then forget to design the buttons. Seriously, documentation helps keep the workflow flowing and prevents tasks from being forgotten.

Navigational standards also include the location of these elements. If you have the 'OK' button on the bottom right on one screen, the top left on another, and so on, you confuse and slow down the user. I have seen many Web sites where every page is completely different. Location, color, size—all different. Talk about irritating and confusing. In Unreal Tournament, the screens are artistic, but follow a convention (see Figures 5.9 through 5.12).

Figure 5.9

The Unreal Tournament menu system follows a specific convention for the placement of navigational items. This Control menu shows the current assignments of shortcut keys to game controls.

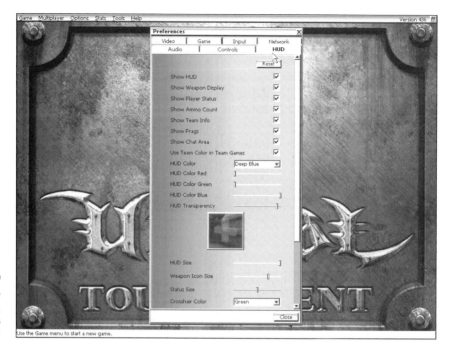

Figure 5.10
The HUD control gives the game player full control over the look, feel, and display of Unreal's heads-up display.

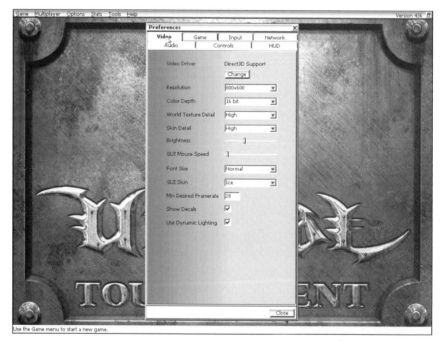

Figure 5.11
The Video Preferences menu enables the player to fine-tune the game's video options to match the "gaming computer" on which Unreal will run.

The most important thing to be consistent about, especially in the beginning stages of design, is anticipating user expectations. The best way to know what the users want is to ask them, watch them, and study them at play. And don't tell the users how to navigate the menu; watch them and see where they blaze and where they stall. Take note and fix the problems.

Figure 5.12
Here, you see a very effective dialog box design for player weapons information and selection.

Finally, "standard" doesn't mean that all windows and navigational items must look exactly the same. In a game where you have an inventory system, if the window that displays inventory looks exactly the same as the window where you sell inventory and manage it, the players may get confused momentarily as to what mode they are in. A simple convention such as a backpack icon or a gold coin icon on the screen can convey mode simply and creatively.

Remove Barriers between the User and the Game

The menu and the other interface elements are barriers between the player and the game. The more you can remove the need for a menu and other interface elements between the user and the world, the better the game will be. Here, you have to look past the organizational flow chart of the menu and let the audience out in your menu on their own. Don't just mail a CD-ROM to a bunch of beta testers and ask them if they had trouble with the menu; watch them work through the menu and take your own notes. The best method I have used for this was to set the computer up in a room and videotape the users (looking over their shoulders tends to make them uncomfortable). Later on, you can watch the results and see where the users stalled out in the menu or game interface.

The game parts you can streamline may be very subtle, such as cutting extra mouse clicks where you can. Think about this example: A user navigating between the character menu and the purchasing menu for their character is thrown back to the main character menu every time they buy an item. During the design of the menu, you may have laid out a process that was more efficient for you, the designer, the artists, and the programmer and even more efficient for the computer to process, but that is bad design. If the user wants to buy multiple items and each time they click on an item they are brought back to the purchasing menu, they have to click on the button again and repeat the process. The better way would be to have the items all highlighted as you select them and then have the user click the "purchase" button once.

It is a lot easier to put the work off on the user, but that is what you don't want to do if you can help it.

Provide Baby Steps First

No matter how complex the game or how advanced the audience, you are always better off paving many roads for your users rather than just one. Have the big shiny button menu that offers the basic three-to-five choice set, and then add layers of complexity. Offer shortcuts, an advanced version of the menu, a control window for advanced users, and even a scripting language. Give a wide variety of users' choices—from baby steps to marathon races. The adage of game design is that a good game is easy to learn but hard to master, and that applies to menus and interfaces as well.

5. Error Prevention

Even better than good error messages is a careful design that prevents a problem from occurring in the first place.

Game and interface designers need to anticipate probable or possible user mistakes and then find ways to prevent users from making them. For example, don't let users create new characters with the same name as the old—and thus overwrite the old character. There's not much you can do as an artist in the way of error prevention, but you can be aware of this principle and make sure that it is considered in the design of the game. Unreal Tournament has several error-prevention steps, mainly in the setup of the game. In Figure 5.13 you can see that the user is allowed to view the new video settings before committing to them, and in the process possibly choosing bad settings.

6. Recognition Rather Than Recall

Make objects, actions, and options visible. The user should not have to remember information from one part of the dialogue to another. Instructions for use of the system should be visible or easily retrievable whenever appropriate.

In the game, you need to plan each aspect of your interface to present to the players what is needed at the time they are using it. There should be Quit, Go Back, and Go Forward mechanisms, as well as access to any information or functions the players will need at that menu—but no more than needed. As in most applications, you can press Escape in a game to quit out of the current menu. In games, the Go Forward and Go Back mechanisms are usually dictated by your progress through the game.

7. Flexibility and Efficiency of Use

Accelerators (unseen by the novice user) may often speed the interaction for the expert user so that the system can cater to both inexperienced and experienced users. Allow users to tailor frequent actions.

If possible, give your players an easy start with the big buttons, but offer many roads, as mentioned above. Have the big shiny button menu and the layers of complexity. Shortcuts and advanced versions of the menu should be standard, and a control window and scripting language should be considered. Give users a wide variety of power levels. The adage (once again) of game design is that a good game is easy to learn but hard to master and this technique of interface design is but one to help achieve that end.

Even though your players will learn quickly and gain mastery quickly, they will also not feel free in the total absence of boundaries (Yallum, 1980). A little child will cry equally when held too tight or when left to wander in a large and empty warehouse. Gamers will also feel the most comfortable in an environment that is neither confining nor infinite. Too confining and you cut out audience members. Unreal Tournament allows for the easy start of a game and easy play (run and shoot) but there is almost no end to the level of control you have with the drop-down System Console (see Figure 5.14). By using this feature, you can type all manner of shortcut keys, change levels, affect the world, and so on.

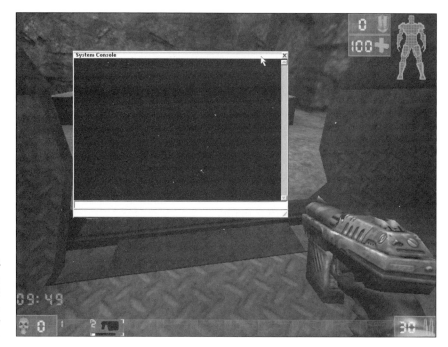

Figure 5.14
The Unreal Tournament System Console allows for an advanced degree of control over the game, but the game itself is easy to start playing.

8. Aesthetic and Minimalist Design

Dialogues should not contain information that is irrelevant or rarely needed. Every extra unit of information in a dialogue [or dialog box] competes with the relevant units of information and diminishes their relative visibility.

The menus and other interface elements should look good (aesthetic), but they are not the focus of the game, so they should be out of the way as much as possible (minimalist). As mentioned previously in this chapter, a complex interface may or may not be part of game play. Know what function your menus and other elements are to play, and design them accordingly. The act of navigating an interface is simply the user trying to get to the game. Even in the game with the extensive inventory system, while it may be needed and expected, the interface should still be designed to operate using the minimum of time, screen real estate, and user effort.

A good example of this exists in the game Diablo 2. Rather than making the user employ the four arrow keys to navigate the world, Diablo 2 allows the player to use the mouse. All the player has to do is put the cursor ahead of the character on screen, and the character will walk in that direction. This setup is much easier, and it reduces the number of fingers used to navigate from four to one. Rather than having an entire hand effectively devoted to moving the character, when the mouse is used the fingers on that hand can also be used to press mouse buttons and perform actions with the three or four (or more) buttons more commonly found on mice these days.

The Big Shiny Button

Okay, even though you were told that you are supposed to design to minimize the menu and interface's interference with the user, you also have to realize that a button the size of a pinhead is not simply *minimalist;* it is darn hard to use. Minimalist doesn't mean use tiny buttons; it means get rid of buttons that don't need to be there. Buttons, text, and other menu objects need to be readable. Text should contrast with backgrounds (dark text with light backgrounds and vice versa). Fonts and lettering should be large enough to read.

Remember Fitt's Law, which states "The time to acquire a target is a function of the distance to and size of the target." Think about this: the bigger the target and the closer it is, the easier it is to hit.

9. Error Recognition and Recovery

Help users recognize, diagnose, and recover from errors. Error messages should be expressed in plain language (no codes), precisely indicate the problem, and constructively suggest a solution.

This responsibility goes back to the designers and programmers, but once again you should be aware of this principle so you can be part of the interface design process. The most you can do here, as an artist, is to make sure the error messages are readable and understandable. The Unreal Tournament engine goes as far as to know if the game didn't work the last time you ran it and offers several options to help you fix the problem, as is shown in Figure 5.15.

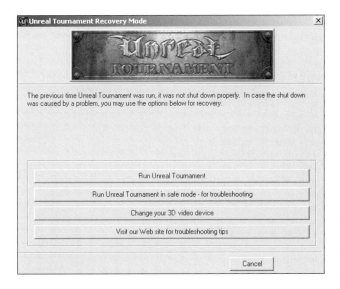

Figure 5.15

If the game Unreal Tournament crashes on you, it remembers and offers several options to help you fix the problem.

10. Help and Documentation

Even though it is better if the system can be used without documentation, it may be necessary to provide help and documentation. Any such information should be easy to search, focused on the user's task, list concrete steps to be carried out, and not be too large.

Three factors control how much online help and documentation you need to provide to your users. In any of these three cases, you always want to strive to keep the amount of documentation to a minimum. The three factors are shown in the following list:

- The complexity of the game or application for which you are creating the interfaces

- The level of the audience for which you are designing

- The quality of the job that the design team does on the menus and other interface elements in the application or game

Of the three factors, you, as a game artist, can exert control only over the third. You can especially exert control if a great deal of the design and flow of the menu is left up to you. The goal is an application so well designed in accordance with the other heuristics that no documentation is needed. Chances are, however, that some documentation will be needed and actually desired because some users actually like written documentation.

These "10 Usability Heuristics" are the basic rules that apply to any menu or other interface element you may devise. So, let's get creative with Photoshop and make some user interfaces.

Creating the Typical 3D Shooter Menu

Now, you will actually create a game menu. For the first exercise, you will assume that you have to make a menu for a very basic 3D shooter. As the game artist, you will most likely have designed the logo for the game, so that will be incorporated into the menu. By the time you are called to design a menu, you will have a color scheme developed for the game as well as an understanding of the look and feel of the game based on the design documentation. These types of menus are usually a simply background, with a font for the menu choices (with multiple states such as idle, rollover, and activated—you will look at these states later), plus the logo or other identifying mark. In Chapter 4, you created the logo for the fictitious game, Acid; you will now create the menu.

If you need to break out the parts of a menu for your own project, the parts of the game menu from the artist's perspective are as follows:

- Fonts, letters, or writing that need to be read by the users

- Cursors or pointers

- Color scheme

- Screen format and layout

- Menus and toolbars, buttons and icons

- Dialog boxes

- Size of objects (Although not really a menu *part,* sizing allows all the other objects on screen to "fit" with one another.)
- Sound effects
- Background art

For this exercise, you will be breaking out only the following elements:

- Color scheme
- Background art
- Fonts, letters, or writing that need to be read by the users
- Screen layout

Color Scheme

First, address the concept of color scheme. Since the logo is black and green, that will be your color scheme. The green will be used as a nuclear glow and the black as a nice dramatic contrast. Color scheme was simple because you are basing your design on a logo. In most cases, menu and interface design is being done for games and products with existing color schemes, and those are the color schemes used.

Background Art

Now that color scheme is settled, let's approach background art. Because the fictitious game Acid is a first-person shooter set in the near-future post-holocaust world (pretty original, huh?), you will want that futuristic-apocalyptic look that people just can't get enough of in games and movies. In the game, when it rains, the rain is made of (come on, take a guess) acid. And guess what else? It rains a lot in the game world—off and on and totally unpredictably. So, you have to fight some evil creature or robot that is immune to the acid rain, and every time it rains, you have to run for cover or die.

1. Start by opening the image "acid.psd" (see Figure 5.16) from this book's companion CD-ROM and duplicating it so you can save your changes to your hard drive. You can also use the File|Save As command to save a copy where you would like it to be on your hard drive.

2. Right-click on the header of the image, or on the title bar, to open the context menu, and choose Canvas Size. Make the canvas size 800 pixels wide and 600 pixels tall. This size is proportional to a computer screen.

3. Open the image "steelfloor.jpg" and copy it into a layer named "steel floor".

4. Copy the "steel floor" layer. Name the copy "green", and color it green (Image|Adjust|Hue/Saturation, and then click on the Colorize checkbox). Add the layer effects Bevel and Emboss, and erase portions of the layer by using the select color range option of the magic wand.

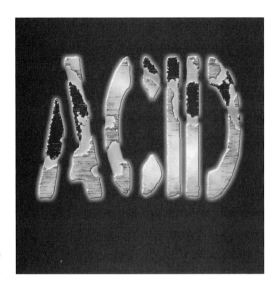

Figure 5.16
The ACID logo from Chapter 4.

5. Add a layer called "stains" between the steel floor and the steel floor copy (green). Set the new layer to Color Burn, Opacity 46%, and add the stains.

6. Make sure that the "steel floor copy" layer is cleaned from around the logo and the stains beneath the logo.

7. Type a capital S and use the Wingdings fonts and the Outer Glow effect for the glowing green drops effect.

8. Add the "rain is pain" tag line (see Figure 5.17).

Figure 5.17
The Acid Logo in a portion of the menu with byline added.

Menu Choices

After the color scheme and the background art are set, you can create the menu options by taking the following steps:

1. For a basic shooter game, the menu choices will be limited to "Start Game", "Load Game", "Save Game", "Options", and "Quit". Create your first menu text by setting the colors to their defaults (press the D key) and typing the text for the options.

2. Apply the following effects for the button states:

- *Normal*—Inner Bevel with the default settings.

- *Rollover*—The same as Normal but the color of the text is lighter.

- *Selected*—Copy the Normal state, make the font white, and add the Outer Glow effect to the text. Settings: Mode Normal, Color Green, Opacity 75%, Blur 26, and Intensity 193.

The following three states represent the three modes a button will need to be in at various times:

- *Normal* is a bit understated, even hard to see, but it is supposed to be that way because it is there simply so the user knows what options they may choose from.

- *Rollover* highlights the option, letting the user know that the option is active and ready to be selected. It is also easier to read in the highlighted state.

- *Selected* is the energized state, glowing with power as the selection is activated. This state is seen only for a brief instant as the menu options change to the new screen or function. It is a strong visual indicator to the user as to what they just selected, as is shown in Figure 5.18.

You have just created three images for each button, one for each state of the button. Your game engine will handle the swapping of these images.

Now, you will move on to make a menu that involves more data from a more complex game.

Figure 5.18

The completed Acid menu. In their normal state, the buttons are a bit hard to see, but as the user rolls over them, they really jump out.

PROJECT Taking the RPG Menu All the Way

In this project, you will create a menu for a complex RPG (role-playing game). In the menu, you will use the "spell book logo" you created in Chapter 4. Because this is a complex RPG, you will specifically focus on one aspect of the menu, although you'll be designing the look and feel used throughout the interfaces. First, make the Character Creation screen that is so common in these types of games. The Character Creation screen usually contains the options that allow for the creation of various aspects of a character such as strength, intelligence, and other abilities.

1. Start by opening the image named "rpg_menu.psd" from the companion CD-ROM.

2. Look at the background layer. This is a picture of an old church that will look great as the background to our menu (see Figure 5.19).

Figure 5.19

The background image for the RPG menu.

3. Next, you need to decide which elements you want to place on this screen, and then you need to lay them out. Look at the "Screen Layout" layer, and you will see that I did a quick-and-dirty layout, using the text tool to place the elements over the image you will be using as a background. For this type of game, this screen will contain the character attributes as mentioned, but you will also add the option to Cancel or Accept the changes, add a title to the screen, add a description window that will contain descriptive text for each rollover state of the menu, and add a window for an image of the character. See Figure 5.20.

Figure 5.20
The layout of the needed elements of the menu set over the
background image.

4. Now that the elements of the menu are laid out, make a button. I made
   a stone texture similar to the one in Chapter 2 and used that. Add the
   Bevel and Emboss effects to the stone. Wherever you have text, put this
   chiseled stone behind the text. I also used the plain old Arial Bold font
   for the lettering. This makes it easy to read, and a menu must be easy
   to read. Set the effects for each text layer to Emboss. See Figure 5.21 for
   a sample of the screen title with the stone effect applied.

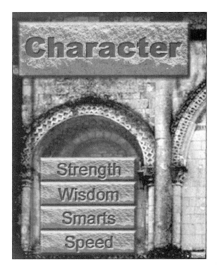

Figure 5.21
The text of the menu screen with
the stone background.

5. After laying out the buttons and the text, move on to the Character Description and the Rollover Description. These are simply areas where the text for the Character Description and the Rollover Description are displayed. Use the Arial font and make it white.

6. The middle arch (Figure 5.22) is the place where the character's image can be placed so the players can see the character they are working on.

Figure 5.22
The character image window.

7. Finally, place your fantasy game logo in the center of the church doorway. The final menu can be seen in Figure 5.23.

Figure 5.23
The final role-playing game menu. You may notice that in the lower-left corner of the figure, the word "weapons" appears and should be "weapon" (singular). Having someone proofread all the text elements in your interface is a good idea.

Moving On

In this chapter, you learned not only how to make game menus but also the science behind the technique. As you can see, it involves a great deal more than just laying out some pretty pictures. In this chapter, I discussed the rules of menu and interface design as well as the process of breaking out and creating game menus. This understanding of proper interface design and the rules of interface design are not only helpful, but also imperative for a good game. Remember, this chapter calls the menu the gateway to a world, but—as I said previously—it is only a gateway if it is a good menu that's well designed and implemented; otherwise, it is a locked gate.

In Chapter 6, you will look at ways to automate your texture creation and speed up your work a great deal.

Chapter 6

Automating Texture Creation

So you've learned how to create many base textures, but aren't you tired of doing the same 10 or 20 (or more) steps over and over? Texture automation will speed things up for you considerably.

Introduction

Creating textures, especially base textures, can become tedious after you have done them many times. Aside from just creating textures in Photoshop, other functions can become tedious as well, and that is why Photoshop provides many tools and techniques to help speed up your workflow.

So if you find yourself performing the same tasks repeatedly, clicking the mouse eight times to perform a function, or simply thinking, "there has to be a quicker way than this," this chapter is for you. Chances are, anything you do in Photoshop can be done faster in a variety of ways.

This chapter discusses several ways you can work more efficiently when you're creating textures in Photoshop:

- *Learning keyboard shortcuts*—Quite possibly the fastest and easiest way to speed up your workflow.

- *Working with unflattened images*—This technique can save you hours of production time by saving you from redoing work.

- *Using Picture Package, Web Photo Gallery, and Contact Sheet II*—These commands assemble images into commonly needed formats.

- *Creating custom brushes*—A very easy way to customize Photoshop brushes.

- *Working with Photoshop Actions*—A very powerful way to get work done. As with macros in other programs, these actions can do anything you tell them to.

Using Keyboard Shortcuts

Quite possibly the quickest and easiest thing you can do to speed up your work is to learn the keyboard shortcut keys. If you reach the stage where you can work on your image with all toolbars, menus, and palettes closed, you will truly be a Jedi Master of Photoshop. Not only will you be fast, but you will effectively increase your screen size as well.

The following list describes the major parts of Photoshop that employ shortcut keys:

- *Tools*—The most commonly used functions of the Toolbar such as the Airbrush, Selection, and Crop tools.

- *Layers*—Shortcuts that will help you navigate the layers faster.

- *Editing*—The most common editing functions such as Cut, Copy, and Paste.

- *Selections*—Manipulating and controlling the selection area.

- *File operations*—Common file functions such as Open, Save, and New.

- *Views*—Views are very important, and the quicker you can navigate your image (move around it, zoom in and out), the faster you can work.

- *Blending modes*—Used a great deal in texture creation to get many of the effects that add realism to your images.

- *Color adjustment*—Color adjustment aids in balancing and blending your images.

- *Palettes*—Opening and closing palette windows as they are needed frees up screen space, allowing you more screen space to work on.

If you have all your toolbars and palettes opened, they are taking up precious screen space. In Table 6.1, I break the shortcuts down into some common categories. Please remember that there are more categories and many more shortcut keys; here, I'm showing you just the most commonly used ones.

Working with Unflattened Images

In Chapter 3, I discussed the texture library and the advantages of working with unflattened Photoshop images. If you save your images as unflattened, you can return later and adjust many aspects of the image to create variations of it. This not only makes all the images created from the original have a consistent look and feel, but it also makes creating them much faster. As examples, you can see that the shooting targets in Figure 6.1 are all different; the versions range from clean to torn, stained, and used for shooting practice.

Making Many Targets

Making the versions of the targets is quick and easy. I started with the target texture that I made by employing techniques from Chapters 2 and 3.

You can find this file (target.psd) on this book's companion CD-ROM if you would like to examine the image in its unflattened state. To do so, take the following steps:

1. Open the target image and, if they are not off already, turn off all the layers. All the images I mention in this exercise are already in the PSD file on this book's companion CD-ROM.

2. Start by looking at the "background" layer. Here, I started with a white background and added some noise (Add Noise|Noise; Gaussian, Monochromatic, and Amount 12).

Table 6.1   Commonly used Photoshop 5 keyboard shortcuts.

Tools	Shortcut
Airbrush	J
Crop	C
Default Colors	D
Dodge	O
Eraser	E
Eyedropper	I
Hand	H
Lasso	L
Magic Wand	W
Move	V
Paint Bucket	K
Paintbrush	B
Pencil	N
Rubber Stamp	S
Switch Colors	X
Type	T
Zoom	Z

Layer Operations	Shortcut
Group with Previous	Ctrl+G
Layer via Copy	Ctrl+J
Merge Down	Ctrl+E
Merge Visible	Ctrl+Shift+E
New Layer	Ctrl+Shift+N

Editing Operations	Shortcut
Copy	Ctrl+C
Cut	Ctrl+X
Fill with Background Color	Ctrl+DEL
Fill with Foreground Color	Alt+DEL
Free Transform	Ctrl+T
Apply Last Filter	Ctrl+F
Paste	Ctrl+V
Undo	Ctrl+Z

Selections	Shortcut
Deselect	Ctrl+D
Feather Selection	Ctrl+Alt+D
Invert Selection	Ctrl+Shift+I
Select All	Ctrl+A

File Operations	Shortcut
Close	Ctrl+W
New Document	Ctrl+N
Open	Ctrl+O
Print	Ctrl+P
Save	Ctrl+S
Save As	Ctrl+Shift+S

Views	Shortcut
Fit to Screen	Ctrl+0 (zero)
Toggle Screen Modes	F
Show/Hide Menu bar	Shift+F
Show/Hide Grid	Ctrl+"
Show/Hide Guides	Ctrl+;
Snap to Grid	Ctrl+Shift+"
Snap to Guides	Ctrl+Shift+;
Zoom In/Zoom Out	Ctrl++/- (plus/minus)
Zoom In/Out & Resize Window	Ctrl+Alt++/- (plus/minus)

Blending Mode	Shortcut
Color	Shift+Alt+C
Color Burn	Shift+Alt+B
Color Dodge	Shift+Alt+D
Darken	Shift+Alt+K
Difference	Shift+Alt+E
Dissolve	Shift+Alt+I
Exclusion	Shift+Alt+X
Hard Light	Shift+Alt+H
Hue	Shift+Alt+U
Lighten	Shift+Alt+G
Luminosity	Shift+Alt+Y
Multiply	Shift+Alt+M
Normal	Shift+Alt+N
Overlay	Shift+Alt+O
Saturation	Shift+Alt+T
Screen	Shift+Alt+S
Soft Light	Shift+Alt+F

Color Adjustments	Shortcut
Color Balance	Command+B
Desaturate	Ctrl+Shift+U
Hue/Saturation	Ctrl+U
Invert	Ctrl+I

Palettes	Shortcut
Show All Palettes	Enter
Show/Hide Actions Palette	F9
Show/Hide Brushes Palette	F5
Show/Hide Color Palette	F6
Show/Hide Info Palette	F8
Show/Hide Layers Palette	F7

Figure 6.1

These are three versions of the shooting target I was able to crank out at inhuman speed, thanks to layers. They look different, but all were made from the same image (*far left*).

3. Now turn on the "man" layer. This is nothing more than a target pattern I got off the Internet. I had to enlarge it quite a bit, so I used Unsharp Mask on it. If you have to do this, too, your image may need to have the text redone as well. If it does, just choose the Text tool and make the font color white. After placing the new text over the old, erase the old text by painting over it with the same shade of black as the target.

4. Add some texture to this layer (Texture|Grain; Intensity 30, Contrast 50, and Clumped).

5. Because I was making this target for an official U.S. Army pistol range, I added the text "Target Silhouette, Army/target, pistol" in the corners. I took this text from another target that was used on a target range.

6. Add some nails, using the Bevel Emboss layer effects and a small brush. This is the first version of the target that is considered new, not yet shot or damaged by weather. See Figure 6.2.

7. Then I had to create a version that was shot and marked up by an instructor. Creating this bullet-holed version was easy; I just created two new layers—one for the bullet holes and one for the instructor's writing. The bullet holes are like the nails, but use Outer Bevel and the Down direction. The writing is simply a layer that uses the Hard Light and Opacity 66 percent settings, and the airbrush was used to do the writing. For the text, I just wrote with the mouse and a red small airbrush.

Figure 6.2

The first—new—version of the target.

8. Finally, I began work on the final version of the target: old, weathered, stained, and torn. To create this environmentally aged version, I created a layer for the stains, pasted in the "dirty pan.jpg" image, and set the mode to Multiply and the Opacity to 60 percent. I created another layer for the "wrinkles" and pasted in another image—named "wrinkles.jpg"—from my library. I changed the layer Mode to Multiply for this image. Finally, I made the layer for the rips and tears; that was nothing more than painting black on the topmost layer, which I later converted to an alpha channel so the tears would be transparent in the game.

9. Then I had to come back to this image and create a version of the target that had no nails so it could be laid on a table in the game. I also created various versions with different writing, with various degrees of dirt, colored and contrasted differently to make the texture look good in the game, and (of course) different sizes.

Having the image layered allowed me to do all these variations very quickly. Figure 6.3 shows the final version of the target.

Cranking Out Signs

You may find yourself needing to crank out a large number of textures that share a common look—for example, a set of signs. I had to crank out a lot of signs for a 3D space I was working on. (Chapter 3 includes a tutorial on making the base sign, and Figure 6.4 shows the three versions of that sign.) In Figure 6.4 you can see that the various versions include different weathering and different lettering. The letters were simply stored as text layers with the Bevel Emboss effects applied.

Figure 6.3
This is the final version
of the target.

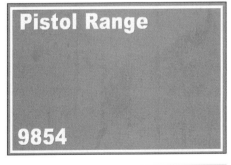

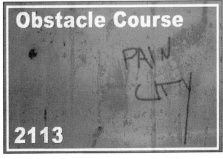

Figure 6.4
The various versions of the sign,
each with different lettering.

Building Walls with Variations

Here are some examples of a base wall texture that has different details added to it in different versions of the image (see Figure 6.5). This image can be used to tile seamlessly along a wall surface, using the detailed versions when needed.

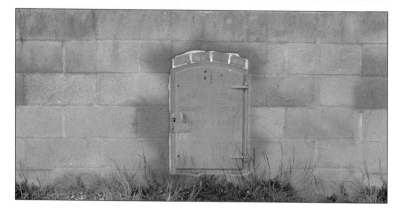

Figure 6.5
Three examples of an identical wall texture, with details added for a consistent world surface.

Using Automation Commands

Photoshop 5.5 also includes some powerful automation features accessed through the File menu. They are:

- Picture Package command

- Web Photo Gallery command

- Batch processing

- Contact Sheet II plug-in (an updated version of Contact Sheet I, of course)

Picture Package

The Picture Package command duplicates and lays out images in the way that school photographs are often delivered. Photographers normally must duplicate, rotate, and scale photos to fit several versions of the same picture on one sheet of film. The dialog box is very simple, as you can see in Figure 6.6.

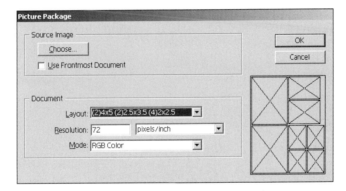

Figure 6.6
The Picture Package dialog box.

Creating a picture package is easy. To do so, follow these steps:

1. Open Photoshop and choose File|Automate|Picture Package.

2. Select the image you want made into the Picture Package. Select Choose to tell Photoshop what image you want to use. If you want to use an image that is already open in Photoshop, select the Use Frontmost Document option.

3. Now select the layout you want to use. There are many options here. The dimensions are in inches, and you can see what the layout looks like in the dialog box.

4. Enter a resolution for the package.

5. Then just click OK to create the package. Figure 6.7 shows a picture package applied to the author's image.

Note: If you are planning to print the page for photographic purposes, please note that the final resolution and final image-mode settings are set at 72 dpi by Photoshop and thus are very low resolution.

Figure 6.7
The author's image with the Picture Package command applied.

Web Photo Gallery

The Web Photo Gallery command exports your images as a Web site. The home page of the site has thumbnails of the selected images, and these thumbnails are all linked to the individual JPEG images, each on its own page. Photoshop automatically creates the images, HTML code, and page layouts. This is great for photographers as well as artists online. Figure 6.8 shows the dialog box for the Web Photo Gallery command.

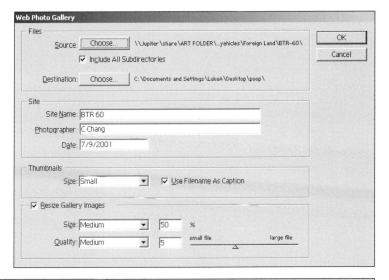

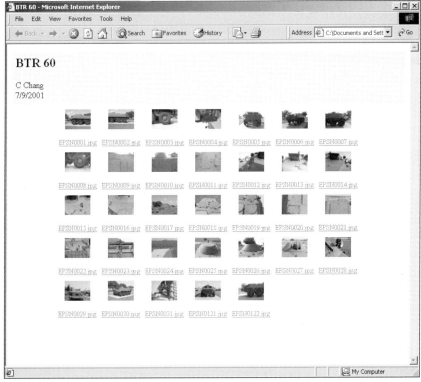

Figure 6.8
The Web Photo Gallery dialog
box and Web page.

To create a Web site in Photoshop, take the following steps:

1. Open Photoshop and choose File|Automate|Web Photo Gallery. Choose
   the Source option's Choose button to select the folder that contains the
   images you want to process. Select the Include All Subdirectories option
   if you want to include all the images inside all the subfolders below the
   folder you chose.

2. You also need to choose the folder you want all the files created in. Click the Destination option's Choose button, and specify the folder you want the HTML files sent to.

3. You can also customize the Web page with the following information:

   • The Site Name.

   • The Photographer (the name of the person who originally created the site).

   • The Date the site was created. Photoshop will place the current date here for you.

4. Set the Thumbnails options:

   • The Size option (the size of thumbnail preview on the home page of the Web site).

   • The Use Filename As Caption option will use each image's file name as the name of the image. If you don't select this option, the file name will not appear on the home page, but it will still appear on each page of the site.

5. Selecting the Resize Gallery Images option will resize all of the images, according to the settings you specify, when they are placed on their individual pages. The resizing options are Size and Quality. The better the quality, the larger the file size will be.

6. Clicking OK will create the site and then open it for you in your Web browser. You will notice that each page has little navigation arrows to take you to the next or previous page on the Web site, as well as back to the main page.

Batch Processing

Later in this chapter, you will learn about actions, or the capability Photoshop gives you to run many commands with one button (or hot key combination) as with macros in Word. But the Batch command is accessed from the File menu, so you should look at it here. The Batch command lets you run actions on a folder of images, so you don't have to run the actions on each image individually.

The flexibility of the batch processing option enables you to leave the files open, to close and save the files after they are changed, or to save modified versions of the files. All of these options are performed from the Batch dialog box (see Figure 6.9).

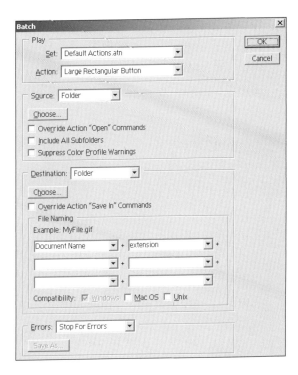

Figure 6.9
The Batch dialog box.

Batch processing of files is easy. To do so, take the following steps:

1. Open Photoshop. Choose File|Automate|Batch to open the Batch dialog box.

2. Select the Action Set containing the action you want to run, and select the Action you want to run.

3. The Source option will allow you to choose the folder containing the images that you want to process.

4. If you select the Override Action "Open" Commands option, all open commands that were recorded as part of the original action are ignored. Using this option is useful because you may have the images already opened, and this would cause errors.

5. You can also choose a destination for your processed images.

   • The None option leaves the files open without saving changes (unless the action included a Save command).

   • The Save and the Close options will save the files in their current location.

   • The Folder option will save the processed files to the specified location. The Choose option lets you specify that folder. If you choose this option, make sure that you also select the Override Action "Save In" Commands option so that the processed files are saved to the specified destination folder and not to a location recorded with the action being run.

6. You can approach error-handling during batch processing in two ways. You can select the Stop For Errors option to suspend the batch until you deal with the error found, or you can select the Log Errors To File option to record any errors to a file without stopping the batch. If there are errors, a message will appear after the batch processing is complete.

Contact Sheet II

The Contact Sheet II plug-in builds pages of thumbnail images. This is handy for cataloging image sets for game artists and photographers. Using Contact Sheet II is easy; it has a simple dialog box like the other automation tools (see Figure 6.10).

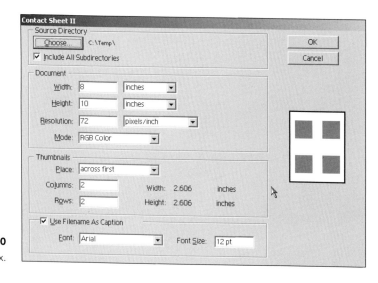

Figure 6.10
The Contact Sheet II dialog box.

To create your contact sheets, take the following steps:

1. Open Photoshop and choose File|Automate|Contact Sheet II. Use the Choose button to specify the folder containing the images that you want to use. Select the Include All Subdirectories option if you want all the images in folders below the level of the source folder to be used.

2. The Document area of the dialog box allows you to set the dimensions, resolution, and color mode of the contact sheet.

3. The Thumbnails area of the dialog box allows you to specify the layout for the contact sheets. The Place option lets you choose whether Photoshop will arrange the thumbnails horizontally (from left to right, then top to bottom) or vertically (from top to bottom, then left to right).

You can also specify the number of columns and rows that you want per contact sheet, as well as the maximum dimensions for each thumbnail. You can also see a preview of the layout to the right. You can tell Photoshop to use the file name as the caption. Not using the file names will result in a contact sheet with no text under the images. Finally, you can specify a caption font as well.

Creating Custom Brushes

Tired of the tried and true round brushes? You can create your own custom brushes. If you find yourself making a lot of bolt heads, bullet holes, and other repetitive but distinct shapes, then make brushes for them. It is very easy to do with the Define Brush command in the Brush palette.

When you create a brush, it is best to use black-and-white images with clean lines; you can use other colors, but they will be converted to grayscale. Even though the brushes are in black and white, you can still use a color with them, just as with regular brushes.

You can get some really cool effects by experimenting and making your own brushes. To do so, follow these steps:

1. Make a new image in Photoshop. Fill it with whatever you like, but keep in mind that the brush will be the size of the image, so you will need to reduce the image size accordingly before making it a brush. You can use this method to create a set of brushes in many sizes.

2. When you have the image the way you want it to be as a brush, use the Rectangular Marquee tool to select it.

3. Go to the Brush palette (see Figure 6.11). Click on the black arrow in the top right corner of the window to access the drop-down menu. Select the Define Brush option, and you will see your brush appear in the Brush palette.

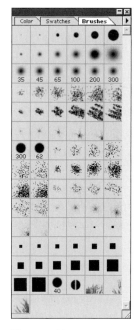

Figure 6.11
The Brush palette.

Easy, right? You can also use the two square bracket ("[" and "]") keys to toggle between brushes in Photoshop. In this way, you can create a brush for an effect, rotate the image and create another brush at a different angle, and cycle back and forth between brushes to detail an image.

I used this technique for leaves and pine needles. I wanted the same leaves but at various angles, so I created several brushes of the same leaf, rotated. The pine needle brush can be seen in the top image in Figure 6.12 in three steps: the branch, the branch with some needles, the branch with many needles at many angles. The bottom image in Figure 6.12 shows the pine branches created with the pine-needle brush.

Figure 6.12
The pine-needle brush I created to paint needles on branches (top), and the pine-needle brush in action on some pine branches (bottom).

Using Action Sets

After you have all the most often-used commands in Photoshop memorized (because you are doing them so often, of course), it is time for you to introduce yourself to the great world of Photoshop Actions. Photoshop Actions are sets of commands that you record and run. In this respect, they are just like macros in Word or other programs.

The Actions capability is useful for many processes, such as any repetitive task that needs to be done. For example, if you work with Web sites, when you are finished working on images, you might always repeat a certain set of commands, such as Duplicate Image|Flatten Image|Color Mode Indexed|Save As JPG. If you do this all day, having one button or a shortcut key to do it all in one stroke is a huge time saver.

Photoshop allows you to group your actions in sets. If you do not create a new set by using the Create Set command, then you will have to place your new action in an existing set of actions. Using sets, you can place your text-manipulating actions in one set, your texture-creation actions in another, and so on.

The following sections show the breakdown of the Actions palette and menu. Actions are a great deal more complex than the other automation techniques, but they are also very powerful tools.

The Actions Palette

The Actions palette is shared with the History palette. Click on the Action tab and then on the black arrow in the upper-right corner to access the pull-down menu. Make sure that the Button Mode option is unchecked. The result should look a lot like Figure 6.13.

Figure 6.13
The Actions palette and pull-down menu.

Here is a description of what those icons on the bottom of the Actions palette (and exactly what the four icons in the Action window) do:

- *On/Off*—Check or uncheck this box to turn on and off an effect within an action. This is useful if you have created a complex action and want to run only parts of it.

- *Dialog*—If you leave this icon unchecked (when you click the icon, it changes so that it looks checked), Photoshop will run the command using the default values. If you turn it on, Photoshop will stop the action and request user input in the dialog boxes for the function you specify. This option is useful if you automate text creation and want the user to type different text each time.

  Suppose, for example, that you are starting the construction of a Web site for which you have developed a really cool effect on the fonts of the header bars and menu bars of the page. (For example, you have tweaked the bevel and emboss settings, matched the color and font, and now have the look set up as you like it.) Each time you have to update the page, you can run your action, and then Photoshop prompts you for the new text. Finally, you have your new text, styled consistently with the rest of the site.

- *Commands*—You may edit your action by selecting a command from this list and choosing Record Again from the Actions menu.

- *Stop Record*—When you are finished creating your action or inserting a stop item (often a step that needs to be manually entered by the user, such as text, and so on), click on this button. This is the first of the VCR type buttons that you'll use in Actions.

- *Record*—This button starts recording or resumes recording an action. This is the second of the VCR type buttons that you'll use in Actions.

- *Play*—This option begins playing an action or set of actions. This is the third of the VCR type buttons that you'll use in Actions.

- *New Set*—This option opens a new set in which you can place the actions that you create.

* *New Action*—This option starts a new action within the selected set.

* *Delete Action*—This option deletes the selected action, or you can delete steps within an action by dragging and dropping the steps to this icon.

* *Action Menu*—This option opens the Actions menu, where you may edit, insert commands, save action sets, and so on.

The Actions Menu

The Actions pull-down menu allows you to create, edit, load, and save actions. This menu is accessed from the arrow in the upper-right corner of the Actions palette. This menu is divided into sections, and most of these options were described previously in the "Actions Palette" section.

Here are two important functions not accessible from the icon bar and not easily understood by those with a Windows-using background:

- *Load Actions*—You can load action sets here. Several Internet sites offer action sets that you can download (you can get Photoshop Actions that do everything off the Internet from several different sites). Go to your favorite search engine and type "Photoshop actions" to find these sites.

- *Button Mode* versus *Edit/List Mode*—Button mode displays the large, pretty buttons that you can click on, as shown in Figure 6.14. Turning off this mode shows you the tree view of the Actions palette. In Button mode, you cannot adjust the command settings. Edit/List mode is the more complicated but also gives you greater control. To create, edit, or save actions, you must be in Edit/List mode. Actions are displayed in List mode by default.

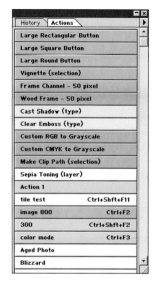

Figure 6.14

The big, pretty buttons of Button mode. These actions are not standard Photoshop Actions.

PROJECT Creating an Action to Make That Rusted Metal You Always Need

In this section, you will learn how to make an action that makes that rusted-metal texture from Chapter 2; however, this time, you can create rust with the push of a button (or tap of some keys), and it will take only a few seconds. The beauty of this project is that you will use the power of Photoshop Actions feature to make the texture in a fraction of the time that you previously did.

To make the "rusted metal" action, take the following steps:

1. Create a new action set by selecting the New Set command from the Action palette's pull-down menu, and name the set "textures." You do not need to have an image open to do this.

2. Now go back to the menu and select New Action and name it "Rust." Select the "Texture" set and press Record.

   If you desire, you can assign a function key (Photoshop will not allow you to use any key combination already assigned elsewhere) and a color to the new action. Colors come in handy when you have a lot of actions that you need to organize in sets.

3. Now, you'll start making the rusted-metal texture. Create a new image that is 600×600 pixels.

4. Fill the background with RGB 158, 139, 117.

5. Add Noise by selecting the following options: Noise|Add Noise; Amount 40, Gaussian, and Monochromatic.

6. Blur this layer by selecting the following options: Blur|Motion Blur; Angle 45, and Distance 45.

7. Distort the layer by choosing the following options: Distort|Ocean Ripple; Size 9 and Magnitude 9.

8. Create a new layer, and select a darker shade of brown (RGB 104, 66, 24).

9. Use the Paintbrush with a really soft brush, and paint some random lines back and forth. Change this layer's mode to Color Burn and set the Opacity down to 66 percent.

Note: When you are assigning function keys, you can use the F1 thru F12 keys, or combinations of keys including the Control (PC) Key, Command (MAC OS) Key, and the Shift key. This two-key combination capability will give you 60 possible keyboard shortcuts.

10. Create another layer, and set the background color to black (press D and then press X). Render some clouds (Filter|Render|Clouds). Change the mode to Color Burn, and turn down the layer opacity to about half.

11. Create another layer. Fill it with the brown color again and add some noise. Change the layer mode to Soft Light.

12. Stop recording the action.

13. When you replay the action, you'll notice that this action won't do the airbrush process for you that was covered in Step 9. However, it will create the layer for you to go back and airbrush in later. If you feel that having the same airbrush pattern available is important, just save the airbrushed pattern you want burned in as an image, and then open the image as part of the action. Just make sure that any image that you call by using Photoshop's Actions feature is in the right place on your hard drive, or you will get errors.

Here is the rust texture created with an action. It looks just like the rust texture in Chapter 2, but it took only seconds, and one click of a button, to create the effect (see Figure 6.15).

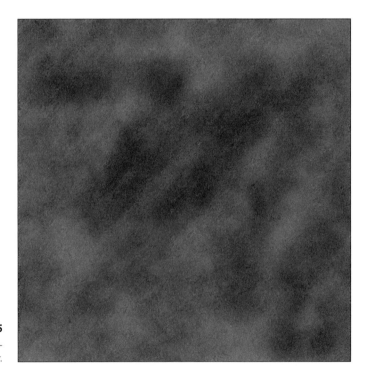

Figure 6.15

The rust texture makes a come-back in actions—faster than ever.

Moving On

In this chapter, you learned how to automate the creation of textures. You learned how to use Photoshop's Actions feature to make this task a breeze.

Now that you have learned how to create textures, plan texture sets, design interfaces, work really fast, and so much more, you are ready to begin the process of creating a 3D world. In Part II of this book, you will create a 3D game world covered in textures that you also will create.

3D Game Art Studio

This Color Studio presents a view of game art as it should be seen—in color, using the tools and techniques presented in projects and tutorials throughout the chapters of this book.

Sign with Hot Spot   Here is the untouched digital image of a sign with a hot spot or "flash burn" on it. Often, an on-camera flash pointing directly at a subject can produce an unwanted bright spot (called a hot spot) on flat or reflective surfaces within a photograph. Before you, as an artist, can use these images, you first must remove the offending flare. For more information about how to perform the hot spot removal process, see Chapter 3.

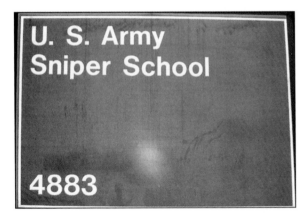

Sign Cropped with Hot Spot   This is the sign after it has been cropped. Notice how crooked the edges are. This occurs when the camera and the subject are not perfectly aligned. You'll have some work to do on almost every image because few photographs are "perfect."

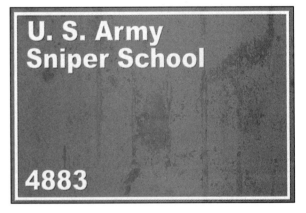

Sign Rebuilt with No Hot Spot and Straight Edges   This is the sign after it has been rebuilt and after the hot spot has been removed.

The Sign, Rebuilt and Used in a Game   Here's an in-game example of using the prepared sign. For more information about how to prepare photographs for game art use, see Chapter 3.

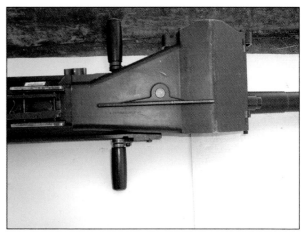
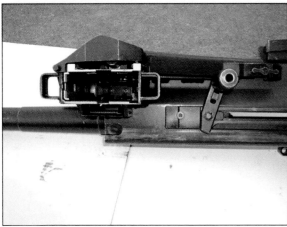
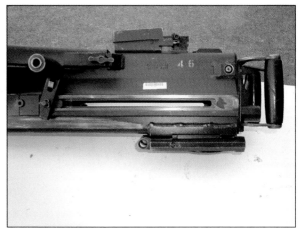

MK-19 Photo Reference These are the digital images of the MK-19 (or, for you civilians, a grenade launcher) and the reference shots that you'll need so that you can create a game version of it. In the line-art drawing, notice the scale of the MK-19 as the man carries it.

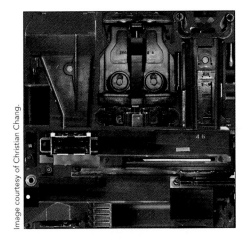

Image courtesy of Christian Chang.

MK-19 Texture for a 3D Model This is the texture "ripped" to be mapped on a game model, meaning the pictures have been taken apart and flattened so they can be wrapped around a 3D model.

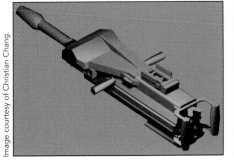

Image courtesy of Christian Chang.

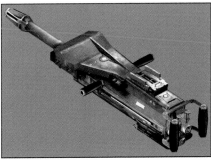

MK-19 3D Model, with and without Texture Here is the 3D model of the MK19 (left) and the same model with the textures applied (right).

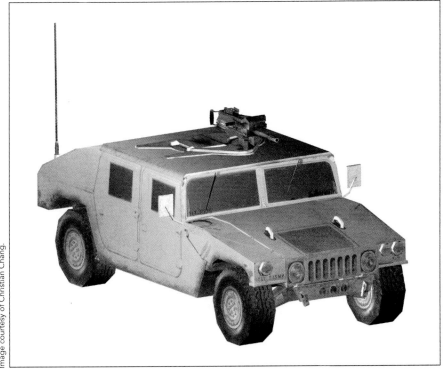

Image courtesy of Christian Chang.

MK-19 3D Model Used in a Game Here the MK-19 sits on its mount on the back of a vehicle. The model and texture are both low polygon count and are actually in game models, but see how good the image looks when you use the original photographs as a reference. The process for moving photographs and digital artwork into 3D game art is covered in Chapter 1.

Real-World Scene of a Castle   Game developers and artists are given typical images, such as this one, and are told by their superiors to "Make a level out of this!"

Game Textures, Castle Scene   The texture set has been created using techniques covered in Chapter 2—cropping, tiling, color balancing, and so on.

Image courtesy of Scott Maclean.

Castle Scene in a Game, the Vanilla Version   The textures have been applied to the geometry built for the scene, but the scene still looks too plain. For pointers on giving your levels a professional look, see Chapter 7.

Image courtesy of Scott Maclean.

Castle Scene in a Game, Deluxe   Here, the textures have been refined, the lighting applied, and a sky added. What a difference it makes when you take time to tweak a scene!

The Office Scene Textures   Similar to the castle scene, these base materials were broken out for the typical modern office scene—a very simple set of materials too.

The Office Scene, with Textures   Here, the textures have been applied to the office scene. Now it looks like a furniture showroom, and it's just a little too clean to be "real-world."

The Office Scene with Dirty Textures   Taking the office scene from Chapter 3 a little farther, some dirt and grime were added, and the lights were dimmed—and suddenly, the atmosphere changes.

The Office Scene with Dirty Textures and Detailed   Finally, after adding some details to the scene, you (as the player) will have questions. Why is the chair turned over? What happened here? Where did the person go? In short, you've developed part of the storyline with graphical tweaks.

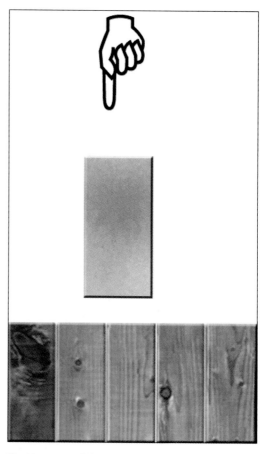

The Deluxe Castle Door   Here is the Deluxe Castle Door—in full color—that you learn to make in Chapter 3. Although the final result is complex, the construction process is actually easy.

The Textures of the Deluxe Castle Door   Notice that even this cool looking castle door is composed of only a few materials.

The Progression of the Deluxe Castle Door   These images show the construction sequence of the deluxe castle door.

The Deluxe Castle Door in a Scene Here is a "final" scene, shown both with and without the Deluxe Castle Door texture. To learn more about the techniques employed to create this door, see the project at the end of Chapter 3.

The Start of the Spell Book Logo Creating a logo can be much simpler than it appears. After a few simple steps, you have a plain but cool book cover.

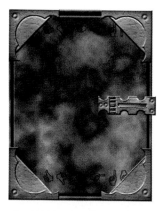

The Mid Point of the Spell Book Logo After few more steps, you have a metal-capped and locked spell book.

The Completed Spell Book Logo By the end of the project in Chapter 4, you have the completed spell book logo.

The Spell Book Logo in a Mocked Up Box Cover and Ad After you have created textures, assets, and art works for a project, you can begin to combine them as was done in this ad for the fictitious game "Spell Book." Notice the logos, the textures, and the level are all taken from projects throughout this book.

The Role-Playing Menu Background Creating menus requires some forethought, such as what to do for a background. This is the background we will use for the role-playing game menu.

The Role-Playing Menu Background with Layout This is the background, with simple notes on where to place the various menu elements. Planning ahead to the point of being able to place the menu objects saves time later on by avoiding potential redesign.

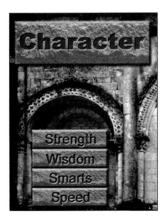

The Role-Playing Menu Background Buttons These buttons are composed using simple textures and techniques learned in Chapters 2 and 3.

The Complete Role-Playing Menu Here is the final role-playing menu, combining elements of all you can learn in the book: textures, effects, logos, and menu layout. The best menus are intuitive and nearly invisible to the player. To learn more about creating menus for 3D games, see Chapter 5.

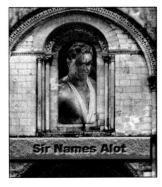

The Character Image Layout This is a closeup of the character window.

Stalingrad Mod images, courtesy of Christian Chang.

Digital Images Chosen to Be in a Game (Stalingrad Mod)   These digital images were chosen to be used as a texture in the Stalingrad Mod game. These images are typical of the type used as a base for textures in games. Thanks to Christian Chang for creating these images.

Image courtesy of Christian Chang.

Image courtesy of Christian Chang.

Digital Image, Cropped   At this stage, the image was cropped, focusing on the portion to be used in the game. Notice that not only was the window used from the first image, but the decoration above the window to the left in the second image was also used. This decoration had to be cut and processed using techniques from Chapters 2 and 3 of this book.

Digital Image, Cleaned and Straightened
After perspective correction work, the digital images have been straightened, cleaned, and blended into each other, and the colors have been balanced. This image is ready to be turned into a building.

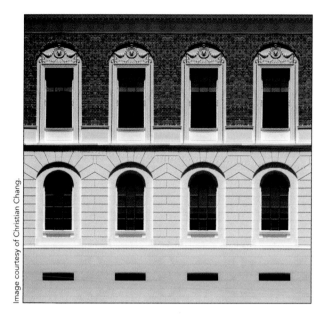

Image courtesy of Christian Chang.

Digital Image, Tiled as a Building   This image was so well done, it can now be flawlessly tiled onto a building front. It is, however, too clean.

Image courtesy of Christian Chang.

Digital Image, Tiled as a Dirty Building   Because the Stalingrad Mod takes place in the city of Stalingrad after brutal bombings, this building should be dirtied up a bit. Here is the building with some smoke and dirt added, to add a feeling of darkness, chaos, and war.

Image courtesy of Christian Chang.

The Final Digital Image in the Game   Here is the final building texture in the game, shown in the Stalingrad Modification of Quake 3.

Images courtesy of Christian Chang.

Balancing Art and Technology   This image shows how the developers of the Stalingrad Mod embody the principles of level design, as is laid out in Chapter 7. This image shows the "Balancing of Art and Technology." Notice the low polygon count of the scenes (of the vehicles wheels in particular); the low count is by design because the game world will be very large.

Image courtesy of Christian Chang.

A Far Shot   This image shows the level from a far shot, and you can see the rubble, perfect for sniping and hiding—the purpose of the level. This level was designed for a multiplayer death-match experience. This image also confirms the world setting—Stalingrad, during World War II.

Images courtesy of Christian Chang.

Historical/Locale Preparation   Developers have access to few pictures that show the location, period, and atmosphere of World War II Stalingrad. The architecture, weathering, aging, and other elements that affect the textures, geometry —even how the sky looks—were all guessed at and taken from other photos. Technically, there is no large terrain, and the buildings are so simple it seems as if the developers were modeling an indoor, not an outdoor, level. This is similar to what you do with Genesis3D when putting a skybox in a room to "open" the level. This image looks like an alleyway but technically, it is a hallway with a skybox.

Part II

World Building: Genesis3D and Reality Factory

Chapter 7

World Building

There is a difference between level design and level construction. Level design requires an in-depth knowledge of the specific game, game world, genre, and audience. This chapter focuses on level construction—building a level that looks good and runs efficiently.

Understanding Level Construction

Level design covers the actual game-play issues that a designer needs to be concerned about, such as mission design, story line, game balance, AI (artificial intelligence) paths, and other aspects of designing a level as a world in which a specific game will be played. Level design requires an in-depth knowledge of the specific game and its game world, genre, target audience, and other related facts on a per-project basis. This chapter concentrates on *level construction*—building levels that both look good and run efficiently.

Balancing Art and Technology

Looks good and runs well: This sums up the balancing act that you'll be involved in when you build game levels. Level construction involves the constant tradeoff of art and technology. Typically, you will begin to design a level by gathering your ideas (i.e., sketching the layout of the level for game play and aesthetic reasons). You will draw a top-down map of the area to be built, detailing buildings, streets, hallways, major obstacles, and objects.

In this chapter, you will start by sketching the levels that I have planned for this part of the book. In this stage, you can let your imagination run wild. Brainstorm freely now, and later you can adapt your ideas to the limits mandated by the game's technology.

The tradeoffs begin when the game level's plan is fairly well developed and you start translating your "analog" sketches and ideas into a digitized game level. When you are planning a map—even for a demo level such as this—you will need to consider the technology to be used and your budget for assets. The word *budget*, as used here, means the total amount of game assets you can have in your level—textures (artwork), objects (or geometry), special effects, and any other aspect of the game level that will affect the performance of the computer. (Later, you will learn some of the optimization tricks and techniques for larger and more complex levels.) For example, a large level may look wonderful architecturally, but the amount of artwork covering all the surfaces may have to be limited to a few low-resolution images. This may work well in a game world set in a city where it is common to have tiling images of the same material.

On the other hand, if your setting is an ornate throne room with paintings and with highly structured floors and walls where many textures are used to cover complex geometric surfaces, you may have to make the rooms smaller and divide them with hallways so the computer only has to draw one elaborate room at a time. Compromises are a constant juggle: Do you use a few high-resolution textures or many low-resolution textures? Do you design small, geometrically structured rooms or large, simple ones? Any aspect of your game that takes system resources to handle will need to be balanced because even though you want as much substantial material in your level as possible, you don't want to ruin the game play with choppy frame rates.

Knowing the Level's Purpose

Of course, in level design, you will primarily need to know the purpose of the level before you can even begin planning it. Is the level a death-match level, a single-player level, a capture-the-flag level, or even a tutorial level? Many game designers include simple levels in the beginning of the game to teach players the game play and functionality of the title; the design of these introductory levels differs considerably in both operation and complexity from the advanced in-game levels.

For this book, a small level was designed to showcase the tools and techniques of 3D game and level construction. In order to use the cool textures we built in Part I, I constructed a small castle level. Technically, this is an indoor level, but some sky will also be in evidence in an open courtyard. Building the castle will introduce you to the basics of Genesis3D and to some of the finer points of level construction, such as texture planning, object placement, and basic lighting. The simple act of walking through your first level is an achievement that will make you feel great.

Deciding on the World Setting

Location, time period, and *atmosphere* are some of the most critical elements of a level for a designer, providing you with the information you will need to start the artistic design of a level. You can then begin to think of details such as the architecture of the world, ornamentation, weathering, and aging, as well as other elements that will affect the textures, geometry, and even the way the sky looks. But before you start on the details, you need to know the basics:

- *Will the level be an indoor or outdoor level?* Most game engines can't handle large outdoor terrain, and if you plan to have any terrain, you will be sacrificing detail in many areas.

- *Will it be a medieval fortress or village, a modern city, or a futuristic spaceport?* Historically (or fictionally), time period and culture can dictate the complexity of buildings and objects, help determine the colors (and the amount of color) used, and give the designer clues on how to use that setting to best advantage. Egyptian settings, for example, can be made of large, blocky walls that are covered in a base sandstone texture. Complex temples or statues can be placed far enough apart that the computer can draw them separately, rather than drawing all of them at the same time.

- *Will you be building a realistic environment or a fantasy creation?* This part of the creation process is one area in which what you see can be used to your advantage. In a realistic setting, such as a mall, there may be a clean view far into the well-lit building, but in a dark dungeon of the same size, you would not be able to see nearly as far. Because the computer doesn't draw what is in darkness, your level can have a few highly detailed pools of light interspersed with dark areas to break up the apparent size of the world that you are creating.

Adapting Your Art to Fit the Game World's Perspective

As you start building the background and objects in a level, you will soon discover that some of the tasks that you thought would be simple will turn out to be somewhat more complicated than you originally anticipated. For example, even the size of a door, which may seem like a simple detail to obtain in the real world, is a challenge that requires much experimentation and input to determine. For example, in the game *Unreal* (created by Epic Games, Inc.; see www.epicgames.com), the characters are cartoonish, the doors are large for quick fighting in the first-person shooter (FPS) style, and the architecture of much of *Unreal* is very science-fictional. If you're trying to build a modern building as a setting for a game by using the *Unreal* game engine, you will be faced with characters that are too large and that may not fit through the doors you build. And the perspective of a door that is built to real-world proportions may not look right as viewed from the eyes of a game character in *Unreal*. The view from the "eyes" (what the player sees on screen) of most FPS characters is a bit wide-angled to make up for the fact that the player is looking at a flat screen and has no peripheral vision because the scene ends at the monitor screen's edge. Eventually, you will realize that you need to do a lot of experimenting with the door's dimensions to find the proper size.

Walls fall under the same limitations. You may find a wall height that looks great in the level editor and the game, but from a texturing point of view, when you are trying to lay the texture on the wall (which will most likely have to be a power of two, as discussed previously in Chapter 1), you find the texture doesn't line up correctly without plenty of resizing by the level editors. So, back to the drawing board you go—to try and make a power-of-two texture that fits nicely on a door when applied, and the act of balancing art with technical limitations goes on.

- *What will the color scheme, the mood, and even the weather be like?* Every detail of the world can be either a challenge or used as a trick to help the designers. You can compress textures more with a color scheme that is muted and low-color. With fast-paced games, you are showing the player more of the world more rapidly and the computer has to keep up, but if the game you are designing is a slower-paced walking game, then you can afford to introduce more to the player in the level and the computer will have an easier time keeping up with the demand. Additionally, weather, which can be hard to create in a computer, can help engine speed. As with darkness, you can use fog to both set a mood and to obscure what the player can see. In this way, the computer has to draw only what is close to the player (rather than what is all around him, at every distance) in the world.

Planning the Level

After you know the level's purpose and general environment (location, time period, atmosphere, and so on), you can start designing and planning. For the castle project, you begin by making a few rough sketches of the castle's exterior, the floor plan, and a couple of detail views just to see if your ideas work on paper before you dedicate a great deal of time to developing them. An added benefit: Even the roughest and most preliminary sketching helps to keep you from drifting in your design. Although, as you can see, the sketches made for this small project are not very detailed (see Figure 7.1), nonetheless, they will aid you in laying out a set of rooms.

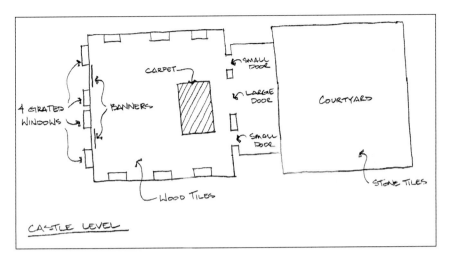

Figure 7.1
The hand-drawn quick-sketch floor plan of the castle level. Notice the rough simplicity of the sketched plans.

The Precision Factor

This phase is important. When working on screen in the level editor, most people operate in a different mental arena; onscreen work calls for you to be so much more patient and precise than you need to be on paper. Your best ideas for the level may not surface if you don't get them on paper. Even the roughest of sketches will improve what you build in the level editor because, when you're sketching on paper, you can explore ideas unfettered by the tedium and the limits of the level editor.

Experimenting while sketching an idea on paper is easier as well, because you are not investing as much time and effort as you would be if you were building your level directly in the editor. Every minute you spend in planning, sketching, and giving thought to your level or room will be reflected in how much better your level will look in the game. And, as you will see in the forthcoming chapters, as you go through the process of building a level from the ground up, the difference in actual level-editing time between a polished, professional-looking level and a rough, amateurish level is sometimes only a matter of a few minutes of effort.

In addition to giving you more freedom to explore your ideas, sketching them on paper before going digital can make your final level easier to build. When you are working from a well-thought-out sketch, you can sometimes put together a level very rapidly. Because you are not thinking of many things simultaneously, you can think in a one-track fashion; the ideas have already been detailed, so you can focus your attention on implementing them.

The Castle Plan

This part of the process deals with the floor plan of the castle level you will be creating for this book. A few rough sketches convey the layout, and as you can see in Figure 7.1, the floor plan is rather simple. But even this simple layout benefits from planning. After this level is completed—when it's textured, when architectural details have been added, and when lighting is completed—it will look great.

Understanding the Level Development Cycle

It is important to keep in mind that developing a level is only part of developing a game. Level design and development has a language all its own (as do most of the various arts of game development) and, in fact, most sizable development teams keep a glossary of terms as part of the design document. Because game-development teams frequently consist of individuals straight out of school, from other professions, and from small and large development teams that have all developed many diverse types of games, we all have our own terms for different concepts and processes. The steps below are as general as I can make them, but they are still somewhat subjective because they are based on my own experience.

Typically, you will develop a level by following this process:

1. With basic information known about the level from the design document (its purpose, its general environment, the weather, and the story surrounding the level), designers start sketching and storyboarding. Ideas are refined and decisions are documented. Procedures and processes, documents and worksheets are created that will make the level-creation process smoother and faster later in the development stage and will also make the levels play more consistently within the game.

2. The level is mocked up (on the computer) from the documentation. The initial prototype is produced, people applaud, and then everyone starts suggesting changes. The processes are refined and should be solid by this point.

3. The base texture set is created or added to the level as are other assets such as base sounds, animations, and models.

4. The level is tested, fixed where necessary, and approved (this process is repeated as needed). At this stage, it is also common for levels to be reworked a great deal, redone totally, and sometimes even scrapped altogether. It is also not unusual for a poorly designed project to hit major trouble at this stage of implementation, when it is discovered that nothing works as planned and the whole project has to be re-evaluated. (Sadly, when this happens to small developers, they usually don't have the money to start over or the time to spend in redesigning the game.)

5. The level is finalized. Lighting, entities, optimizations, and continuity checks are complete. There is not much applauding at this stage as people are working hard. Suggestions are (hopefully) minimal by now.

6. The final level is compiled, tested, recompiled, and released.

Note: Remember, level construction is only part of the overall level development. Even before a formal testing stage occurs, the level designers, programmers, and artists may all have a level they call a test level, used for benchmarking and testing various aspects of the tools and technologies they are using.

Ideally, before a level is constructed, a great deal of the game is already understood on paper. Sometimes, however, artists, modelers, and level builders may be put to work building levels while the design document is still being written. This happens frequently, usually because the development company has the technology ready to go and wants to keep the team busy, but it can also happen when the game is not being properly developed. The best way to construct a level is to be given a folder that presents a wealth of information that is essential to good level construction—the storyline, setting, mission goals, art budgets, timelines, maps, and sketches. Often, however, a level builder's work consists of redoing work, adding elements after the fact, and even redoing whole levels (if they are not dropped from the game). These last-minute additions and changes should be avoided, if possible.

Prototype Level

Usually, a prototype level is built from one idea that has been laid out on paper, following the documentation that was previously generated. This layout may be solely the creation of the level designer—based on notes and the design documentation—or the level designer may be given sketches, floor plans, and a mountain of information both textual and visual that must be assembled into a game-world level. This process can require several stages of development, depending on the size of the level, the size of the development company, and the degree of structure the company uses. Some development teams have one person doing all the "level" work, and other teams have level designers, level editors, and even specialists in lighting and game play. Regardless of how level design and construction are done before or during the actual construction of the world, the process is an evolutionary one.

Usually, prototype levels use assets that are placeholders and sometimes levels are without textures and only contain box mock-ups of the playing area. However, even if a designed level is complete, it should be constantly reviewed during development. You do want to avoid redoing work at all costs, but after you have used the tools for a year, bonded with the team, gotten a better understanding of the game, and improved your skills, the level you built at the beginning of development will most likely pale next to the one you built at the middle or end of development, and you need to strive for consistency.

Actually, even though "levels built" is a milestone or goal in most development schedules and the process looks linear on paper, in actual practice, it shouldn't be. To keep the team and the levels fresh, it's a good idea to have a good bit of *coordinated* level hopping. If one level presented a challenge that the team worked on for weeks and the challenge was met but the level is not complete, it may be wise to let the team members get a breather and switch gears to a different, and therefore more interesting, level. This also ensures that all levels are kept up to date. But remember, this process must be organized and controlled, or there will be chaos as your team members go in separate directions.

Test Level

After most of the paper design has been digitized, tested, and discussed, bugs have been fixed, and other major obstacles have been addressed that may cause redevelopment later on, a test level is built that should closely emulate the final game. The paper design is updated, the levels are laid out in detail, and construction begins. At this point, no more questions should exist about the game and its design, atmosphere, setting, mood, and so on. The only task remaining is to produce and polish the game, to make it work as defined, and to add as little as necessary to the mix.

At this point, the process for building and testing levels should be set in stone. How assets are created, named, and stored should be standardized and documented. However, it is almost impossible for even the most experienced level designer to think everything through up front. Very often, even after the game is running and playable, mistakes are found, dead spots in levels are discovered, and other areas that must be addressed become known. All changes must be reflected across-the-board in development.

Level development should always be subject to a process that ensures the level is consistent and running at its best, and that the workflow is paced to keep the team from becoming bored or being overworked.

Consistency within a level involves more than making sure that textures and other elements are similar from one scene to the next—that castle floors, for example, don't change from aged stone to new brick. Consistency can also involve items from the game's storyline—you need a continuity specialist (or at least, a team member whose job it is to check and track special elements). Suppose that, for example, the story says, "Legend has it that the castle with the green stone walls contains powerful magic." Someone has to ensure that the walls of the magic castle are, in fact, green.

The Demo Level

The demo level is the level that testing firms, reviewers, and sometimes the general public get to see. It should have no obvious or critical bugs or problem areas, and it should represent the game well. You must resist pressure to push a demo out the door before it's of at least "beta" quality. It should be close as possible to release-candidate quality because a buggy demo will generate a mountain of bad publicity for the game or product.

Mistakes to Avoid in Mapping Your Levels

To begin, there is an excellent article on level design, "The Art and Science of Level Design," by Cliff Bleszinski of Epic Games at **www.cliffyb.com/art-sci-ld.html** that all level designers must read. In this article, Bleszinski says the following, "In addition to having dedicated world-texture artists and environment concept designers, the need will soon emerge for dedicated "prop" people; artists who create content that will fill up previously static and barren environments. Most architecture is relatively simple, much of the detail in the real world comes from the "clutter," the chairs, tables, and decorations that fill these places up." We are already there. Currently, there is a hot scramble to hire more specialists who can model certain types of world objects and texture them.

Bleszinski goes on to say that "It is very likely that the level designer will be like a chef, taking various "ingredients" from other talented people and mixing them into something special while following the "recipe" of a design document. Right now, there are companies that have artists lighting levels, as well as doing custom texture work on a per-surface basis. The level designer will evolve to the role of the glue of a project, the hub at which everything comes together." This is exactly how the current project I am working on is set up, as are many other development efforts that are just beginning.

In this same article, Bleszinski also lists his "Design Commandments," which I will summarize in the next few sections.

Designer, Evaluate Thyself

The best level designers are never afraid to reevaluate their content and take breaks from it as well. If you become burned out or sick of your own level, you are in danger of doing shoddy work.

Thou Shalt Seek Peer Criticism

A great designer accepts criticism from his peers. In fact, a great designer is the sum of himself plus his peers. Prima donnas are often the weakest link in a design team. The ideal designer seeks criticism even from those he may consider "less talented" than he, because even if he believes that the critic in question has no skills, the commentary will be fresh and from a new perspective.

Thou Shalt Value Rivalries

In addition to taking suggestions from one another, it's key for level designers to feel a desire to "one up" each other. Healthy competition in any area of a development team means improved results.

Do Thy Homework

As much of this work is moving into the realm of the Art Director and art team, the designers remain the Digital Architects, and they will still be responsible for much of the look and feel of the levels. Therefore, if a project needs an accurate Roman Empire, everyone had better be doing his or her homework. Having a shared directory of R&D images on a server as well as an art bible that is referred to by all designers and artists will contribute to a more consistent look and feel.

Thy Framerate Shall Not Suck

If the designers are working with a technology that can push 100 million polys, they will try to make the technology look like it can push 3 times that. Although much of the framerate issue falls upon the programmers, with optimizations and level of detail technology, it is extremely important that designers have hard-coded guidelines for framerates, detail levels, and RAM usage.

Thou Shalt Deceive

Pay no attention to the man behind the curtain. If a designer can simulate a newer technology with some trickery, then by all means allow and encourage this. If the programmers are exclaiming things such as "I don't remember programming that!" or "How did you do that?" then something special is going on. If a scene can look more detailed with creative texturing, then go for it. If bump mapping or specular highlighting can be faked even though the engine doesn't "truly" support it, then why not do it? Only the hardest of the hardcore gamers will know the difference.

The Three Sins of the Beginner

Many beginner-made levels suffer from everyday ailments, things that a few minutes of tweaking or extra work could fix. The most common of these mistakes include bad textures or texture placement, blocky construction, and bad lighting. These sins will be discussed in the sections that follow, but if you have read Part I of this book, bad textures should not be a problem for you.

Bad Textures

Often, textures created by amateurs are not created properly and/or they are not placed properly on the world surfaces. Fortunately, you learned how to do both earlier in the book. Textures are very important; they are second only to lighting, and that is only because lighting controls so much of the color and atmosphere of the level. Textures are abundant on the Internet, as are tutorials and tools to make textures. (Remember not to use other people's textures without their permission.)

Taking the time to place textures properly in the game world pays off in a big way, as you will see. You may notice that a truly amateur level will feature textures that are simply colorized noise, hard lines, and other techniques, typically produced by people that have no texture-creation training. The other problem with amateur texturing is the lack of attention to detail. Seams that don't meet, stretched or squashed textures, and textures with no detail that have been placed quickly look terrible. Figure 7.2 features examples of bad textures and bad lighting in the same scene.

Driver: (D3D)Primary Display Driver 640x480

LukeA: 0

HEALTH   ARMOR   BLASTER   GRENADE   ROCKET   SHREDDER
100   0   Inf   0   0   0

Figure 7.2
Bad textures. These texture examples lack both detail and depth.

Blocky Construction

Levels with blocky construction give the impression that the world was built rapidly, with no attention to detail. Simply dropping cubes about a map is not level building; making the cubes look like objects you would find in a real or imagined world, is. The fact that Genesis3D has no vertex manipulation—or the capability to drag out individual points on an object—makes blocky construction an obstacle. You can taper and skew cubes, for example, and make a cool base to a column by typing in different parameters when creating the cube, but these techniques are not vertex manipulation. However, you can find ways around this limitation, and using light and composition is one of them. As an artist, I skew or slant the columns inward; this adds a sense of the dramatic beyond having simple, straight square (i.e., non-tapered) columns. See Figure 7.3 for an example of a level with the same objects arranged and lit in two different ways.

Vertex manipulation, as we said, is the capability to drag out points of a 3D object (see Figure 7.4) and change the shape of the object. While Genesis3D does not allow this, there are a few things you can do to get around this limit. Another way of getting around Genesis3D's lack of vertex manipulation capability is to type in different values. In Figure 7.5, you can see a cube of normal proportions, and then a cube created by typing in the top X and Y values to force it into a tapered shape—you will look at this technique more closely in Chapter 9. Figure 7.5 also shows the same two cubes with texture and lighting, so that you can see how much better this simple trick makes them look.

Figure 7.3
Here, you see an example of a room with the same columns—only now, one set is slanted to give the room a more interesting look. Composition is an important aspect in making levels look good, especially as you are working with fewer, simpler objects.

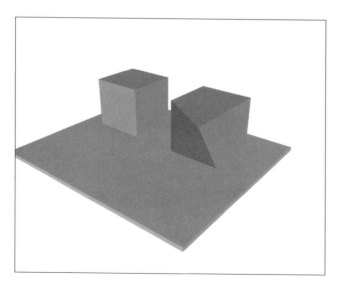

Figure 7.4
A normal cube (left) and a cube tapered (right).

Figure 7.5
The same cubes (although the tapered cube on the right has been re-manipulated), now with texture and lighting added.

Bad Lighting

It is possible to make a well-lit series of rooms with *no* textures look, or rather feel, better than a poorly lit room with good textures. With poor lighting, your level will look like a bunch of painted cardboard boxes. For a good (or should I say, bad) example of this, see Figure 7.6.

As you can see, the default light level in Genesis3D (as in many game engines) is harsh, and it flattens the colors and depth of the scene. The only benefit to this default setting is that level designers won't find themselves in the dark if they forget to place lights in their world. One of the most powerful aspects of Genesis3D is the ability to control the lighting and its many parameters. Lighting in Genesis3D is a huge bag of tricks that should be explored and exploited. Unfortunately, many beginners leave the default setting of light in their world and touch no other lights. Figure 7.7 shows the difference lighting can make to a scene.

Texture Planning for the Castle

As you have seen in Part I of this book, many ways exist in which you can create 2D textures. They can be scanned in, they can come from a digital camera that then can be rendered in a 3D program, or they can be made completely in Photoshop. Some of the textures in the remainder of this book in all the exercises starting with Chapter 9 were created using digital images (from a digital camera), which were then touched up (a great deal) in Photoshop, and the remaining images were created by using the techniques presented in Part I.

Note: You can find all assets for the tutorials in this book on the companion CD-ROM in the Tutorials folder.

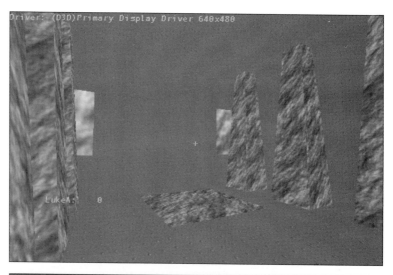

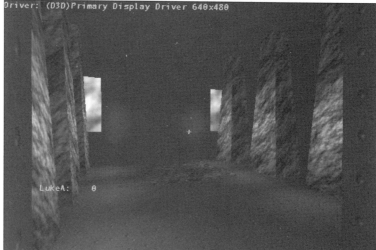

Figure 7.6

Here is a level with bad textures and poor lighting (the top image) and the same level with the same textures and good lighting (the bottom image).

Going back to our initial level design, the sketches, and the small discussion we had about the project previously, you will see that we have to create a few types of textures for the castle environment. We need to create the stone walls that will cover 99 percent of the level as well as the floor, create wood for beams, and create detail and specialty textures such as the banners and any ornamentation in the level.

Because the castle is ancient and abandoned, the texture on the walls will be aged stone. This texture was made from a digital image taken of stone from an old building near my home. I had to make the image tile well, which was a challenge because the stone was irregular (refer to Chapter 2 for tiling tips). While the stone had to be cleaned up and modified in Photoshop to tile well, it also had to continue to look dirty and old. So although the stone image was cleaned up to tile well, with imperfections that would stand out and make the pattern of our tiling texture visible removed, the stone image also was weathered and aged. Making the texture not look tiled or too plain is not only texture

Figure 7.7

In this example, you see two shots. In the top image, the default lighting was left on. In the bottom image, the default lighting was turned way down and a few lights were hand-placed in the scene, about 30 seconds of work.

work but is also part lighting and part usage of the texture in construction. See Figure 7.8 for examples of three textures: one that is too plain, one that is obviously a tile, and one that is just right.

The Castle Texture Set

Called the *texture library* in this book, but often also called the *texture set* or the *texture palette*, these terms refer to the set of textures in your library of textures that will be used to map the level's surfaces, as you learned about in Chapter 3. In Chapters 2 and 3, ways of breaking the texture sets out of a scene were discussed, but, as artists, we frequently are simply handed a list of what textures to make for a level and, more often than not, that list is incomplete. But most of the time, a texture artist works from a checklist. Unfortunately, just working blindly from a list and not understanding the process that it took to generate that list prevents you from contributing and helping to refine the process of texturing the world. Reading Chapter 3 will help you gain that understanding. To put some of the discussion from Part I into effect here, I'll break out the texture set for the castle level.

Figure 7.8

Here are examples of textures that are too plain (bottom texture), obviously tiled (middle texture), and finally, just right (top texture).

The Castle's Checklist

To show you what an invaluable tool a good checklist is, I created one for the castle. This section breaks down that list into base textures, ornamental textures, and special elements. You'll need to have textures ready for each of these elements before you can complete the castle project.

The castle's base textures will consist of the following:

- Stone tiling for walls

- Stone tiles for courtyard (dirtier and more worn than walls)

- Wooden tiles for the floors

- Wood, slatted for the ceiling

- Base wood (four-way tile) for beams and stairs

The castle's ornamental textures will consist of the following:

- Carpet

- Banner 1

- Banner 2

- Door 1—Massive portal

- Door 2—Smaller side door

- Grate 1— Between beams

- Grate 2—Between holes in floor

Other elements of the texture set include:

- Skybox textures.
- If you use lava, water, or any other special surfaces, you would include them here in your checklist.

Some of these textures were made in Part I of this book, and the rest we will look at in the upcoming chapters, as they come into play. In any case, you can get the complete textures from this book's companion CD-ROM if your interest lies in building the level and not creating the textures for it.

Your Job as Texture Artist

If this texture set request were handed to you as a texture artist, the list would contain a great deal more information. As an example, I have included the following instruction set which has a great deal of information about creating a carpet for ornamental textures, but even this sample does not contain all the information a texture artist will need to create it properly in the context of a complex game:

Sample Instructions: Ornamental Textures

```
Texture name: orn_int_crpt_001.bmp
Format: BMP
File size: 256x256, indexed
Level: Old Castle
Description: This texture is an old carpet* that lies in the
ruined castle entrance. The texture must have crossed chains in
the pattern that prominently appear to the gamer, but other than
that, you can get creative. The chains should not be too
overstated. Keep in mind that this castle was once the dwelling
of a good king, so maybe the carpet should reflect this.
* This carpet covers a secret door.
```

As you can see, just making this small simple castle level in the context of a larger, more complex game can get demanding. In addition to the creation of the textures, we have the technology, storylines, and other aspects to pay attention to. For instance, it was mentioned in the example above that this was once the castle of a good king, but now maybe it is a run-down castle inhabited by evil monsters. The castle design and textures will have to reflect both the good king who once lived here, and the new monster inhabitants. To achieve this, the carpet in the example may have the pattern and look of a once-nice piece, but will now be stained and torn. The tiles on the floors will also reflect this aging and disuse, having once been part of an opulent palace that is now a dark and smelly dwelling for monsters.

You may have noticed that the texture set contains some grates. These will be a few textures you will create that use transparency to help break the blocky look of the level. A grate, a chain or two, and some cobwebs will add some "delicacy" to the objects in the world. See Figure 7.9.

Figure 7.9
A few well-placed objects using transparency and good textures can help break the solid blocky look in a game level.

A Final Note about Organization

If you make your own images, save all of them in a folder where you can find them again. Remember to back up all your work and save the larger high-color versions of these images. For Genesis3D, you will be creating images that are 256×256 and Adaptive Color. If you don't feel like creating the images, don't worry. All the images are included on the companion CD-ROM, as well as in the Texture Library format ready to use with Genesis3D.

Moving On

In this chapter, you looked at the basics of how to design and develop a level that will look and play professionally, and have seen that planning and proper implementation are vitally important. One major theme of this book is that, quite often, the difference between an amateur result and a professional result is a few more moments of work, a few more touches to your work, a little more thought and planning up front.

In the next chapter, you will start looking at Genesis3D tool set. You will find a quick overview of what Genesis3D is, how you install it on your computer, and how to get it up and running.

Chapter 8

The Game World Editor

Once you have planned a game world, planned your
texture library, and created those beautiful textures,
you probably can't wait to see that world come to life.
This is where the Genesis3D game studio comes in.

What Is Genesis3D?

In this chapter, you will be introduced to an Open Source game engine and the game-world editing tools that come with it. With these tools, you will be able to build a game world and put textures in that world from a texture library that you will create (using textures you have made in Part I, or from this book's companion CD-ROM). The tools are collectively known as Genesis3D, and they are the best way for a beginner to get started in 3D world building. Genesis is a top-notch engine, easily usable by both professionals and beginners. As a plus, Genesis3D has a large and helpful online community that is accessible to you through its online forums.

Note: Please search the forums on the Genesis site (**www.genesis3d.com**) before posting a question to it. Chances are that your question already has been asked and answered.

Genesis3D and Its Relatives

If you start seriously getting active on the Genesis forums, you will face some confusion about the companies and product versions involved with Genesis3D. Here is an overview of some of the companies and product versions:

- *WildTangent, Inc.*—This firm acquired the assets, technology, and most of the employees from Eclipse Entertainment, the developers of Genesis3D. Eclipse is still its own company and retains the capability to license the existing Genesis3D source code for non-Internet applications. WildTangent has written a game driver that specializes in Web play; this driver will be a superset of the Genesis and WildTangent technologies. WildTangent is developing Genesis3D 2, but it will not be Open Source, which means that if you use the WildTangent technology for commercial purposes, you have to pay for it. (A personal use license, however, will still be free.) For a breakdown of the costs involved in using the WildTangent technology, go to **www.wildtangent.com/sales**.

- *Genesis3D 1.1*—This application is the original Genesis3D Open Source engine. Currently, it is still the most popular and widely used Open Source game engine in the world. There is now a push in the current Genesis3D community for Genesis3D to be further developed as Genesis3D Classic. Eclipse Entertainment recently handed over the development and maintenance of Genesis3D Open Source technology to Cheyenne Cloud, Inc. This effort is currently under development.

- *Jet3D*—Eclipse Entertainment's Jet3D gives a glimpse of what is coming in the future for Genesis3D Open Source technology. Jet3D project is mostly dead.

What is Open Source Software?

Open Source software is software whose code is available to any developer who wants to see it, work with it, modify it, improve it, and redistribute it. The idea behind Open Source software is this: The more people who work on a product's source code, the better the code becomes, and the faster the product improves. For information about Open Source software, visit the Web site of the Open Source Initiative (**www.opensource.org**).

- *Reality Factory*—This product is not only an upgraded and improved version of Genesis3D, it also has had a great many enhancements. Rabid Games built Reality Factory on top of the latest version of Genesis3D 1.1. The best option right now is to learn the basics of Genesis, and then after you've mastered 1.1, move to the Reality Factory suite of game- and multimedia-development tools.

In Chapter 13, you will look at Reality Factory, after you learn the basics of Genesis3D. Rabid Games has made significant improvements to the code, editor, and usefulness of the original Genesis3D tools.

For the latest and most accurate information, please visit the Web sites of the following companies at:

- **www.wildtangent.com**—WildTangent Game Driver and Genesis3D

- **www.jet3d.com**—Jet3D

- **www.rabidgames.com**—Reality Factory

What Comes with Genesis3D?

Genesis3D is a set of game development tools and APIs (application programming interfaces). The application comes with the following components: libraries and drivers for building your application; a sample game (GTtest) and related code for showing you the game engine's basic capabilities; documentation; and tools for building your games. You can also download a demonstration called GDemo1 from the Genesis3D Web site.

Genesis3D includes the following game-building tools:

- *The world editor*—Also called the "level editor," "the editor," or "GEdit"; the tool that you'll use to create your game levels, geometry, textures, and lighting effects.

- *Actor Studio, Actor Builder, and Actor Viewer*—Tools that you'll employ to create and view *actors* for your games. Actors are objects in a game that have behaviors assigned to them.

- *The Texture Packer*—A tool that you can use to build the texture libraries that the editor and level compilation tools employ.

- *3DS Max exporters*—Exporters for 3DS Max versions 2.5 and 3; these tools are needed to export geometry for building with the Actor tools.

- *GTest*—A death-match arena created to demonstrate and test the functionality of the Genesis3D engine. You can use GTest to run the levels that you build and compile in the world editor.

As you work with the various tools in Genesis3D, you'll need to be familiar with the following file type extensions:

- *3dt*—These files are created by the Genesis Level Editor. They contain the geometry, lighting, and all the information associated with the level.

- *txl*—These are the texture library files. The TPACK utility creates these files and the editor reads them.

- *bmp*—This extension represents the image file type that the TPACK utility can import. This is the standard indexed color Windows format.

- *wav*—These are the sound file types used by the game for effects such as weapons, explosions, and player noises.

From the level builder point of view, we will only deal with these types of files. There are other file types associated with Genesis3D, but don't concern yourself with these files when you are building levels.

What Do I Need to Run Genesis3D?

To run Genesis3D, your computer should meet certain minimum requirements. Keep in mind that the requirements are suggestions only. You can probably force the Genesis3D application to run on a slower system, but if you plan on running huge levels with a high degree of complex geometry and many large textures, you will need to get a faster computer. Also keep in mind that these are only the requirements to run Genesis3D, and not the other development tools that you may also want open at the same time. Tools such as Photoshop 5 or 6 (for texture editing), 3D programs (such as 3D Studio Max), sound editing software, program compilers, and even word processors all devour system resources. You may need to get a better computer based on how involved your development will go. This is the list of suggested requirements:

- Genesis3D can run in software-only mode, but does not perform very well. A good 3D accelerator card is best. They cost about $100.00 or more and should support Direct3D.

- Any good sound card that is Windows-compatible will do.

- RAM, or system memory, the more the better. 64MB or higher will do nicely.

- Your chip speed should be at least 166MHz (greater speed, of course, is recommended). A PII 233 or higher with MMX will do very nicely in this context.

What Can I Do with Genesis3D?

Genesis is designed primarily for rendering games (for the most part, those set indoors) with moderate polygon counts, so that the game can operate at a very high performance level. Genesis can also be used to build outdoor scenes, but you must be careful to plan and build outdoor scenes correctly. (In Chapter 7, I discuss the tradeoffs of art and technology when building levels in greater detail.) Of the advances that Reality Factory has made to Genesis, the ability to use fog and a clipping plane allows you to build much larger scenes and also outdoor scenes, and provides better level optimization. You will look at the capabilities of Reality Factory in Chapter 13.

The Genesis3D level editor, which comes with the Genesis3D tool set, is a top-notch editor. This Genesis editor uses a standard CSG (Constructive Solid Geometry, or building things with solid shapes) concept coupled with an easy-to-use interface for modeling the architecture of levels. With it, you can quickly build levels and run them in the engine to see what your world looks like in its complete form. The user interface has been designed to be simple, yet it provides enough power to allow you to do a truly professional job. At the end of this chapter, you will look more closely at the editor, and you will use it in this chapter and in Chapters 9 through 12 to create levels that employ the powerful features of both the editor and the engine. You will even use a built-in keyframe animation system that allows you to animate world geometry, which you will learn to manipulate in Chapter 12.

Genesis3D Features

Using Genesis3D tools, you can develop and test levels, import and apply textures, apply various lighting to your scenes, compile your level, and prepare it for distribution. Keep in mind that, although Genesis3D has limitations, it is a cutting-edge 3D game construction engine that is free to use. This is a major step in independent game development, especially if you consider that a comparable set of game development tools and source code costs anywhere from $50,000 to $500,000 and offers the same level of code use. Genesis3D provides the development tools of advanced lighting, networked play, and more. The following list describes some of the strong features of the Genesis3D Engine:

- *True RGB dynamic lights*—Dynamic RGB lighting means that lights can be any RGB color and can dynamically affect the game world in realtime. A light can move through a room, casting light and shadows across all surfaces. Shadows are half of what makes lighting work but—until Genesis3D—no 3D engine has supported dynamic shadows for world geometry. 3D polygonal characters cast shadows, too. You will learn more about light types and working with them in the editor in Chapter 12.

- *Fog lights*—Genesis3D supports a mode of light called the fog light, which generates a radius of fog around the light.

- *Mirrors*—Being able to have a mirror or reflective surface in a game provides an extra touch of reality and depth. Mirrored surfaces can be made to reflect the world at 100 percent, like a polished wall mirror, or the effect can be applied to a floor of polished marble and toned down to the point that you will see the marble texture and the reflected world. All lights, shadows, and geometry are perfectly reflected by the surface with the mirror attribute. This capability will be explored further in Chapter 10.

- *Realtime water surface distortion*—You can create a surface, apply a water texture, and then make the geometry to which the water surface is applied distort and wave, just like the surface of real water, whether you want it to look like a pond, a lake, a stream, or a river. You can also combine a water shimmer effect with a light entity to make the light on the walls around the water shimmer as if the light were reflecting off the water's surface onto the walls (you will find more information about this technique in Chapter 12). You also can make the water surface translucent; that way, you can see through the water and view the underwater world below, and the world geometry will also be waving and shimmering.

Use of 3D Studio Models
Genesis supports 3D models exported from 3D Studio Max (3ds max 4, in its latest incarnation). Motion attached to these models is also exported, allowing the engine to animate the character in Genesis3D in realtime, just as it is animated in Max. By using texture morphing, you can employ Genesis to enable a 3D model to morph from stone to flesh. Soft skin of polygonal objects can also morph. It is possible to build a "mimetic poly-alloy" character in the style of the *T-2* villain (surely, you have seen the movie *Terminator 2: Judgment Day*, where the latest version of Terminator is constructed of liquid metal) that morphs from liquid to solid, animating the texture as well as the mesh.

Render Options
Genesis has currently been implemented to support a software rasterizer, Direct 3D, and 3DFX Glide. An OPENGL version is under consideration. The interface to Genesis is a standard API set. The performance of your application code is limited only by your scale and not by a proprietary PCODE layer or interpreter (i.e., Genesis3D will run well on a wide variety of computers).

Physics System
Genesis has an advanced physics system that allows you to set up a series of models that respond to physical stimuli from the player. For example, you can create a platform on a pivot that will start to tilt over when a player jumps on it (with a pool of hot, deadly lava below, of course) and if the player doesn't jump to the next platform right away he will fall off the platform.

Installing Genesis3D
Genesis3D is a straightforward installation. Go to the Genesis folder on the CD-ROM and open it. Click on the Genesis3D120.exe file, and follow the installation instructions. You will be prompted with several standard screens; the most important are the Software License Agreement and the Destination Location screens, as seen in Figures 8.1 and 8.2.

It is important that you read the license agreement. It is also important that you either install Genesis to the default folder or take note of where it is installed if you change the install location. It is assumed by the Genesis3D application that you are not changing the default installation parameters; if

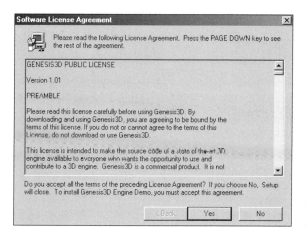

Figure 8.1
The Software License Agreement screen.

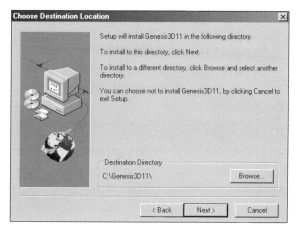

Figure 8.2
The Destination Location screen.

you do change the default installation location from C:\Genesis3D11\ to another drive letter and folder, then you must compensate for this later. (When the need to compensate arises, it will be mentioned in the text.)

Troubleshooting Genesis Startup

With any installation, something can always go wrong; it's the nature of software and computers. The following list describes some of the errors you might encounter and the methods for fixing them:

- *"Error in Ctl3d32.dll"*—If this error message appears on screen, the file Ctl3d32.dll is not in your Windows system folder. You can copy this file from the Redist folder (in the Genesis application folder) to the Windows system folder.

- *"Could not find glide2x.dll in the path"*—Make sure that you have the latest Glide drivers installed. If you do not have these drivers installed, check the Web site of the manufacturer of your video card and download them.

- *"Failed to decompress %'s"*—You might not have enough free disk space in the TEMP folder. Check to see that you have enough hard drive space.

- *"Check your 'autoexec.bat' file"*—Your temp folder should be set in the line SET TEMP=C:\TEMP, and it is also good to have the line SET TEMP=C:\TEMP in the autoexec.bat file. Here are some possible fixes for this:

  - Make sure that the folder C:\TEMP actually exists.

  - Clean out the C:\TEMP folder of all files.

  - Make sure that none of the files in the Genesis3D folder are set to the read-only attribute. To determine this, right-click on each file, choose Properties, and deselect the Read-Only attribute checkbox, if it is checked.

  - Finally, it is possible that your video driver could be causing the install program to go bad. Switch to VGA mode and try installing again.

- *"GTest in D3D mode does not work properly"*—Make sure that you have the latest version of Microsoft DirectX installed and that your video card supports the D3D rendering API. You can determine this by reading the documentation on the card. You may also want to update your card's drivers.

> **Note:** You will need to restart your system after trying these changes before they can take effect.

Backing Up the Default Genesis Files

Before you start working on your first world, it is important that you make a copy of the Genesis files you will be using and place them in a separate folder so you can start over if needed. Primarily, you will be altering the following folders (substitute the appropriate drive letters, if you installed Genesis on a drive other than your C: drive):

- C:\Genesis3D11\BMP

- C:\Genesis3D11\LEVELS

You can use WinZip to compress these folders into a file and save them in another folder. If you need to use them later, I strongly suggest that you unzip and restore them (copy the original files back into their correct folders) rather than attempting to reinstall Genesis3D because, if you keep your work in the same folder, the installation process will wipe out all of the work you did. You don't need to make backups of the entire Genesis3D installation.

The Texture Packer

The Texture Packer, or TPACK (tpack.exe), is an essential utility that takes all of your images and puts them into the TXL file format. Because the level editor reads only TXL formatted files, you need to use this utility before you can work with your files in Genesis3D.

Loading the Tutorial Texture Library

To prepare to work with companion CD-ROM castle textures for this book's project, take the following steps:

1. In Windows Explorer, go to the folder in which you have installed Genesis, find the file tpack.exe, and double-click on it.

2. After TPACK is opened, choose File|Open. This will place you by default into the Genesis3D11 program folder. Go to the Tutorials folder on this book's companion CD-ROM and open castle.txl (see Figure 8.3).

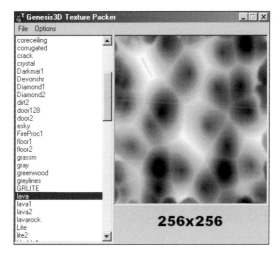

Figure 8.3
The Genesis3D Texture Packer.

3. Now choose File|Save As. Save the file "castle.txl" in the levels folder of the Genesis program folder. You'll need your working files to be in this folder later on, so that Genesis3D will be able to access them.

While you are running TPACK, you can click on a file name, and you will see the image in the window on the right side of the Genesis3D Texture Packer screen. You will also see the image size: 128×128, 256×256, and so on.

You can also delete images from the library by pressing the Delete key. Also, you can extract your library to the folder that already contains TPACK. This will unpack every image in the file into the folder—you are not given the option of where to unpack the files, so be careful if you don't want image files mixed with every other file in the folder. Extracting images will not delete or alter the original texture file.

Creating Your Own Texture Library

Creating your own texture libraries for Genesis3D is easy. There are just a few steps to understand and follow and a few guidelines you have to observe:

1. Images must be power-of-two images (64×64, 128×128, 256×256, and so on). You can resize images in Photoshop by right-mouse-clicking on

Preparing a File for Editing

When you use the Copy or a Save As options on the file castle.txl from the companion CD-ROM, the file that you're converting may be set as a Read Only file. You need to use Windows Explorer to go to the file, right-click on it, choose Properties, and deselect the Read Only checkbox of this attribute before you will be able to edit the castle.txl file. It's always a good idea to make this procedure a part of your initial preparations when you start creating a level.

Note: If you add images to the library on your own, be careful. When you drag the image files to TPACK, they are added, and it is subtle; your image will not appear in the window. You will have to scroll the list and look for the name of your image and *then* click on the name to see the image.

Note: Make sure that your images are of the correct size and color depth. The TPACK option will allow you to put the wrong-size images into it, but Genesis3D will not let you use them.

the header bar and using the Image Size option. Type the image size you want and make sure that the Constrain Proportions box is checked, so that your image will scale proportionally.

2. All images must be in the 256-indexed color mode. When you are reducing files (by selecting Image|Adjust|Mode; Indexed), use the Perceptual option for the best results.

3. Images must be in the Windows Bitmap (BMP) format.

4. You can have the same name for different images, but this is not advised because using the same name can become confusing for both you and the computer. The file name of the image will be the same name in the texture window in the editor. For example, "dirt.bmp" will become "dirt" in the editor. You cannot rename textures in the editor.

5. TPACK can import images that were improperly sized and are the wrong color depth. If you do this, your system may crash, and you may see oddly colored images, you could encounter texture stretching, or—at the least—you may get no response from the editor. Make sure that you check your image format before dragging and dropping your images. Finally, you can corrupt the TXL file. If this happens, you will have to rebuild your TXL file.

6. The default texture file used by the editor is named gedit.txl, and you must change the file association within the editor before you can use your TXL (as we did in the previous section).

Importing Your Images

To get your images into TPACK, take the following steps:

1. Open the TPACK utility. Position it as close as possible to the left edge of your screen.

2. In Windows Explorer, open the folder in which you placed all your images. You can turn on the Windows Explorer's thumbnail view to see small representations of the images.

3. You can click and drag one image at a time, or you can highlight and drag many images at the same time.

4. Save the file before closing. It is also a good idea to name this file (the TXL file created by TPACK) the same name as the 3DT file (the map file created by the editor). As they don't share the same extension, you can do this. It will help you find the files more easily, as you will eventually have multiple texture and map files in your project.

Now it's time to move from the preparation stage to the actual working stage. Close TPACK and open the world editor, GEdit.

The World Editor

The first time that you open the world editor, you will see a standard-style Windows interface (see Figure 8.4). Across the top of this interface, you will see the following:

- The menu bar

- The toolbar cluster just below the menu bar, with all of its icons

- The four view windows

- The Command Panel with the Option tabs

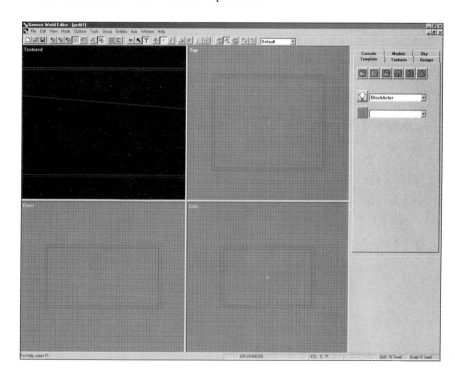

Figure 8.4
The main screen of the world editor. Note the most important parts of this screen: the menu bar, the toolbar, and the four view windows.

In the following sections of this chapter, you will briefly go over the basics and learn the function of each window. Then—starting with Chapter 9 and continuing through Chapter 12—you'll learn about the specific functions and options for each item in the tutorials. Along the way, you'll also exercise your newfound knowledge by completing projects of varying difficulty.

The menu bar contains all of the options available in the world editor. The toolbar has a cluster of icon bars that contain icons that are shortcuts to the most commonly used functions in the editor (see Figure 8.5). Although this toolbar looks as though it's only one bar, it's really three bars: The world editor calls the first section the Toolbar (also referred to as the General toolbar), the second section is named the Mode bar, and the third section is called the Group bar. These three bars can be displayed together, rearranged, or hidden independently of each other by using the View menu.

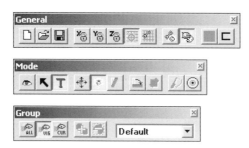

The four large view windows that make up most of the Genesis3D GEdit's (or World Editor's) user interface are the most important parts (see Figure 8.6). Here, you lay out your level, add geometry and entities, and view your level.

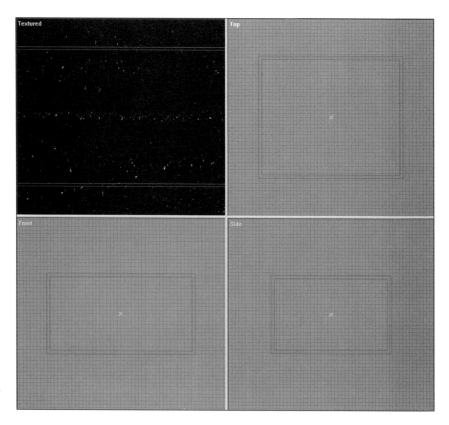

Figure 8.6
The four view windows in GEdit.

The Command Panel and its tabs (called *option pages*) offer access to different modes and tools in the editor (see Figure 8.7).

The Four View Windows

The world editor's main screen has four windows that let you see your level from different views:

- Textured View (or Camera view, as it is sometimes referred to)

- Top

Figure 8.7
The Command Panel tabs.

- Front

- Side

In the Textured view, you can look at the game level with textures on or off. The Textured view is also used for face editing (you'll learn more about this in Chapter 10). If you can't see the textures or the changes you made in this view, you can click on the Quick Compile button to refresh the view. In Chapter 10, you will also learn how to navigate this view so that you can get a better all-around vision of the world.

You will do your entire geometry and entity placement in the top, front, and side three views. Because you are editing a 3D space in a 2D view, you need to look at it from all three views in order to do accurate editing.

> **Note:** Although this view is close to what your level will look like in the game, it is *not* representative of what the level will look like after you've placed it in the game. There are many reasons for this, but primarily the game engine is not displaying the level at this point, the level editor is. You will eventually get used to this and start to know what the level you are building will look like.

The Command Panel

The command panel is displayed to the right of the views in the editor window. The tabs of the command panel are as follows:

- Template

- Textures

- Groups

- Console

- Models

- Sky

The Template Tab

The Template tab has three areas (see Figure 8.8). One allows you to place geometry (or brushes), the next allows the insertion of entities, and the third is blank. The third area is where your loaded prefabricated game objects are accessed. Chapter 10 explores the concept of importing "prefabs" into your world.

Figure 8.8
The Template tab.

The basic geometric shapes (*brushes*) are accessible from here. You can assign certain properties to them and then place them in your level.

There are six geometric shapes: Cube, Spheroid, Cylinder, Staircase, Arch, and Cone. Each of these primitives has parameters and functions, described in Chapter 9.

Entities is the term for objects that you place in your level. Although all entities are represented as a small "x" in the level editor, they are actually objects that perform many different functions in the game. They are things such as lights, models, and level starting points. We will look at each entity in detail as it occurs, in upcoming chapters pertaining to the topics of lighting, models, and basic game world building.

Note: The entity will be placed 16 texels from the surface on which you click.

The Textures Tab

When you click on the Textures tab, you can view all the textures in the assigned TXL file. For the purposes this book, you will be viewing the "castle.txl" file. This is where you place a texture on a piece of geometry or a face if you are in Face Editing mode. Also, the texture you have selected will be applied to any newly created geometry (see Figure 8.9).

Figure 8.9
The Textures tab.

The Groups Tab

You can group your level's geometry and entities and name them. This is helpful when a level gets large. You can hide and unhide groups to make your work easier; this will also allow the editor to run faster, because it won't be displaying everything in the level. In this tab, you can also assign colors to groups. This is another helpful tool; you will often zoom into a level to tweak brush placement, and all you will see are many lines on the screen. It helps if the lines are different colors (see Figure 8.10).

The Console Tab

If you click on the Console tab when you first start the editor, it will be blank. This area is where the editor spits out messages as it compiles your level for running in the game engine. The console will be helpful for some errors such as lost textures, leaks, and missing assets (see Figure 8.11).

The Models Tab

In Genesis3D, you can make models by using one or more brushes. Then, you can animate them to make doors, elevators, and even atmospheric movement, such as ceiling fans and waterwheels (see Figure 8.12).

The Sky Tab

The Sky option lets you assign textures to the skybox that surrounds your level and set the speed at which your sky moves. You can't see the skybox in the editor; you can see it only in the game (see Figure 8.13).

Note: *This is important!* Anything hidden is not used when compiling the level. This means that the time required to compile the level can be greatly reduced by hiding large parts of the level, but it also means that the compile may fail if you hide a brush that subsequently creates a hole in your level and causes a leak. I'll talk about the importance of sealing a level when we start building one in Chapter 10.

Note: Most error messages are very familiar to the folks on the Genesis forum, so fret not. You can log on and send them the console errors.

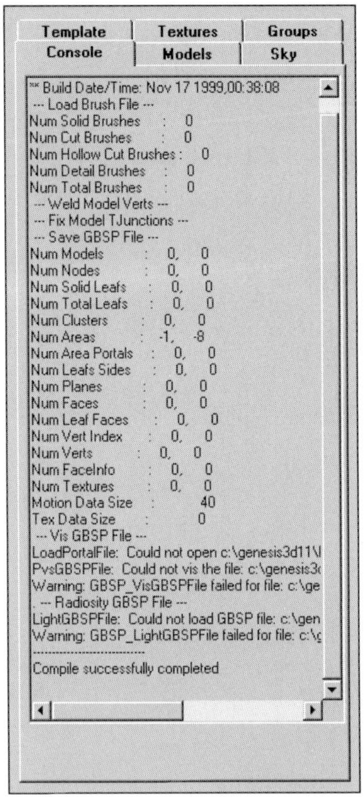

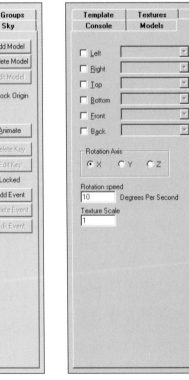

Figure 8.10
(Left) The Groups tab.

Figure 8.11
(Right) The Console tab.

Figure 8.12
(Left) The Models tab.

Figure 8.13
(Right) The Sky tab.

Moving On

In this chapter, you learned about some of the great things you can do with Genesis3D. You learned how to install the software and how to get it up and running. You learned how to prepare files for use in Genesis3D's World Editor. You also learned the basic moves of the world editor.

Now that you are essentially familiar with the world editor, Chapter 9 will provide a more in-depth look at the tools at your disposal. You will learn about the building blocks of your world—its geometry—and the various things you can do to your geometry to make a world that looks better and is more interactive and more interesting. There are many parameters and options that allow a great deal of flexibility in what you can build into virtual worlds with Genesis3D.

Chapter 9

Game World Geometry

Even the most basic shapes of geometry can be made to look good, given the right amount of time, tweaking, and the proper use of the tools. This chapter explains the basic geometric shapes and tools in Genesis.

Chapter Overview

In this chapter, we'll look at using the most basic geometric shapes, or primitives, available for creating maps. (Basic geometric shapes are called *primitives* because they are so simple; these shapes are what you're limited to using in Genesis.) Some people get frustrated because they are limited to such basic geometry to create the walls and objects in their game worlds. However, the nature of 3D games is that they must run in "real time," generating a 2D image of a 3D world many times a second. The images must run very fast in order for the game to both look good and have smooth movement. The more geometry (and textures, models, or any other element of a game) you have, the more the computer must do to generate that 2D image.

Think of it this way: A movie is simply a long string of 2D images that are played in rapid succession to give the illusion of movement. Now, you can play that movie forward and backward, but you are not interacting with the movie world; you are watching the events of that world at one moment in time being played forwards and backwards. A 3D game works on the same principle, but the difference is that the 2D image is generated from the user's point of view as quickly as possible in real time, as it is happening. If, for example, you are walking down a hall in a 3D game, for every second you move, the computer must look at all the information within that "world" and generate a series of 2D film frames, up to a speed of 60 times a second, so that you will feel as though you are walking down the hall. This creation of immersion within the game, or "a sense of reality," is known as *verisimilitude*. Add to this scenario other players in the world, their bullets, dynamic lighting, and other programming issues, and you begin to understand the complexity of creating a 3D game that feels real to the player. To do this, you have to make a few cubes look good. You can do this with great textures, lighting, and composition—tools you must exploit whenever possible.

To begin, we'll look at the settings that allow us to go a little beyond the primitive to make a wide variety of shapes to further customize a level. Then we'll look at the attributes that can be assigned to select pieces of geometry to make brushes function in various ways in the game world being built.

Basic Brush Shapes

The most fundamental aspect of building a level involves creating, placing, and manipulating brushes. A *brush* is a piece of geometry that has different properties assigned to it. The basic brushes you can create are listed here:

- Cube

- Sphere

- Cylinder

- Stairs

- Arch

- Cone

When you are in Template mode and you select any of these shapes, a menu pops up that allows you to set several variables, which allows you to create a wide range of shapes. Generally, when you're creating a brush, you can also set a few parameters, such as the height, the width, and the top and bottom size of the shape. These parameters can help you create more pleasing shapes. Simply tapering a column, for example, can do wonders for the spirits of a level builder. Now let's look at the basic shapes and what we can do with each one to break free of the primitive prison we all start in as level builders.

Cube

The lowly cube; how many items in games are made from the much-maligned cube? Crates, health power-ups, even entire buildings—so be kind to the cube. You use the cube tool (see Figure 9.1) to create a solid or hollow cube. You can set the cube's height and the size of the cube's top and bottom. Using these options, you can create tapered columns and rooms that have slanted walls.

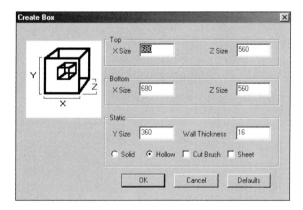

Figure 9.1
The Create Box dialog box.

You can even create building roofs by using a hollow cube. Set the Top X size to a very small size, set the Bottom X size wide, and make the Z size the same (wide). The resulting shape is that of a prism. If you use a hollow brush, you can use a cut brush to open up the attic space under the roof.

Sphere

Creating a sphere is a fairly straightforward process (see Figure 9.2). In addition to setting the sphere's radius, you can choose the number of vertical and horizontal *stripes* (see Figure 9.3), and specify the wall thickness. The term "stripes" refers to the number polygons used to create the sphere, and the more polygons you use, the smoother the resulting sphere will be. Stripes simply refer to the fact that, when polygons are lined up to form a spheroid shape, they appear to be stripes running the length of the sphere.

Note: Do not try to make a smooth sphere with many sides. At best, it is horribly inefficient in the game; at worst, it often crashes the level editor.

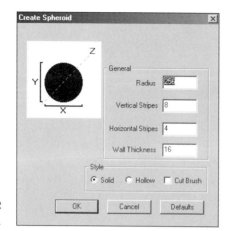

Figure 9.2
The Create Spheroid dialog box.

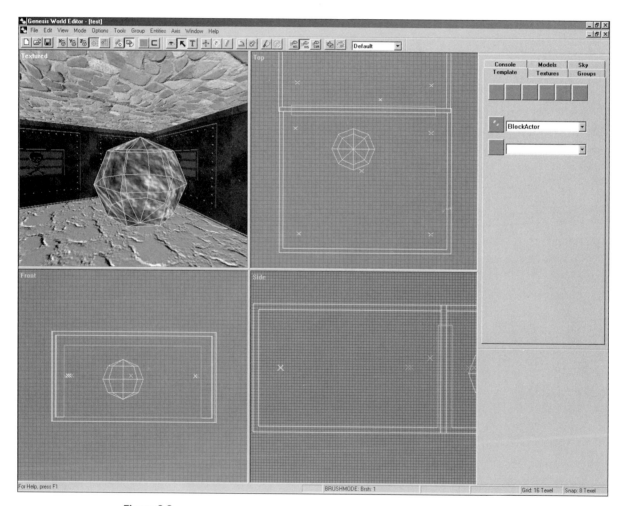

Figure 9.3
The vertical and horizontal stripes in a spheroid.

Cylinders

When you use the Create Cylinder dialog box to create a cylinder, you can set the size and the offset of the cylinder's top and bottom (see Figure 9.4), but these variables are actually easier to change visually by using the Size and

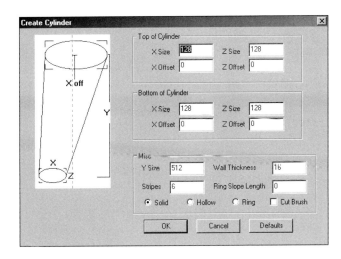

Figure 9.4
The Create Cylinder dialog box.

Skew options in the level editor. You can set the number of stripes in a cylinder, as you can for the sphere, for a smoother curve on your cylinder.

Other options include the hollow cylinder or a ring. A ring has no ends and is great for pipes, tubes, and tunnels.

Stairs

You use the Create Staircase dialog box to create stairs and ramps. You can set the height, width, and length of your staircase. Most important, you can set the number of stairs. You can also make a ramp (use the Make Ramp option), which has no stairs, of course (see Figure 9.5). For more information about creating stairs and ramps, refer to Chapter 8.

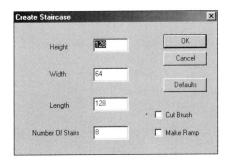

Figure 9.5
The Create Staircase dialog box.
Notice the Make Ramp option.

Arches

Creating an arch is easy, and you can set many parameters to customize it (see Figure 9.6). As with the other brushes, some of these parameters can be easily changed in the level editor; others are "set in stone" as soon as you press Enter. Table 9.1 describes the range of arch options you can set.

When you set the arch's style to Ring, you can use an arch as a tunnel. See Figure 9.7 for examples of using the various arch options.

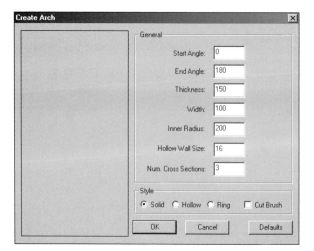

Figure 9.6
The Create Arch dialog box.

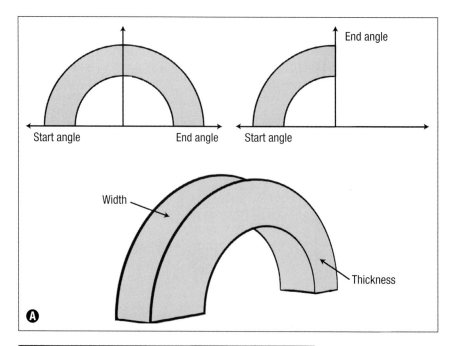

Figure 9.7
These two images show an artist's drawing (A) and the end result (B) of using the arch brush.

Table 9.1   Genesis 3D arch parameters.

Parameter	Description
Start Angle and End Angle	Set the places where the arch begins and ends. The defaults are 0 and 180 to create the traditional arch. If you changed the Start Angle to 90, the arch would start halfway to the End Angle.
Thickness	Sets the thickness of the arch's cross sections, as viewed from the side.
Width	Sets the thickness of the arch as viewed from the top.
Inner Radius	Sets the height of the inner arch and the overall size of the arch.
Hollow Wall Size	Sets the hull thickness of the walls in a hollow brush.
Number Of Cross Sections	Sets the number of sections composing an arch.
Style	Specifies whether the arch is solid, hollow, ring, or cut brush.

Cones

The cone can have a vertical number of stripes assigned (see Figure 9.8); there-fore, a cone with four stripes (or sides) is a pyramid. You can also turn a cone into a funnel. A funnel has an open bottom, and when a funnel is inverted, it makes a great brazier for hot coals and fire, a great four-sided roof, or even a pyramid, of all things.

Note: Don't be afraid to experiment with brush creation. You can always click on the Defaults button to restore all the original settings of the brush.

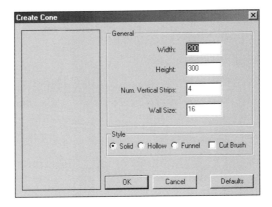

Figure 9.8
The Create Cone dialog box.

Brush Types

After you create a brush, you can also change how it functions. The following brush types do not change the brush's geometry (the shape); rather, they change the geometry's behavior.

Solid Brush

Solid brushes block passage and visibility; hence the term "solid." They will compose your world's obstacles, such as columns, doors, platforms, and any-thing else that you want to build. Although it can be hard to get detailed in your construction, you can build simple and convincing objects with solid brushes. See Figure 9.9 for examples of objects in a game world made from simple solid brushes.

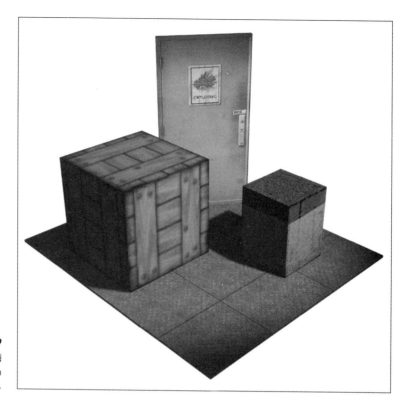

Use Hollow Brushes for Efficiency

Whenever possible, use hollow brushes rather than cut brushes. The level editor and the engine do distinguish between the two, and cut brushes are more inefficient than hollow brushes.

Hollow Brush

Hollow brushes are the same shape as solid brushes, but they are hollow inside. They are used to create the rooms and major areas of a level. You can change the wall thickness (called the *hull size*) of the hollow brush. As you resize the brush, the hull size remains constant. Hull size consistency is important when you begin using the hollow brushes to make levels and you want to make a room bigger without having the walls swell as you resize the room (see Figure 9.10).

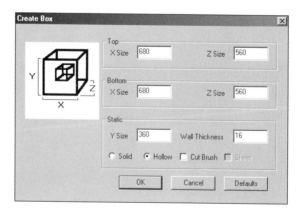

Figure 9.10
Choosing a hollow brush for a cube.

Cut Brush

Cut brushes are brushes that carve their shape out of other geometry created with solid brushes. You can use cut brushes to hollow out solid objects, to cut doors and windows into walls, or to build fairly detailed forms of geometry. See Figure 9.11 for an example of using the cut brush. In Figure 9.11, the green lines are outlining the cut brush, which is invisible. See how it cuts away the solid shape it comes into contact with.

Figure 9.11
Using a cut brush to hollow out part of a cube.

There are several ways to make a cut brush. These possible options are described in the following list:

- Select the Cut Brush checkbox when you create the brush from the template tab.

- Select an existing brush and click on the Carve toolbar button.

- Select Cut from the brush's property box.

Sheet Brush

A sheet brush is a one-faced brush, meaning you can't see the brush from both sides. In 3D programs, it is possible to have a polygon face that exists only from the front and not the back. If you could see both sides, then you are actually looking at a 2-sided polygon. This brush type is useful for placing decals and images against the walls for posters, gunshots, stains, and so on.

To create a decal, you want to place a sheet brush one *texel* (the base unit of textured graphics, texels define a three-dimensional object's surface; the base unit of the surface of a 3D door or wall is a texel—two-dimensional objects are made up of pixels) from the surface. When you do this, however, the engine

Using Multiple Cut Brushes

It is possible to create a cut brush that overlaps several objects. If you want some, but not all, of these objects to be affected by the cut brush then you simply select the objects that you want to remain unaffected and use the Make Newest command. Because a cut brush affects only brushes that have gone before it, you can control what does and does not get cut this way.

will have a hard time displaying the flat planes so close to one another, so you should have the Flocking option checked. I'll discuss this option later in the "Brush Attributes" section of this chapter.

A *face* is a side of a brush. A solid cube, for example, has six faces: top, bottom, left, right, front, and back. A hollow cube has twelve faces: six outside and six inside (see Figure 9.12).

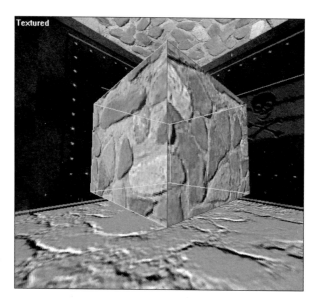

Figure 9.12
A solid brush with one face selected.

Figure 9.13
The Brush Attributes dialog box.

Brush Attributes

The designers of Genesis 3D created additional dialog boxes that allow you to select some options, called attributes, when you create a brush. After you place a brush in the world, you can click on the Brush Attribute icon or use the menu options (by selecting Tools|Brush|Attributes) and alter the brush in some interesting ways. Figure 9.13 shows the Brush Attributes dialog box.

- *Solid*—You can make a brush a solid brush by selecting this option.

- *Cut*—You can turn a brush into a cut brush from here if you didn't create it as one originally.

- *Empty*—An empty brush is visible but can be passed through. This brush attribute is useful for creating pools of water and lava. Later in this chapter, you will learn how to make reflective and translucent liquids.

- *Window*—A window brush is a translucent piece of geometry that allows visibility but blocks the gamer from passing through it.

- *Clip*—A clip brush is an invisible piece of geometry that blocks passage. Clip brushes are useful for preventing access to parts of a level without having to build a solid wall. They differ from the window brush and other brushes because clip brushes cannot have textures or other properties assigned to them, and clip brushes are more efficient to use if all you want to do is block passage with a perfectly clear field.

- *Hint*—A hint brush is invisible and doesn't block passage; it is unseen during game play. Hint brushes are supposed to instruct the level compiler so it will compile a more efficient level, but Hint Brushes are not working in Genesis 3D.

- *Hollow*—A hollow brush is a piece of geometry with a hole cut out of it. You aren't allowed to set this attribute in the Brush Attributes dialog box (you can set it only from the brush template dialogs), but you are allowed to change the hull thickness for hollow brushes.

- *Wavy*—If you enable the Wavy attribute for an empty brush, the texture with which the brush is filled will "wave" or animate to simulate moving liquid.

- *Detail*—The Detail attribute helps the compiler run more efficiently by removing some pieces of geometry from visibility and lighting calculations. You should use Detail brushes for geometry that you know will not block visibility. A wall between rooms would be a poor choice for a detail brush, but a column or beams going across the room, or any small fixture that doesn't block the visibility of the room, would be an excellent choice.

- *Area*—The Area option is for brushes that seal off areas of your level (such as doors). This attribute allows the game engine to completely ignore very large portions of the world if the area brush is visible, and this makes rendering much faster.

- *Flocking*—If you want to place decals on your walls (such as cracks, posters, signs, or other flat art that you want to look as if it is either part of the wall or flat against it), you need to make sure that the Flocking option is checked. If it isn't, the level editor, when compiling the level, may try to remove the flat plane. This option makes sure that the sheet brush you placed stays there, and that it is displayed properly. One exception to this rule: If you use transparency with your decal, check the Detail option and leave the Flocking option unchecked (see Figure 9.14).

- *Sheet*—The Sheet attribute turns the selected brush into a sheet brush.

- *Hull Thickness*—The Hull Thickness option allows you to change the Hull Thickness of a hollow brush.

- *Water* and *Lava*—The Water and Lava options allow you to change an empty brush into water or lava. When players enter water, they can swim, but if players run into lava, they are injured.

Figure 9.14
The same decal appears twice: once with the Flocking option turned on (right) and once with the Flocking turned off (left).

Setting up GEDIT

After you have GEDIT installed and you are familiar with it, you need to set it up before you can use it. You need to point the editor to a texture library and turn on the grid.

Textures

To set up a texture library for later use as we begin to build a game level, take the following steps:

1. Choose Options|Level Options to open the Level Options dialog box (see Figure 9.15).

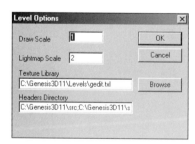

Figure 9.15
The Level Options dialog box.

2. Click on the Browse button. Find the folder you installed Genesis into, and then open the Levels folder. Select the castle.txl file. If you haven't copied this file onto your computer already, refer to Chapter 8, "The Texture Packer" for instructions on how to do this. If you go to the Texture Tab in the Windows Control Panel, you will see the textures used in the Castle level.

The Grid

Choose Options|Grid Settings to open the Grid Settings dialog box (see Figure 9.16). For this project, set the Grid Snap option to 32 texels. We do this so we can lay out the room quickly and precisely, but when we zoom in later, we'll still be able to align objects to the one-texel level. Our goal is to tweak a level not only so it looks good, but also so it runs efficiently. When you are precise and organized, your level will run better.

> **Note:** Placing all geometry pieces one texel away from each other, when possible, helps reduce the polygon count in the game world and increases the game's efficiency.

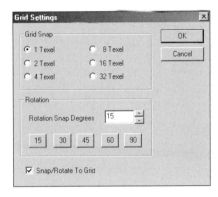

Figure 9.16
The Grid Settings dialog box.

Moving On

In this chapter, you learned about brushes and their attributes and how you use them to help create your worlds. You also leaned about GEDIT, and how to set up a texture library.

Now that you have a firm understanding of the basics of the Genesis tools, in Chapter 10 you will start building a castle room and applying some of these tools. Soon, you will see what can be done with Genesis, its brushes, and other options, and you will create a level that you can call your own.

Chapter 10

Creating a Game World

Using an editor is easy. If you can create one boxy room and get that running, you are well on your way to creating rich and complex game worlds.

The World You'll Be Creating

Now that you are familiar with the Genesis3D tools and the editor, it's time to load it up and make your first map. Keep in mind that this is only a tutorial exercise, which is designed to teach you the basics of world construction in games and virtual environments. If you were building a map for a real world, a great deal of planning, going into all aspects of the level, would precede this step.

These planning steps would include the layout and dimensions of all the geometry as well as the color scheme and consistency with the back-story of the game. After you become more comfortable building small rooms and corridors, you can then start building larger ones until you are creating full levels. Remember, however, that it is easy to go from building a room to building a full level, but it's hard to build a level that is fresh, that is smoothly functional in terms of technology and game play, and that fits into the whole of a larger game world.

In this chapter and in Chapters 11 and 12, you will learn how to create a game world, add models to it, and light it. All of the skills you learn while doing the tutorials for this extended project will help you with your own projects. Take what you learn here, and apply it to your own games.

This chapter teaches you how to create a simple world. While you're doing that, you'll also learn about the options in the Face Attributes dialog box, and you'll learn some basic techniques, such as those shown in the following list:

- Creating a simple cube
- Using the three editing modes
- Placing a texture file where Genesis3D can find it; then applying textures to whole objects and to the individual faces of those objects
- Compiling and previewing this first map (level)
- Cloning the first room to add a second room
- Creating groups to keep related objects together
- Creating a basic sky box
- Applying simple lighting effects
- Adding a banner

You will start with creating a one-room level (as part of the castle project). Then, you will clone it to add a courtyard to the castle. You'll also add a few other touches, and finally, I will give you a few tips on building levels to maximize speed.

Let There Be Cube

Every time you start the World Editor, you are given a new and empty world with one potential hollow cube in it. This potential brush does not exist yet in the world; it is called a template. If you click on one of the view windows to activate the editor and you press Enter, you will hear a "whoosh" (if your computer's speakers are on), and the cube will be made real in the editor, but you will be inside the cube, as is shown in Figure 10.1 (i.e., the camera will be in the center of the cube).

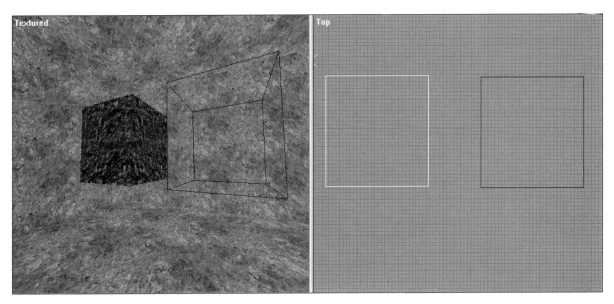

Figure 10.1
The startup screen of Genesis3D, with the potential hollow cube and then the actual cube.

After you have pressed Enter, you have created your first room. Before, however, you change and add to this new room, we have to discuss the editing modes.

The Three Main Editing Modes

The World Editor provides three main modes of editing: Camera mode, Select mode, and Template mode. To change modes, you can use the Mode menu, you can click on the mode buttons on the toolbar, or you can press the keys designated for these modes in the View menu.

Camera Mode

Just like it sounds, Camera mode enables you to look from the camera view and move about the world. By holding down the Shift key and using the mouse button, you can navigate in the Textured window with ease. The movements are described in the following list:

- *Shift+left mouse button*—Look side-to-side and move backward and forward.

- *Shift+right mouse button*—Look up and down and side-to-side. You stay in one place.

> **Note:** Become comfortable with the difference between the potential brush, or template, and the real thing. Frequently, the template's outlines are positioned directly over a created brush and make it hard to see. The potential brush and the real brush are both represented as lines in the World Editor, whereas the real brush is a textured piece of geometry in the camera view, and the potential brush will still be a set of lines.

Alternate Modes

The World Editor also provides two other sets of modes. One set consists of Move/Rotate, Scale, and Shear; the other consists of Face Adjustment and Brush Adjustment. Of those modes, Brush Adjustment is the default; all textures you apply are applied to the whole brush (geometric object). To work with individual faces of an object (called face editing), switch to Face Adjustment mode.

Note: It is all too easy (especially if your sound is turned off) to create multiple brushes, one on top of the other, by pressing Enter multiple times. This can lead to errors and, at the least, confusion when you edit. Be careful to avoid doing this.

Note: If all of the primitive icons are shown as grayed out, you are not in Template mode.

Learn to Use "Hot Keys"

Using "hot keys" (keyboard shortcuts) can speed up your work considerably. For example, you can press T for Template mode, M to move, L to resize, and PgDn (Page Down) to toggle between Face Editing and Brush Editing modes. Using a single key, rather than a series of three or more click-and-select moves, is always the quickest and most efficient way to select tools.

- *Shift+both mouse buttons*—Look straight ahead while you move side-to-side and up and down.

In the other views (Top, Front, and Side), you can hold Shift+left mouse button to move the view up, down, left, and right. Shift+right mouse button allows you to zoom in and out.

To activate Camera view, you can choose Mode|Camera, you can click on the Camera Mode icon (the icon with the image of an eye), or you can simply press the C key.

Select Mode

In Select mode, you can select brushes and entities to move and edit them. To activate Select mode, you can choose Mode|Selection, or click on the Select Mode button on the toolbar (the icon with the arrow on it), or press S.

Template Mode

Template mode allows you to add brushes and entities to your new world. Template mode activates not only the brush options, but also the entity list. To activate Template mode, you have three options: You can choose Mode|Template, you can click on the Template Mode button (the icon with the T on it), or you can just press T.

Creating the First Room

You will begin by creating a basic room. After you learn how to do this, you will be able to add, subtract, and modify any space to create your world.

1. If it's not already active, activate Template mode (either click on the Template Mode button in the Toolbar, go to the Options Panel, and select Template, or press T).

2. By default, when you start the editor, you should have a blank new file with a Hollow Cube template waiting. If you press Enter, you should hear a whoosh and see the Textured view update with you inside a box. (By box, I mean that, when the cube is first created in the 3D world, it is created around you.) You may need to first click on the Textured view before pressing Enter to make sure that the editor is active. (This is a quirk of the World Editor that sometimes prevents the creation of a brush.)

3. The texture on the cube is the default; you'll change this texture next.

4. Before you take any other actions, you need to save this file. Save it with the file name "castle".

Accessing and Applying the Castle Textures

Now that you have your cube, you'll change the texture by using the Castle texture library provided on this book's companion CD-ROM. Before you can use this file easily, it should be in the Levels folder of the Genesis3D program directory. Later, you can locate the TXL files wherever you want on your hard drive, but it's easier to lose them that way.

To get your project's texture file ready to use, take the following steps:

1. Open the Windows Explorer. On the companion CD-ROM, find the "tutorials" folder, and copy the file "castle.txl" to your computer. Copy the tutorials folder to the root folder of the place where you installed Genesis; typically, it will be C:\Genesis3D11. The folder will be easier to find if you place it there.

2. Choose Options|Level Options, and click on the Browse button. Figure 10.2 shows the Level Options dialog box. Select the castle.txl file (either double-click or single-click and click on Open), and then choose OK when you return to the Level Options dialog box.

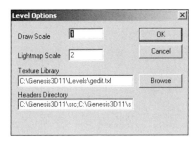

Figure 10.2
The Level Options dialog box.

You may notice that the geometry in the level of your Textured view is now covered in solid colors. What just happened was that you simply switched texture libraries, so the geometry lost its texture map. To fix this, take the following steps:

1. Select the Hollow Brush that makes up your room.

2. Go to the Texture tab, find the "brickblk" texture in the library. Click on Apply. The "brickblk" texture will be applied to every face of our hollow cube room (see Figure 10.3).

Notice that the nice wall texture doesn't look very clean or finished on the walls and floors. You'll fix this in the following exercise.

Texturing Individual Faces

There are many things you can do to the face of your brush. First, however, you will start with learning how to select an individual face and apply a specific texture to it. To do so, take these steps:

1. Click on the Textured view window of the editor. Activating this window will allow you to select the Hollow brush you created. You can work on individual faces only in Face Adjustment mode.

> **Note:** At this point, it may be a good exercise to switch to Camera mode, click on the Textured window, and practice using Shift+the mouse to look and move about the room.

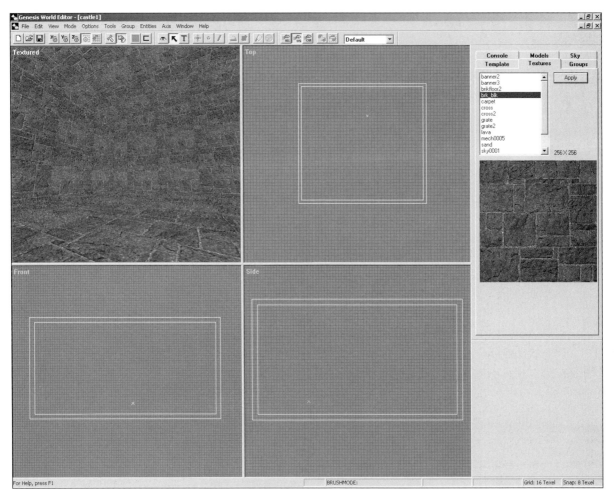

Figure 10.3

The room with the same "brickblk" texture on every face.

Note: Often, the World Editor allows you to select only one face, and not the face you want because of your position (the position of the camera, that is) in the world. You can use the arrow keys to cycle through the faces until the one you want is highlighted.

2. The outline of the brush will appear bright green after you select it. If at this point you were to use the Texture tab to scroll through the textures and start applying them, they would be applied to every face in this mode. (If you do this, make sure that you re-apply the "brickblk" file to the room before you go on.)

3. Before continuing, make sure that the room is still selected in the Textured window.

4. To apply textures on only one face, choose Mode|Face Adjustment (or press PgDn).

5. You will notice that the lines outlining our object turn purple. This indicates that you are in Face Editing mode and that all the faces are selected. Click on the floor; notice that most of the lines again shift back to green, and now the floor is the only face highlighted in purple.

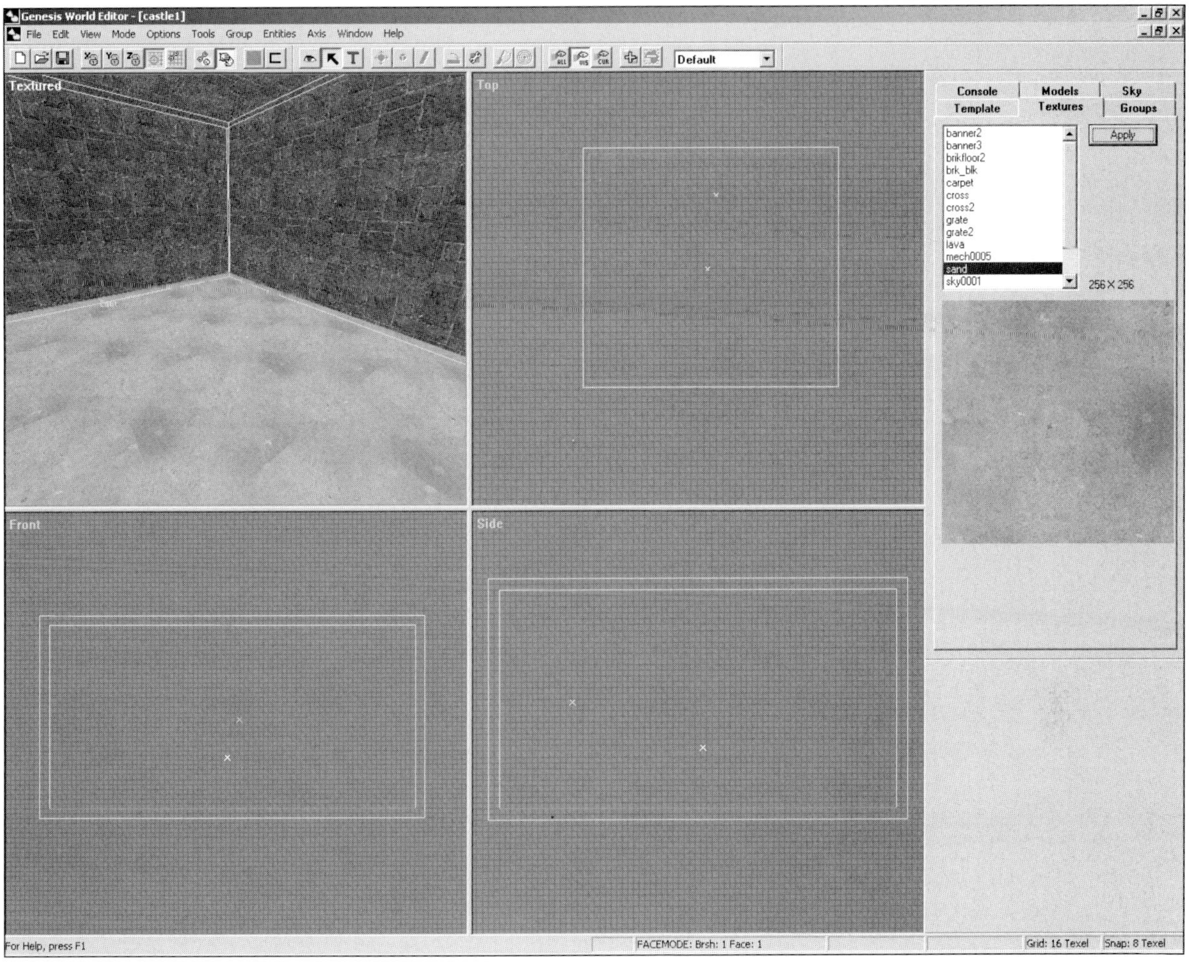

Figure 10.4
The room with a sand floor and stone walls. Notice the green and purple lines that form the outline of the brush because we are in Face mode.

6. Now, with the floor highlighted, go over to the Texture tab, find the "sand" image, and click on Apply.

   You now have a floor tiled, as is shown in Figure 10.4.

7. Click on the ceiling of the room, go over to the Texture tab, select the "mech0005" image, and apply it to the ceiling (see Figure 10.5).

Face Attributes and Texture Alignment

As nice as this little room is starting to look, you can do a lot more with face editing than just placing textures. In Face Editing mode, you have access to the Face Attributes dialog box, which enables you to change the attributes of the selected face.

To view this dialog box, make sure you are still in Face Editing mode (with a face selected in Adjustment mode), and either choose Tools|Face|Attributes, or click on the Face/Brush Attributes toolbar button.

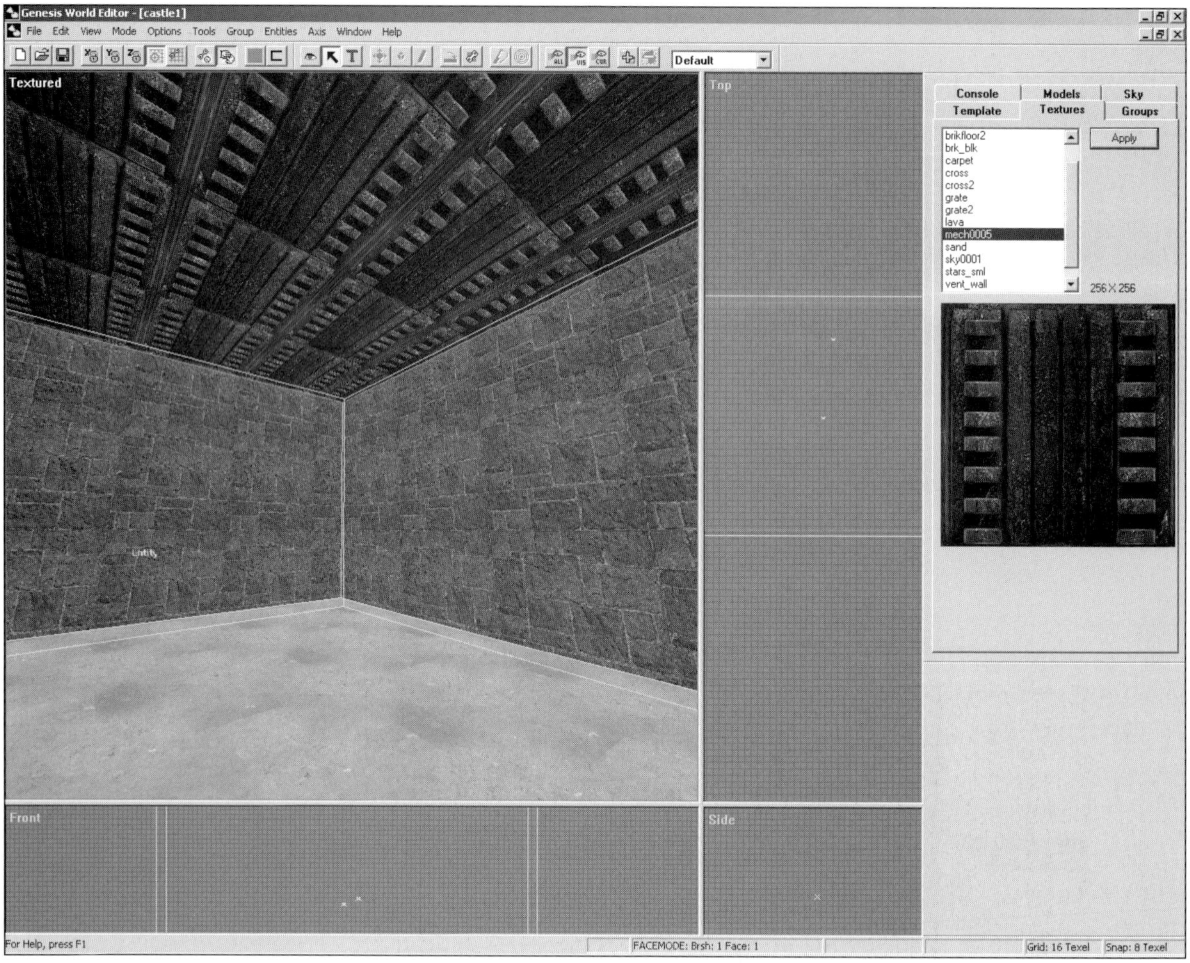

Figure 10.5

The room with walls, a floor, and a ceiling all textured differently.

Navigating While in Face Editing Mode

While you are in Face Editing mode, you can still navigate the world by using the Shift+mouse button combination, but you must click on the Textured window first before pressing Shift. If you don't take these steps, you will simply toggle the Mirror attribute to On, and this setting will cause errors and inefficiencies that will be hard to weed out later in level construction.

The Face Attributes dialog box is a modeless dialog box. That is, you can select different faces and edit their attributes without closing the dialog box. The changes that you make to each face are saved each time you switch faces. This is a major convenience because it enables you to edit many faces without having to repeatedly open and close the dialog box.

Each face of each brush can have a different attribute. These attributes are assigned using the Face Attributes dialog box (see Figure 10.6).

Mirror

Select this attribute if you want the face to be a mirror. (Be careful, however: Using this attribute for a face not intended to be a mirror will cause noncritical errors and hurt the performance of the level.) If you select a face to be a mirror, you must also turn on the Transparent option (in the bottom-right corner of the dialog box) and make adjustments to the transparency value of the face. For samples of the mirror face in action see Figures 10.7 through 10.9. You can see that the settings must be experimented with if they're used at all.

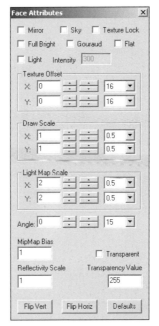

Figure 10.6
The Face Attributes dialog box.

Note: You can select multiple faces by holding down the Control key and clicking on them. The values set in the dialog box at this time are from the first selected face. If you change a value in the dialog box, that value will be applied to all of the selected faces.

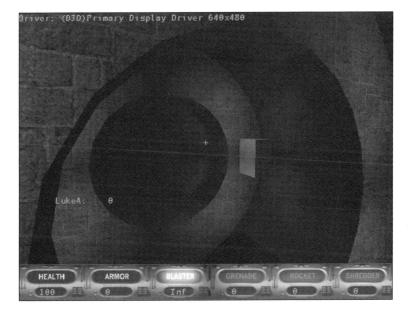

Figure 10.7
The floor has the Transparency Value set to 0. This causes the floor to become a perfect mirror. Every detail about the floor is lost, so this image appears to be two copies of the same room on top of each other.

Sky

When activated, the Sky attribute will make the brush face appear bluish in the level editor, but it will be invisible in the game. This attribute makes the face transparent in the game, thus allowing the skybox to be seen outside the level (see Figures 10.10 and 10.11). Because the skybox is simply a big cube that surrounds the level—with the texture of a sky on the inside of it—this effect, when activated, allows the players to see the sky through faces marked as "sky."

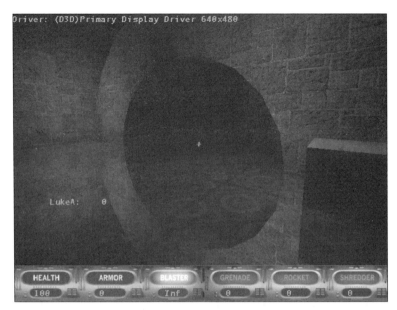

Figure 10.8
The floor has the Transparency Value set to 125. This causes the floor to look highly polished. Some of the floor texture is there (you have to look hard), but you see a great deal of what is above. Not right for our dirty castle.

Figure 10.9
The floor has the Transparency Value set to 200. This causes the floor texture to show through much stronger and diminishes the high polish, or reflecting ability, of the floor to the degree that we don't see the reflection of anything above the floor.

Note: If you are going to use the Texture Lock function, engage it first before using the Offset option to adjust the texture when the brush is moved. Make sure that you use the Quick Compile feature to refresh the window. (Choose Tools|Compile, and in the Compile Manager dialog box, check the Entities Only checkbox.)

Texture Lock

The Texture Lock attribute allows you to lock a texture in place after it has been lined up on a brush (we look at texture alignment in the Offset option). If you do not lock it, the texture will shift and move when you move the brush.

Full Bright

The Full Bright (see Figure 10.12) attribute will make the selected face impervious to darkness during the game. This is great for brushes made to look like lights. You will use this attribute later in this chapter in the section called "Adding Magical Light."

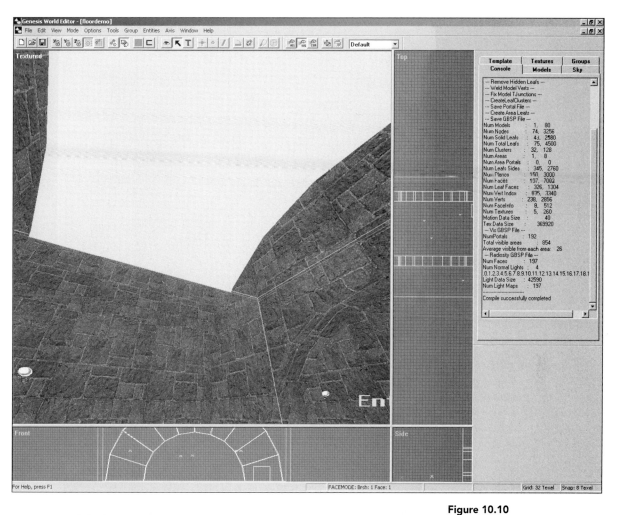

Figure 10.10

This is the sky as it appears in the World Editor.

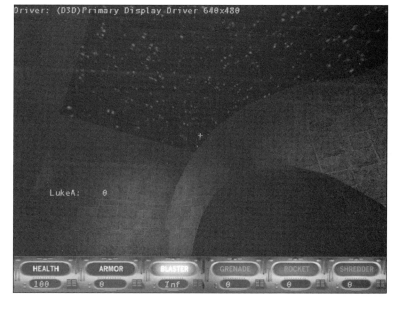

Figure 10.11

This is the sky as it appears in the running game.

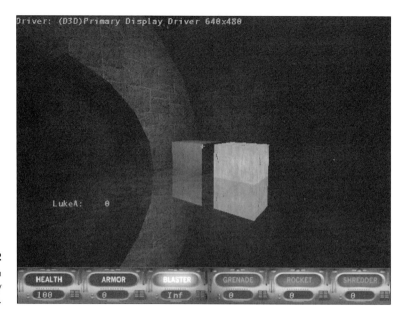

Figure 10.12
One cube has the Full Bright option on. This option makes the face fully lit under all circumstances.

Gouraud and Flat

These two attributes are two other ways of lighting that don't use light maps. They produce a faster lighting with a loss of accuracy. Use this for large levels that need it, or for surfaces that you may want to be lit in these ways.

Light

Set the Light attribute if you want the face to emit light. If you set this attribute, make sure that you also set the light's Intensity value. A consideration in deciding whether to use Light or Full Bright is that Full Bright only makes the face look like it is lit; Light, on the other hand, actually emits light that affects the surrounding area.

Texture Offset

The Texture Offset attribute controls where your texture is drawn on the face. The texture can be moved left to right and up and down in large or small increments by using the two scroll bars. This option moves the texture in pixel increments: 4, 8, 16, 32, 64, and 128 pixels at a time. Remember to engage Texture Lock if you are planning to spend any time adjusting a texture to a face. When you move the brush, the texture will shift.

Draw Scale

The Draw Scale attribute determines the scale or size at which you want the texture drawn. Figure 10.13 shows one block with the draw scale taken down to 0.5, meaning that the texture is drawn half as big as its actual size and therefore it looks smaller.

Figure 10.13
The blocks have the same texture, but two different Draw Scales.

Light Map Scale

The Light Map Scale attribute determines the size of the light map that you want to use for this face. If you set the scale to a larger light map scale, you will produce a more efficient level, but with softer lighting and shadows. You can see in Figure 10.14 how the shadows, cast from the same light and from the same brush, differ from each other due to the settings of the Light Map Scale parameter on the face on which the shadow is cast.

Figure 10.14
The light and the brush casting the shadow are the same, but the faces on which the shadows are cast have different Light Map Scale settings so the shadows appear different. The shadow on the left is harder and has a stair step pattern to it; the shadow on the right is softer.

Angle

Use the Angle attribute to set the angle by which you want to rotate the texture on the face.

MipMap Bias

MipMap Bias is not currently implemented in this version of Genesis3D. Do not make any changes in this box.

Reflectivity Scale

This Reflectivity Scale option determines how much light is bounced per face by using radiosity light. Rather than setting the world's reflectivity scale to 4, you may make special light for different rooms. Doing so results in sharper shadows and a more realistic lighting.

Flip Horizontal and Flip Vertical

The Flip Horizontal and Flip Vertical attributes allow you to flip the texture horizontally or vertically on the face.

Transparent and Transparency Value

By turning on the Transparent attribute and adjusting the value, you can set the face's transparency to be anywhere from completely invisible to solid (opaque). If you use transparency with the Mirror attribute, you can get various effects. By setting the Transparency Value to a very low number, you get more reflection and less of the texture showing through. Adjusting this value can make mirrors and windows look dirty or clean (see Figure 10.15). The transparency scale is based on the number range of 0 to 255 (0 being totally invisible and 255 being completely solid).

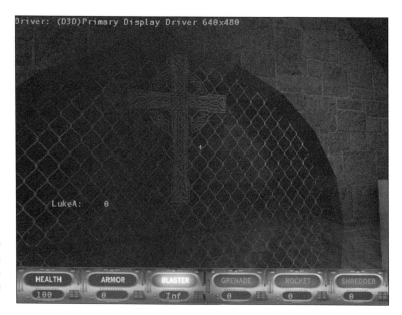

Figure 10.15

By assigning transparency to a face and adjusting the value, you can create effects, such as both the cross and the chain-link fence.

Defaults

This option resets all the values to the defaults (the "factory" settings that you saw when you first started the editor).

Testing the Map

If you have been looking at the Face Attributes dialog, close it now by clicking on the "X" on the upper-right corner of the window. Save the level file, too. Before you can test the map, you must do one last thing.

Placing the Player Start Position

Before you compile a level, you need to place the player-start position. This is where your game's player will be when he or she enters the game. If you do not place this entity here, the level will not run.

To place a player-start position, take the following steps:

1. Switch to Template mode.

2. Select the Template tab on the Command Panel, and select the DeathMatchStart entity from the drop-down list.

3. Click on the yellow lightbulb icon to place the entity in the level (this entity is represented by a blue "X" in the Top, Front, and Side windows and a lightbulb icon in the Texture view). Then press Enter; the entity is not there until you press Enter and hear the whoosh.

4. Choose Tools|Compile, or click on the Compile button on the toolbar.

5. Accept the defaults and let the map compile. Make sure the Preview option is checked; then choose Yes when you are prompted to preview the map.

> **Note:** You can move an entity before you press Enter. After you hear the "whoosh," however, you are in Template mode. You have to change to Select mode before you can select and move the entity. Make sure that entities are not inside of a wall or out of the level by looking at them from every angle while you are in the editor. Make sure that the DeathMatchStart entity has room around it for the player to appear.

Troubleshooting Compile Problems

If you have trouble starting and running the level, try the following suggestions before doing anything else:

1. Did you put the DeathMatchStart entity in? Is it in a wall or off in space? Check all of your views.

2. Run GTest. Even before you load a level from the editor, try to run GTest. If this does not work, you may have a system or configuration problem.

3. If you created more than the one room, you may have made a hole in your level. Your level has to be sealed. Make sure that you don't have a cut brush cutting a hole in your level by accident. You will see this effect in "Placing a Cut Brush to Create a Door Between Rooms."

Adding a Courtyard

If you successfully built a one-room level that runs, then you are ready to create a second room in the castle and build upon your level. You will link the two rooms with a Cut Brush, add a sky, and learn a few tips for making your maps run their best. You will also explore how these basic techniques of brush placement and manipulation will allow you to add a great deal of varying detail to your maps easily by cloning brushes and adding columns.

The next step in the castle is to simply create another room. The easiest way to accomplish this is to clone the first room.

Cloning a Brush to Create a Second Room

Because most construction is very similar throughout, you could redo every step of building your first room to create the second room, or you could simply clone it. Cloning is faster.

To adjust and then clone the first room, take the following steps:

1. Start by making the room you have already created a little bit longer, about twice as long as it is now: Switch to Select mode, and select the brush in the Side view. (You can resize an object in the Top, Front, or Side view windows, but not in the Textured view window.) Choose Mode|Scale (or press L) to activate the Scale mode. Then resize the brush; drag the brush edge out to make the room about twice its original size.

2. Now press the L key again, and you will be back in Select mode.

3. Click on the Top view. Hold down Shift, click on the brush with your left mouse button, and drag. This clones the brush, and you will see the new cloned brush moving. Keep dragging until the brush is roughly next to the original brush. You will make fine adjustments later.

4. In the Top view, hold Shift+left mouse button and line up the brushes end to end. Then use Shift+right mouse button to Zoom up to the one-texel level (see Figure 10.16).

5. Turn the off Grid Snap (choose Options|Snap To Grid—it's on by default). Place the two brushes together, as in Figure 10.17. Hold Shift+right mouse button and zoom back out when you are done.

Placing a Cut Brush to Create a Door Between Rooms

In this section, you will learn how to use the Cut Brush to cut a hole in your cubes to make a hall between them.

1. First, go to Template mode and select the Cube brush. The Create Box dialog box opens. Change the parameters to Solid and Cut Brush and click on OK. The template is there, but the cut brush is not, so press Enter.

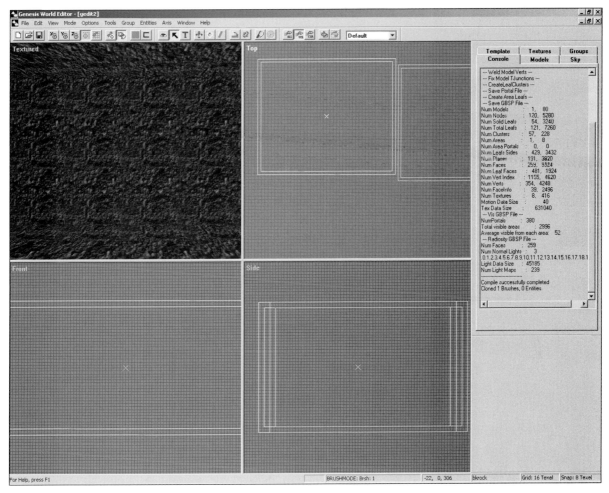

Figure 10.16
The two brushes—side-by-side, but not completely aligned yet.

2. Switch to Select mode and select the newly created cut brush. Activate Scale mode (choose Mode|Scale or press L) to prepare to resize the new brush.

3. Zoom in from the Side view, and match the cut brush with the floor of the two hollow cubes. Bring the top of the cut out a bit lower and the sides in as well to form a hole that's roughly the size of a door. Make sure that the cut brush does not cut through the hollow brushes to the outside of the rooms anywhere and cause a leak in the level.

More Face Editing

You may notice that the faces of the cut brush contain the wrong textures. This can be fixed quite simply.

1. Go into Face Editing mode (press the PgDn key).

2. Select the face you wish to change textures on.

3. Go to the Texture tab and find the texture on the list that belongs on the face you have selected. They should be "mech0005" for the top of

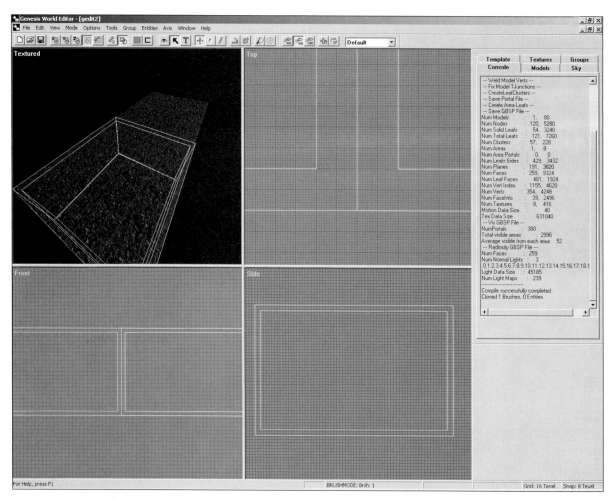

Figure 10.17
The two brushes placed precisely.

the brush, "brickblk" for the sides, and "sand" for the floor. Apply each texture to the appropriate faces.

Using Groups

You may notice that every time you add anything in the level, it is represented in three of the four views as lines. So, as you add rooms below, above, and next to each other, and those rooms become more complex, you will have many lines going everywhere. The best solution for this problem is to select all the items in a room and create a group. To create a group, take the following steps:

1. Make sure that you are in Select mode.

2. Go to the view window that offers the best view of the brushes that you want to select.

3. Select the brushes, and then go to the Groups option in the toolbar. Choose Create New. You can select multiple brushes either by clicking, by holding down the mouse button and dragging a selection around the brushes, or by holding down Ctrl and clicking on the brushes.

4. You will be prompted for a name of the group. Enter a descriptive name such as "Main Hall".

Note: If you create a group and hide it, you must unhide all the groups before compiling and running your map. If you do not do this first, you will get errors.

You will notice the other options that allow you to add and remove objects from a group. From the Groups tab, you can then hide groups for easier working. You can also color groups as well.

Next, you'll give your room a view of the sky.

Using a Sky Box

The way a sky works in Genesis3D is to render a huge six-sided cube on the outside of your level. If you go to the Sky tab on the Command Panel, you will see six checkboxes, as shown in Figure 10.18.

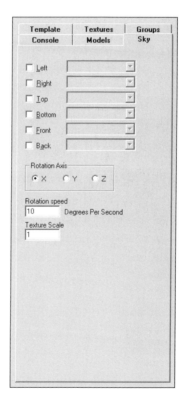

Figure 10.18
The Sky tab in the Command Panel.

Each of the checkboxes allows you to activate a face and then assign a bitmap image to that face from the texture library. Here, you can also assign a rate of rotation and axis. This capability is great for adding storm clouds because you can have the sky moving by very fast, as it does in a storm. For your castle project, you're creating a starry sky, so you won't need this feature.

To prepare a starry sky for your project, take the following steps:

1. Go to the Sky tab on the Command Panel. For each face of the sky, select the "stars" image from the drop-down list.

2. Your stars don't need to rotate, so set the Rotation Rate for the stars to 0.

You have just set up your first sky. Keep in mind that the sky box is not visible from the level editor.

Seeing the Sky from a Level

Now, to use your sky you could simply switch to Face Editing mode, click on the ceiling, and set the face to Sky; then you would see the stars in the game. But to make the level look good, you need to use another approach; add a few brushes to the level to give the illusion that the room you are making is thicker, or more solid.

1. Make sure that you are in Template mode, and go to the Texture tab and select the "blkbrk" texture.

2. Go to the Templates tab, create a Solid Cube, and make it a Cut Brush. While you are here in the Create Box dialog box, make the Top X Size and Z Size values smaller than the Bottom X Size and Z Size values. In this case, I used 350 for both the top values and 400 for the bottoms. This creates an interesting tapered cut brush.

3. Now place the cut brush so that it cuts into your ceiling but does not cut through it. Center it in the room, but leave enough of a border (don't cut too much out of the ceiling) and give your skylight a nice thick edge so that it resembles the one shown in Figure 10.19.

This approach helps give the composition of the room a feeling of a solid structure. Try the simpler approach by making the entire ceiling face a sky face, and you will see how this ruins the illusion of solidity and makes the walls feel paper-thin.

> **Note:** You can set the grid to 32 when laying out rooms. This makes it easy to set walls, columns, doors, and other large items in precise locations. However, when you are setting a cut brush in a wall, as in this example, set the grid to 1 and place the cut brush one texel from the hull edge.

Putting Up a Grate

Next, you will put up a raunchy iron fence across the skylight to give things a really oppressive feeling. To do so, take these steps:

1. Go into Template mode and select the "grate" texture from the Texture tab; create a sheet brush. Place it along the top of the skylight.

2. Activate Face Editing mode, open the Face Attributes dialog box, and turn on Transparency. Leave the value at 255.

3. Compile and run your map to see the effect.

You may want to take the Draw Scale down to 0.5 in the Face Attributes Dialog so that the grate texture will be drawn smaller and look better. You can even drop the Transparency setting down a little from 255 to around 200 so that the grate isn't so hard edged but so that you still cannot see through to the background (see Figure 10.20).

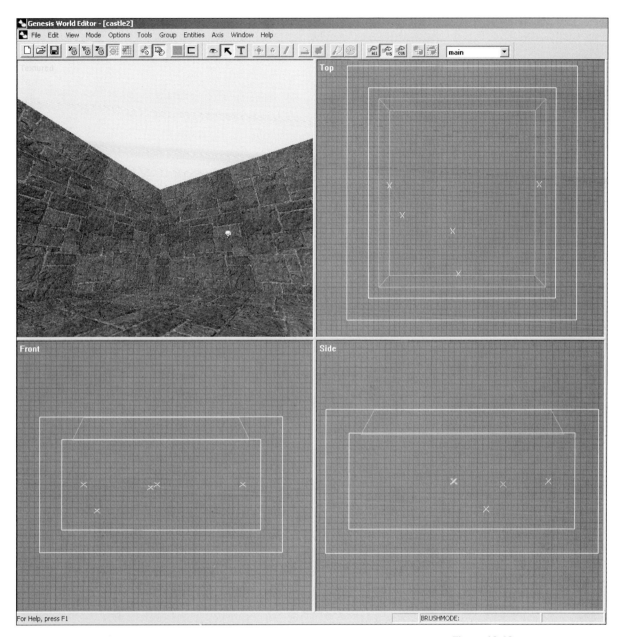

Adding Magical Light

Next, you can add some cool magic lights to the world. Do this by creating a cut brush that is textured in the same material as your castle stone floor and cutting into the floor. The holes that you create will match the material they are cut from, just like the hallway you made previously. You can then use the Face Adjustment tool to retexture the bottom face with a lava texture and make that face full bright (or look like it is giving off 100 percent light). It will appear as if lava is flowing under your level.

Figure 10.19

The alignment of the cut brush for the skylight.

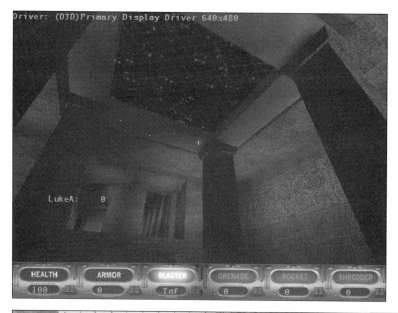

Figure 10.20

The oppressive wooden grate in the editor and in the game.

1. Start in Template Mode and Center the room in your editor windows. Create a Solid Cube brush with the "brkblk" texture on it. Make this brush a cut brush and embed it into the floor, but do not cut all the way through the level (see Figure 10.21). Instead, place the cut brush one texel from actually cutting through the level. You can make your

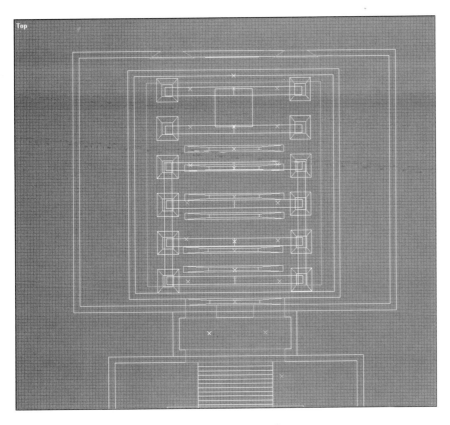

Figure 10.21
The layout and placement of the lava trenches. These trenches are made from cut brushes with a lava texture and the Full Bright option on one face.

cut brush tapered as I have for a much cooler looking effect. Clone and drag these cut brushes along the floor.

2. Now use the Page Down key to enter Face Editing mode. Select the bottom face where the lava flows under the floor of the castle.

3. Go to the Texture tab and assign the "lava" texture to the selected face.

4. Choose Tools|Face|Attributes, select the Full Bright option, and then close the Face Attributes dialog box.

5. Clone a few more lava trenches and fit them about the floor of your level. Remember that if you do the cloning from the Top view, the brushes will stay exactly where they are supposed to be and not cut through the level. You can also turn the grid on to 16 units, and this will make it easier to position the trenches exactly between the pillars and in the center of the room. For effect, face-edit one of the trenches (in Face Editing mode, select the trench and open the Face Attributes dialog box), and turn the Full Bright option off so it will appear that the lava has cooled (see Figure 10.22). You'll learn more about lighting effects in Chapter 12, and add a light entity above the lava and experiment with other lighting effects.

6. Remember to save your file now and often, as you work!

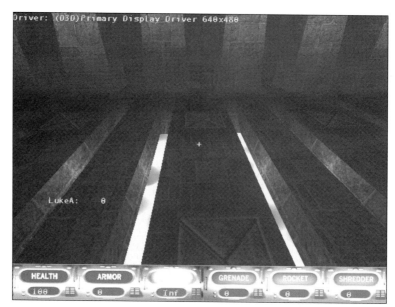

Figure 10.22
Here are the lava trenches
in the game.

Adding Banners

In this section, you will learn how to add a hanging banner of a cross on the wall using the sheet brush, transparency, and the Detail option.

1. Create another Sheet brush; go into Template mode and select the Cube Template and check the "sheet" option on the dialog. Assign the texture "banner2" to it, and place this brush one texel from a wall in the courtyard, about midway up.

2. With this banner, you want to turn on Transparency and Texture Lock. Position the banner and size the brush to fit using the Face Adjustment dialog (Page Down Key). In the Face Attributes dialog box, set the banner's Transparency Value to 155 so the banner will look washed out on the stones. Also, set the Draw Scale up to 2 so the banner will be larger and look like a large, old, and faded mural.

3. Because you are using Transparency on a sheet brush, go to Brush Adjustment mode and make this a Detail Brush to avoid draw errors. Because you are laying your one-faced polygon against another surface, the engine gets confused as to which polygon to draw on top of the other. This option tells the engine always to draw the sheet brush on top.

Note: Sheet brushes often are created "face up" and will need to be rotated.

4. The next detail you can add is the large Celtic decoration. Add another sheet brush and position it in the main room between the two windows. Place the "cross" texture on the brush and set position and size it. See Figure 10.23 for the final result.

Creating a Game World 235

Figure 10.23
The Cross looks painted on the wall in the game. A texture with the transparency on it produced this effect.

As you can see, if you open the version of this map I provided on this book's companion CD-ROM, I added minor details and brushes to get a cool looking level. Try some of the things I did, or experiment on your own. Instead of sticking a column in my level that is a box, I made tapered ones; I even made a column out of two tapered cubes and one straight one. Try sticking three or four shapes together, or try using the arch template instead.

Speed Tips

As you make your maps larger and more complex, you will need to know a few tips for speeding them up and making them more efficient.

Remember the One-Texel Rule

Always distance every brush one texel from all others when possible by setting the grid to "one texel" and zooming in to make the fine adjustment. This procedure prevents the splitting of geometry into more faces. Geometry splitting is when the engine has to draw several pieces of geometry around an object stuck in the floor as opposed to one flat surface.

Set the Light Map Scale

The Texture Offset scale, how big a texture or image is drawn, and Light Map scale are separate. If you have large outdoor areas running slow, you can make your Light Map scale a 5 or 8. In smaller indoor areas, you can bring them down to 1 or 2 for finer shadows. Texture Offset does not affect the render speed.

Use Detail Brushes

Every time you create an object and place a brush in your world, ask yourself if it can be a detail brush, as detail brushes are key to getting fast compiles. If the object is not going to block visibility, then make it a detail brush so the game engine won't have to run a calculation on it to see if it blocks visibility. Only the basic shape of your world should be structural (non-detail). such as the major rooms and halls. Fully "vising" the level will speed up the *radiosity* (shadow map creation) pass, as well as the overall speed of the level in the renderer.

Radiosity is a method of producing realistic lighting in computer images, and it produces some of the most realistic images because it simulates the actual behavior of light. Radiosity is also one of the most computationally expensive ways to create computer images. For "one frame at a time" rendering (as in movies) where it doesn't matter how long a frame takes to render because it will be showN in succession later, this was acceptable; for realtime rendering, however, this process used to take too long for the computer and is just now becoming feasible with the new and faster graphics cards.

You should not set major hallways and the major bounding areas of your rooms to detail. These need to be left as they are because they will be used to generate areas that the computer will not draw if they are not visible. Just by setting brushes to detail, the number of areas the computer will try to keep track of will go down, and you will get a speed increase because the engine doesn't have to check against as many areas to see if it's visible.

Avoid Cut Brushes

The editor and engine do not handle cut brushes very well. The fragments left behind from the current cut method build lots of portals, or areas the computer has to think about to draw. This makes for slow light building times (20 to 30 hours!).

Use Hint Brushes

In tight spaces that should be running fast but are running slowly, put a couple of hint brushes in. Hint brushes should span the entire problem area (like cutting a hallway totally in half). A hint brush is one way to let the engine know that it needs to do a better (tighter) job building light maps around the hint brush area.

Use Area Brushes

Area brushes were described in Chapter 9 and should be used—planned into your level—on doors. Area brushes will tell the computer to stop trying to draw an area sealed off by an area brush.

Moving On

In this chapter, you learned the basics of creating one room in Genesis3D. In creating this room, however, you learned the basics of creating an entire world.

In Chapter 11, you will be looking at making and animating models in Genesis. With this simple, yet powerful tool, you will be able to create doors, elevators, and almost anything you can imagine.

Chapter 11

Adding Models to Your World

By creating models, you can animate brushes or groups of brushes in your level. You can make moving doors, platforms, waterwheels, and vehicles. In this chapter, you will create a simple model with a dramatic effect—with only a few simple steps.

Making Things Move in Your Level

In this chapter, we will make things move in your level, but to do that you must have a level first. If you haven't yet worked through Chapter 10, do so now, and then come back to this chapter. If you've read Chapter 10, you already know that I'm taking several chapters to show you how to create a basic game world (refer to Chapter 10), to add and animate a model (this chapter), and to add lighting (see Chapter 12). All of the skills you learn while going through the tutorials for this extended project will help you with your own projects.

Making things move in your level adds a great many things to your game: life, game play, and immersion in the game world are all increased. For example, a spinning windmill, a moving set of gears, or any moving model that can connote the forces of man or nature adds another dimension to your world. Adding models can also be used as part of game play; for example, you may create a moving platform that the player must jump on and ride to get to another part of your level. Of course, doors and elevators add a lot to a game and they can be modern, high-tech doors or elevators or they could originate completely in a fantasy world.

In this chapter, you will create and animate a windmill as your model. As you do this, you'll learn about the options in the Models options page, and you'll learn some more basic techniques:

- Creating a model

- Specifying a model's animation options

- Attaching entities to models so that the models work in the game

Before you get to work, you'll first need to understand what models are and how they work in Genesis3D.

Overview of Models

> **Note:** The process of making a model in Genesis3D is the process in telling the computer that a certain piece of geometry or set of brushes is a model. The geometry (or brushes) already exists when you do this.

In Genesis3D, a model is any piece of geometry (or any group of geometrical objects) that you've designated as a model (by using the Models tab in the Command Panel). You designate an object as a model so that you can animate it or so that game programmers can attach data (such as special effects) to it when a game operation involves that model.

Creating an animated model is actually a simple process that involves the following basic steps:

1. Create your geometric object (or group of objects).

2. Select the object or set, and designate it as a model. (Click on the Models tab, click on the Add Model button, and name the model.)

3. Specify the model's animation options (keyframes and associated timelines).

4. Assign entities to the models, if needed.

When you first select the Models tab, the only button that you will see available is Add Model (see Figure 11.1). After you add a model, the other buttons become available. The top half of this tab contains what I'll call the basic options; the bottom half contains the animation options.

Using the Basic Options on the Models Tab

On the top half of the Model tab, you see Genesis3D's most basic model features. Figure 11.1 shows the Model tab.

Figure 11.1
The Models tab and its options.

Now, let's take a closer look at the basic options on the Models tab. The following list describes these options:

- *Model Name drop-down list*—This option allows you to select any model on your map from here. This is extremely useful if you have a large map that contains many models.

- *Add Model*—This option creates a model from a brush or from a selected group of brushes. Make sure that you have selected only those brushes you want to become part of a model.

Note: It's important to remember that, if you animate a model and assign it to various entities and then delete it, you will have to redo *all* your work. Even if you add the same brushes to a new model by the same name, you will have to go back and reanimate and reassign the model, even though the model name appears in the entity dialog boxes.

- *Delete Model*—This option deletes the model, but it does not delete the brushes that you used to compose the model.

- *Edit Model*—This option enables you to open (or ungroup) a model and edit its geometry and textures.

- *Select*—By clicking on this option, you select the model you have highlighted in the drop-down list.

- *Deselect*—Use this option to deselect a model that is currently selected.

- *Add Brushes*—If you have created a brush that you would like to make part of a model, because of some detail you thought of at the last minute, you can add it to the model. To do this, select the brush that you want to add to the model, select the model from the drop-down list, and click on Add Brushes.

- *Remove Brushes*—This option allows you to remove brushes from a model. Remove Brushes is a great tool when you are experimenting and find that that the quick-and-dirty model you made has been animated perfectly. Because animating can grow very tedious, it's best to improve the model by first deleting the old brush and then adding a new one, rather than redoing the entire animation on a new brush.

- *Clone Model*—Click on this option to copy the selected model, including its animation. The copy will not be assigned to any entities. You will learn about the entities that you must use for models later in this chapter.

- *Set Origin*—This sets the pivot point of the model. This option is especially useful for doors because most brushes have their pivot points in the center, and doors have theirs on the edge. After selecting the model, select "Set Origin" and drag the small blue "x" around until you have the hinge line—or pivot point—of your model set where you want it. You will look at the pivot point later, at the end of this chapter.

Using the Animation Options on the Models Tab

The bottom half of the Models tab has all the options for animating models. The way animation works in Genesis3D is by defining *keyframes*, or points throughout the animation where you want the model to be. You also assign the time it will take for the model to reach each of those points in the animation. For example, if you animate windmill blades spinning, you can start the animation at 0 (zero seconds), rotate the blades a quarter of the way, and enter the keyframe value of "1". That means that the blades take one second to go from their starting position to a quarter of the way around (see Figure 11.2).

Note: Keyframes are the positions and orientations of the model at specific points in an animation.

Now, you will look a little more closely at the animation options and tools on the Models tab. The following list describes the animation tool options:

- *Animate Key*—This key is depressed when you are ready to start moving and recording your models' animation.

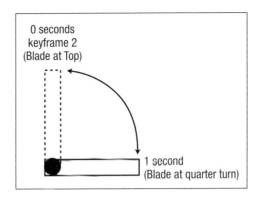

0 seconds
keyframe 2
(Blade at Top)

1 second
(Blade at quarter turn)

Figure 11.2
The concept of a blade spinning and its keyframes.

- *Keyframe window*—This window lists all the keyframes and their times.

- *Delete Key*—This key deletes the selected keyframe.

- *Edit Key*—This key allows for the editing of the keyframe time.

- *Locked*—The button for this option locks the keyframe time so that it cannot be changed.

- *Add Event*—The button for this option is used to add special events to the model, but because it requires the services of a programmer, it will not be touched on in this book. Special events can include special sounds, and so on.

- *Delete Event*—The button for this option allows you to delete the above-added event.

- *Edit Event*—This option allows for the editing of an added event.

Note: There is a row of buttons to the left of the Animate button that are always grayed out. These buttons are not functioning in the current version of the Genesis3D program.

To create a motion for a model, select the desired model from the drop-down list on the Models tab and then press the Animate button. The editor will automatically select the model and also put the editor into Move mode. You can now move and rotate the model to the next position you want it to have in the animation (the next keyframe). When you have the model at the position you want, press the Stop Animating button (this button toggles between Animate and Stop Animating) and enter the keyframe time. Genesis3D interpolates between keyframes to smooth the animation.

After you're done adding keyframes and their timelines, you're still not quite finished with the animation. Before the game engine can recognize that a model has motions attached, you must assign an entity to the model and then edit the entity's properties.

Entities You Can Assign to Your Models

Genesis3D provides entities that you can use to animate your models. Entities are accessed from the Entity drop-down list on the Template tab. There are several types of entities, including one that makes the animation play in a continuous loop. The entities you can use are described in the following list. These are the only entities you can use with a model in the list.

- *Door*—This entity makes the model respond as a door and plays the door sound.

- *Model Controller*—This entity makes the selected model's animation run in a continuous loop.

- *Moving Platform* (MovingPlat)—This entity makes the model respond as an elevator and plays the platform sound.

To use these entities, simply place them in the level and from their properties dialog boxes assign a model to them (see Figure 11.3). You will work through this procedure in detail later in this chapter. Meanwhile, you will learn how to use these entities in the following project, in which you will create a windmill.

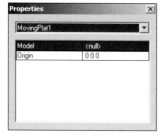

Figure 11.3
The Properties dialog boxes for the Door, Model Controller, and Moving Platform entities.

PROJECT Creating and Animating a Windmill

Now, as an exercise, you will build a simple windmill that will have a surprisingly great effect in your game world due to its size and motion. See Figure 11.4 for the general proportions and layout of the windmill.

To create the structure of the windmill, follow these steps:

1. Create the level: Create a large box for your level. (Open the file "windmill1", if you would like to see how I started my level.) Add the wall and skybox for effect, and texture the ground with the sand texture. Make sure that you have the castle texture library loaded from the previous chapters.

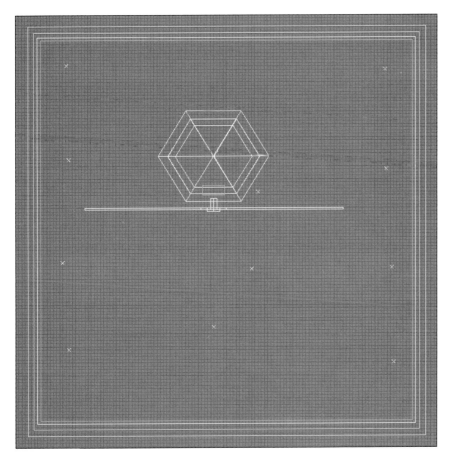

Figure 11.4
The general proportions of the simple windmill (top view).

2. Now start building the windmill: In Template mode, make a huge cylinder (eyeball this; it isn't critical that you be precise) and select the Ring option to make the cylinder hollow. Apply the "blkbrk" texture to the cylinder.

3. To add the top, create a pyramid object and use the Funnel option. If you make sure that wall thickness and the number of sides are the same as for your ring, then the top can be made to fit the building precisely. I actually made my roof overlap a little on all sides.

Looking at this windmill in the editor, it is not too impressive (see Figure 11.5). However, this example is a solid illustration of how game level construction is part trickery and part illusion. After the level is loaded and the windmill blades are spinning, you will need to add a skybox and lighting (creating effective lighting is discussed in Chapter 12). This adds a great deal of realism to your level.

Creating the Blades

Your new windmill isn't complete (and you won't have anything to animate) until you add blades. To do so, follow these steps:

1. Create the hub for the blades: Create a cylinder, and center it where the blades connect. Copy the cylinder, make it thinner and wider than the original cylinder, and move it to the hub's end to form a cap.

Figure 11.5

The simple windmill in the level editor, not yet very impressive. In the game, however, it looks great.

2. Start creating the blades of the windmill. To create the first blade, drag out a solid brush with the "blades" texture on it. Make this blade roughly the same shape in the figure. You can face-edit the brush (switch to Face Editing mode and open the Face Attributes dialog box), select the Texture Lock option, and line up the blade texture, as you learned in Chapter 10.

3. Duplicate the blade, and drag it over to the opposite side of the hub. Now you can select both of these blades, duplicate them, and rotate them 90 degrees to create the last two of the four blades of the windmill. See Figures 11.6 and 11.7 for an illustration of how this is done.

4. Select all the blades and the hub pieces, making sure that you do not select anything that you do not want to move with the blades.

At this point, the blades are still just brushes; you will need to make them into a model that you can animate. Do this by using the Models tab, following these steps:

1. With the windmill blades and hub pieces selected, click on the Models tab (see Figure 11.8). The blades are now a model.

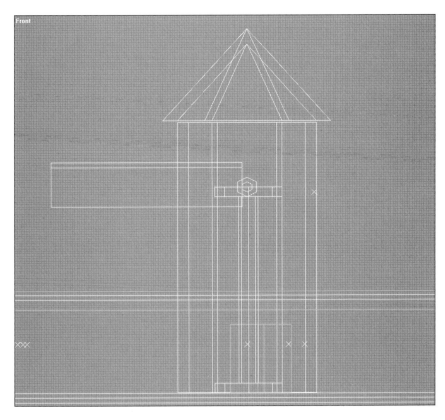

Figure 11.6
The first blade on the windmill.

Figure 11.7
Four blades on the windmill, in textured view.

Figure 11.8
The Models tab.

2. Notice that everything is grayed out in the Models tab except for the Add Model button. To make the selected blades and the hub pieces into a model, click on the Add Model button. You will see a prompt requesting you to name the model. Name it "blades".

Now, check out the Models tab. You can see that all the buttons on the Models tab are available; they're no longer grayed out, because you now have a model with which to work.

Animating the Windmill Blades and Adding a Turning Shaft

In the next part of this project, you'll animate the windmill's blades. To do this, take the following steps:

1. Select the "blades" model.

2. Click on the Animate button. Notice that it toggles and becomes the Stop Animating button.

3. Now, rotate the blades one-quarter turn. You can use the Rotate button in the toolbar to move the blades exactly one quarter of a turn.

4. Click on the Stop Animating button. You will be prompted with the message "Enter Key Time". Enter a "1", which stands for 1 second. Remember that this amount is the number of seconds that the model will take to reach this first keyframe. A spinning windmill blade may take less than

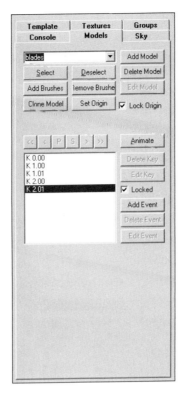

Figure 11.9
The windmill blades animation and its keyframes.

1 second in a high wind, but we want this to look good, and we also want the player to be able to get into the building (see Figure 11.9).

Because Genesis3D interpolates between keyframes to smooth the animation, you need to define an additional keyframe at the same location to help the interpolation process.

5. Click on the Animate button once again, and do *not* move your model. Click on Stop Animating. When you are prompted to enter a Key Time, enter the value of "3.01".

You want your blades to appear as if they are spinning constantly and smoothly. To do this, you can animate the blades turning all the way around once, and then stop it there. In the game, the effect will be the blades spinning constantly because when the animation is done, it loops back to precisely where it started. This gives the appearance of the blades spinning in one constant motion.

Another model that you can add to the windmill is a center shaft, or long pole, inside the building. This shaft will extend from the top of the windmill—where the shaft (in a real-world windmill) is turned by the windmill blades—and will go down to a large wheel (perhaps, to a grindstone) at the base inside the building. Make this shaft by doing the following:

1. First, create a solid cylinder. Then, apply the "woodold" texture to it. Center the shaft within the windmill building, and stretch it so it reaches from the floor to ceiling.

2. Now copy the shaft and flatten it and make it wider, just like you did for the hub of the blades to create "gears." Stick one of these at the top and one at the bottom of the shaft you just created.

3. Group these three objects together and make them a model, and animate it so that the gear shaft is spinning. Here, the trick is to make it look like it's synchronized with the blade's motion: Make the shaft take the same time to complete a revolution (1 second per quarter turn). See Figure 11.10 for the shaft setup. When you run this level, you will see that the two parts seem to be moving together. Before they will move, however, you need to add the entities I mentioned previously.

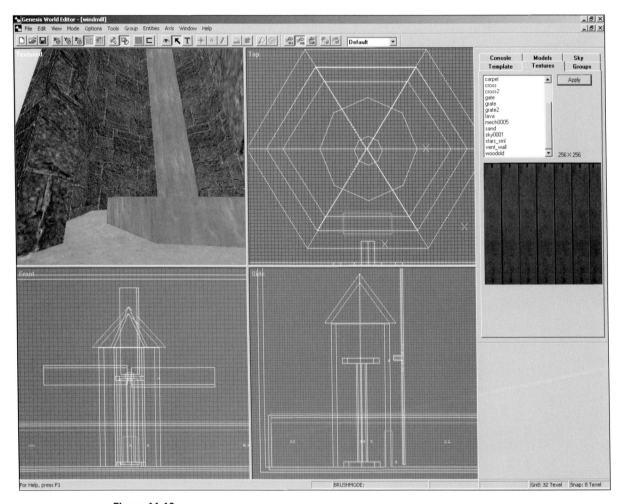

Figure 11.10

The shaft setup.

To add an entity that makes the blades and shaft of the windmill spin, take the following steps:

1. In Template mode, select the "Model Controller" entity from the Entity drop-down list on the Template tab.

2. Place the entity in the level (anywhere you want, but place it where you can find it later). You can perform this in one of the two following ways:

- Click on the Entity button (the lightbulb icon next to the drop-down list). The template entity is displayed in blue in the orthographic views. Move the template entity in any of these view windows and press Enter.

- In the Textured view window, click where you want the entity placed, and press Enter. The entity will be placed 16 texels from the surface on which you clicked.

3. Assign the entity to the model. To do this, open the entity's Properties dialog box and select the model. The easiest way to access the entity's properties is to click on the Entity Dialog icon in the toolbar and use the pull-down list to locate it.

Animating Doors and Platforms

You can also animate doors and rising platforms, such as elevators. You animate them using the same process you did for animating the blades. The major difference here is in what you have the animation *do*. For a door or elevator, you usually want the animation to run in three phases. The door phases are open, pause, and close. The elevator phases are ascend, pause (at the top), and descend. The pause is so that the player has time to get through the door or off the platform. See Figures 11.11 and 11.12 for animations of a door and platform.

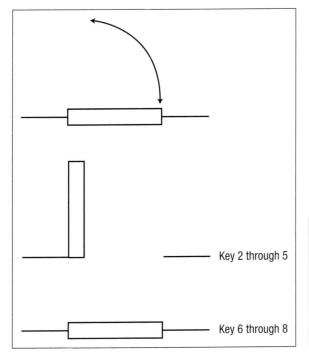

Key 2 through 5

Key 6 through 8

Figure 11.11
The animation of a door in three phases.

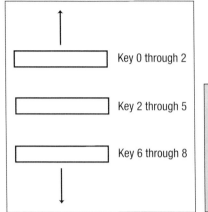

Figure 11.12
The animation of a platform in three phases.

Key 0 through 2

Key 2 through 5

Key 6 through 8

Note: When you're animating models that will return to their original position, be sure to use the Grid Snaps and line things up to the one-texel level, so the model doesn't jump or pop at the end of its animation.

When you're planning and executing the animating of doors and platforms, keep in mind the setting and the "technology" or "magic" behind them. Obviously, a door's setting is established on the texture and model, but a good animation supports the setting. A spaceship or high-tech door may pop open quickly and close a little slower. Heavy doors may be thicker and open with painful slowness—and close even more slowly. Also, although it often destroys the illusion that the computer world is real by having large objects floating in space, this trick can be used if implemented well. A door that, when opened, floats magically away can look good if done well, or it can look ridiculous if done poorly.

You are now ready to compile and test your level. You should be able to see both the windmill blades and the shaft spinning. If you need help in compiling and testing a level, refer to Chapter 10, in the "Testing the Map" section, and take the steps you find in that section. The windmill, as shown in the final game, can be seen in Figure 11.13.

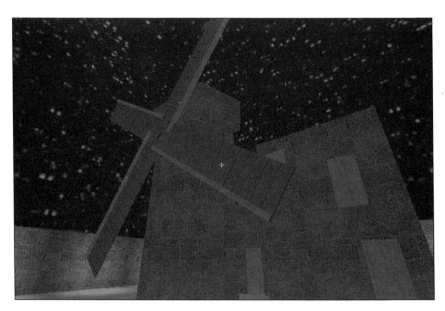

Figure 11.13
The windmill in the final game level.

One item, however, is missing: Sounds, such as the "flapping" of the blades and the grind of the shaft. This is where the many advances of the Reality Factory come in, as you'll see when you read Chapter 13.

Moving On

In this chapter, you learned about the basic options and the animation options by using Genesis3D's Models feature in a project that showed how to create and animate a windmill with moving blades. You also learned how to heighten the windmill's look by adding and animating several mechanical parts, such as gears and shafts.

You may have noticed that the levels you have created in this chapter may seem a bit bland and washed out; they don't look much like game levels that you may have played. This is because they haven't been lit yet using the lights and light entities that can be found in Genesis. You will begin to learn how to light levels in Chapter 12.

Chapter 12

Lighting the World

You can do many things to a game level—add textures, geometry, animations, and more—but when lighting is applied to the level, great things can result. A poor level can be made to look better with good lighting, and sadly, a great level can be made to look terrible with poor lighting.

An Introduction to Lighting

This chapter continues with discussion of the Castle project. Here, you will learn how to change the lighting in your projects to alter the mood, set the atmosphere, or direct the player to investigate areas through subtle manipulation of Genesis 3D's powerful lighting features.

In this chapter, you will learn to light your level, and in the process, you'll look at several lighting entities that allow for special-effect type lighting. These light types can simulate fog, lightning bolts, and more. These entities are not all lights, but they are classified as light entities because they produce the effects commonly associated with light, such as the Electric Bolt and Corona effect, both of which are explained in following sections of this chapter. You will also examine some of the more basic game lighting techniques that will help you achieve the lighting atmosphere that you are trying to achieve. First, however, you need to look at the most important lighting tool in the Genesis3D bag—the Default Light Level.

Default Light Level, or Ambient Lighting

Whatever you choose to call this setting, Default Light Level is *the* light level for the entire world. So far, you have been building your worlds with the default light setting either at full or as it was set in the level that you opened. This setting, however, is not an entity. Rather, this is a parameter that is controlled from the Compile Manager dialog box (see Figure 12.1), and you can set the color and brightness of the light by using RGB values. Unfortunately, you cannot use the color picker (as you can with the light entities), but because the input is RGB color values, you can go into Photoshop or open the color picker for a light entity, find the color that you want to use, write down the RGB values, and transfer those values to Genesis3D in the Compile Manager dialog box, in the Light Settings section.

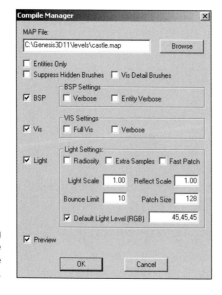

Figure 12.1

The Compile Manager dialog box, where you can set the color and brightness of the world's lightning.

As mentioned in Chapter 7, Genesis has a default light level. But as you will see, the default light level in Genesis (as in many game engines) is harsh and flattens both the colors and the depth of the scene. The only benefit to this default setting is that level designers won't find themselves in the dark if they forget to place lights in the world. You can turn the ambient light off by deselecting the checkbox to the left of the Default Light Setting Text Box. This change makes the world completely black, except for any lights you may have already added to the world. The best settings are low RGB values (equal amounts of RGB) so the world is always partially visible, but the lighting effects you place are clearly dominant.

Basic Lighting Techniques

Also in Chapter 7, I mentioned bad lighting as one of the three most common mistakes often made by a new level designer. Here are a few lighting tricks that a good game designer frequently uses. Do not consider this section to be the definitive guide to lighting or game lighting; you can simply use the few tricks presented here to accomplish whatever design goals you may have. These tricks include setting mood or atmosphere, faking sunlight in Genesis3D, and accenting important game-play points with light that warns players.

Setting Mood or Atmosphere

You can play with the RGB settings of the Default Light Level and change the atmosphere of the world's light. You can create worlds that are bathed in a mostly bluish light for an Artic or ice world, a mostly red light for hell or the inside of a volcano, or a mostly green light for a toxic world, or—perhaps—a world that the player views through night vision gear.

Note: Don't go overboard with color—use colored lighting sparingly. Most level designers agree that colored lighting doesn't equal atmosphere, and colored lighting can also be a strain to the players' eyes.

Faking Sunlight in Genesis3D

You can fake sunlight coming through windows in Genesis by placing light entities inside any window in your world and adjusting the lighting color, radius, and position. Using the capabilities of the lights in Genesis, you can cast shadows by using the windows for this effect (see Figure 12.2).

Accenting Important Game Play Points with Light

As part of your game design, you are required to give the player clues about your world, such as where they should go next or where they should never go. Lighting can be a powerful way to add these game play points. As an example, take a look at Figures 12.3 and 12.4. Notice how the emphasis switches from the carpet to the pyramid simply by moving the light.

There are a few more tricks you can employ that are specific to the entity being used. Here are some examples:

- A door with a toxic green mist about it (fog light) may be avoided or approached carefully by the player. This kind of addition can also be a signal to the player to don a gas mask, if one is part of their inventory.

Figure 12.2
By using lights in each window, you can cast shadows across the floor to fake sunlight.

Figure 12.3
In this shot, the light (and, therefore, the emphasis) is on the rug. The player's eyes will be drawn to this part of the room.

- A huge lighting bolt that shoots from the eyes of a god in a temple, hitting the trap door in the floor before it (the lightning bolt, that is) screams danger.

- A pulsing red light spills from a doorway, but nothing else is visible beyond the portal (fog light)—this screams either evil or intense heat.

Genesis Lights and Light Effects Entities

To add lights in Genesis3D, you use the various light entities provided, and edit their properties. There are several light entities we can use in Genesis3D. The following list describes them:

Figure 12.4
In this scene, the light has been moved over the pyramid. This change switches the emphasis (from the rug, as is shown in Figure 12.3, to the pyramid, as shown here) on where the player will most likely go exploring in this room.

- *Light*—This entity illuminates in a radius, or a globe, and can have effects assigned to it called *styles*. These lights are like omni lights in 3D Studio Max, lighting outward in a globe from the center point to a point where the light stops (a user-designated point). For an example (although here, the colors aren't visible), see Figure 12.5.

Figure 12.5
Light entities in a game level. Notice the various sizes of the light. The colors are, from left to right, blue, green, and red.

- *Dynamic Light*—This light can be assigned behaviors that control the flicker rate and size of the light and attach the light to a model. No figure is provided to illustrate the Dynamic Light Entity because its effects cannot be reproduced for print.

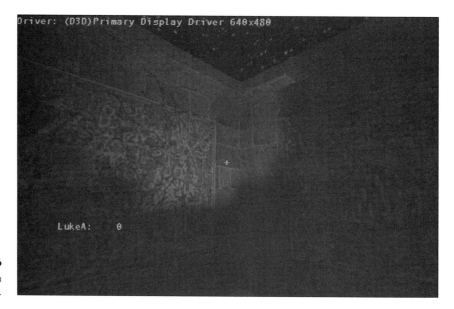

Figure 12.6
The spotlight entity gives you control over areas of light.

- *Spotlight*—This entity gives the user a controlled beam or circle of light with which to work. Like a real-world spotlight, this spotlight gets aimed in only one direction (see Figure 12.6).

- *Fog Light*—This light produces a radius of fogged, hazy light (see Figure 12.7).

Figure 12.7
The fog light entity lets you create balls or areas of fog as in this example, which shows an eerie glow near a doorway.

Note: The difference between the corona and the fog light is that the fog light actually produces a ball of fog; the corona, on the other hand, is a bitmapped image that is scaled and rotated on a point.

- *Corona*—This light creates the effect that looks and behaves like the glow or halo around a streetlight at night. Corona light entities can also be attached to models, as is shown in Figure 12.8.

- *Electric Bolt* and *Electric Bolt Terminus*—These two entities work together. The Electric Bolt is the starting point of the bolt, and the terminus is the end of the bolt. You must have at least one bolt and one terminus, but

Figure 12.8
The corona entity gives a light the effect of a glow, like after you have been swimming and you look at the street lights.

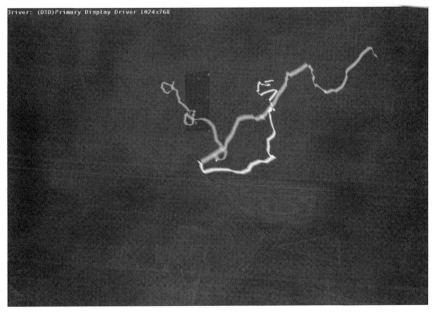

Figure 12.9
This is an example of a bolt created by the Electric Bolt and the Electric Bolt Terminus entity.

you can also have many bolts leading to the same terminus for some pretty cool effects (see Figure 12.9).

Adding a Light Entity

To add a light entity, just take these basic steps:

1. In Template mode, select the light entity you want from the Entity drop-down list on the Template tab. Click on the Entity button (the lightbulb icon to the left of the drop-down list). The template entity is displayed as a blue "X" in the orthographic views (the Top, Front, and Side windows).

2. In any of these view windows, move the template entity to where you want it, and press Enter.

3. Switch to Select mode, and select the entity.

4. Choose Entities|Entity Editor to open the entity's Properties sheet. The properties listed depend on the type of entity you added. To change a property, just double-click on it.

Understanding Light Entity Properties

Now, take a quick look at the properties available for the various light entities. Then you'll add lights to your castle level. The properties for the Light entity are described in the following list:

- *Color*—This is the RGB color of the light. You can bring up a color picker to choose the color of the light. Light color is, of course, extremely important in level design as touched on previously in this chapter.

- *Light*—This setting is the radius of the light in *world units*, or texels, the units the grid is set by. This has a default value of 150.

- *Origin*—This setting is the *xyz* coordinates of the light in the world. Moving the entity will set this value, although you can also type the *xyz* coordinates here, if you need to.

- *Style*—Using numbers from 0 to 11, you can assign different effects to the light. Many are various rates of flicker, but a few styles stand out. The following list shows off some of my favorite light styles:

  - 3—Flickers slowly.

  - 4—Flickers really fast.

  - 5—Fades in and out at medium speed.

  - 6—Flickers more like a torch.

  - 11—This is a throbbing shadowy effect that you really need to see.

Please note that I discovered these styles by spending a great deal of time experimenting in Genesis3D. Many of these styles are very similar to each other.

Dynamic Light Entity Properties

Properties for the Dynamic Light entity are described in the following list:

- *Allow Rotation*—If you anchor a dynamic light to a model, then you can use this parameter to specify whether or not the light follows the rotation of the model.

- *Color*—This is the RGB color of the light. You can bring up a color picker to choose the color of the light.

- *Interpolate Values*—You can turn this on to make a smoother transition between the Radius Function values, discussed next.

- *Max Radius*—The maximum radius of the light in world coordinates, or texels, the grid units.

- *Min Radius*—The minimum radius of the light in world coordinates. If you have a maximum radius of 300 and a minimum of 50, you will see a pulsing light as the light goes from the max to the min size. If you set the max and min values close together, there will be a less noticeable change.

- *Model*—You can attach a dynamic light to a model. You also specify the model here.

- *Origin*—The *xyz* coordinates of the light in the world. Moving the entity will set this, although you can also type in the *xyz* coordinates here if needed.

- *Radius Function*—The Radius Function entity allows you to set a pattern of flicker for your dynamic light by using any letters of the alphabet, from a to z. With this property, the letter "a" represents the Minimum Radius, and "z" represents the Maximum Radius.

  For example, the long string of letters below will make a failing-light effect because the light will appear more random; the portion of the string where the letter "a" is repeated gives the effect of a light that is failing. (The light is getting smaller.)

  `azaazzaazzaaaaaaaaaazzzaazazazazazzazaaaaaaaaa`

- *Radius Speed*—This property sets how fast the program cycles through the Radius Function values; this is measured in seconds. Set this down to half a second (0.5), and the light will appear to flicker.

Spotlight Entity Properties

Properties for the Spotlight entity are described in the following list:

- *Angle*—This property is the direction your light is facing, specified in values between 0 and 359 (like a compass), with 0 being north, 90 being east, 180 being south, and 270 being west. If you change these values and close the Entity Editor, you will notice that the light icon in the world editor will appear, showing the angle.

- *Arc*—Arc is the width of the cone of your light, which is also expressed in degrees. The smaller the number you enter, the tighter the cone of light will be and the larger the number, the wider the cone of light.

- *Color*—The color property can be set in the same way you set the other lights.

- *Light*—This is the distance for which the light is effective, specified in world coordinates.

- *Origin*—The *xyz* coordinates of the light.

- *Style*—Styles can be set in the same way as the Light entity.

Fog Light Entity Properties

Properties for the Fog Light entity are described in the following list:

- *Brightness*—This is set at 0 by default, and you must bring this up to about 300 or more to see the fog effect. This setting seems to have no numerical limit, but the higher you set the number, the brighter the center of the light gets. Because of this lack of information, I decided to experiment. I set a light to 5,000 and it looked great; a setting of 2,500 had much the same look, but the center of the effect was simply brighter.

- *Color*—Use the color picker to set the color of your fog effect.

- *Origin*—This is the location in *xyz* coordinates of the entity.

- *Radius*—This is the radius (the width) of the fog light effect.

Corona Light Entity Properties

This list describes the properties for the Corona entity:

- *Allow Rotation*—Use this property if the corona is attached to a model.

- *Color*—Using the color picker, you can select the hue of the corona.

- *Fade Out*—This allows the corona to fade out when it passes out of visible range. This can happen if the player moves away or the model the corona is attached to moves away from the player.

- *Fade Time*—How long the fade takes to drop to zero visibility, expressed in seconds.

- *Maximum Radius*—The maximum size, expressed in texels, the corona will ever get. In other words, the corona will never grow larger than the size you specify here.

- *Maximum Radius Distance*—This is the distance at which the corona will cease growing larger.

- *Maximum Visible Distance*—This property is the maximum distance the corona is visible.

- *Minimum Radius*—This setting is the smallest the corona will ever get. Radius expressed in texels. The corona will never grow any smaller than the size you specify here.

- *Minimum Radius Distance*—Below this distance, the corona will cease to shrink.

- *Model*—You can attach a corona to a model by selecting the model from the drop-down list.

- *Origin*—This is the *xyz* location of the corona entity.

Electric Bolt and Electric Terminus Entity Properties

Properties for the Electric Bolt entity are described in the following list:

- *Color*—Using the color picker, you can select the color of the corona.

- *Dominant Color*—You can set the dominant color of the bolt here. 0 = Red, 1 = Green, and 2 = Blue.

- *Intermittent*—By choosing 0 or 1, you can determine whether the bolt winks out or is constant.

- *Max Frequency*—If the bolt is intermittent, this property sets the maximum time between bolts, expressed in seconds.

- *Min Frequency*—If the bolt is intermittent, this is the minimum time between bolts.

- *Num Points*—This property sets the number of divisions the bolt can have expressed in the power of 2, which means that you should stick to the bitmap size numbers of 32, 64, and 128. The bolts will be drawn in these bitmapped sizes.

- *Origin*—This is the location in *xyz* coordinates of the entity.

- *Terminus* —You must have created an Electric Bolt Terminus in your world and choose it here so the bolt has a target.

- *Width*—The texel width of the electric bolt.

- *Wildness*—The degree of wildness expressed as a 1 or 0. Wildness is the area and randomness of the bolts.

Electric Bolt Terminus has only one property: Origin. This property is the *xyz* location of the entity.

Lighting the Castle Level

Begin by opening your castle level and lighting it. But before you add any lights to this map, make it a bit larger by following these steps:

1. Select the Hollow Brush that composes the room with the skylight, and make the floor a little lower by dragging it down. Be careful not to move the wall containing the cut brush to the other room, or you will have to go in and make the fine adjustment all over again.

2. You can place some stairs in the opening between the two rooms. Assign the "blkbrk" texture file (from the Chapter 7 tutorial files on the accompanying CD-ROM) to the stairs and press Enter. Move, rotate, and size the stairs in place (see Figure 12.10).

Figure 12.10
The stairs being placed in the enlarged castle room.

If you have already compiled your level and run it (you can learn more about this procedure if you refer to the end of Chapter 11), you will see that default ambient lighting looks harsh and flat. Now, you will place some lights in the castle level. Doing so will make the castle level look really spooky and cool with lighting, and you will also highlight certain details of the level while losing others in shadow, as you read about previously in this chapter.

First, you need to assume that there is no light—or very little light—in the level. The next time you compile the map, you will turn the default lighting way down so that your lighting effects will dominate and the shadows will be darker. Now you will place a few regular light entities in your level.

Using the Light Entity

You'll start by adding the basic Light entity, which you can use for a wide variety of effects, moods, and atmospheres as we looked at previously. To add a Light entity, follow these steps:

1. Go into Template mode and go to the Template tab. From the Entity drop-down list, select the Light entity. See Figure 12.11. Click on the Entity button (the lightbulb icon) to place the Light Entity template on the map.

Note: You can choose the Center Brush/Entity In View button on the Toolbar to center the Light entity in the middle of all views.

Figure 12.11

The Entity drop-down list on the Template tab of the Command Panel.

2. Move the dark blue "X" to the corner of the room and halfway up the wall. Press Enter to place the light entity in the world.

3. Go into Select Mode and select the light you just placed. Open the Properties sheet for this entity (choose Entities|Entity Editor, or use the toolbar button). See Figure 12.12 for the light's Properties sheet.

   Remember that the Light property is the radius of the light, set in world units. This has a default value of 150. For this exercise, change this value to about 300 or 350. (In Figure 12.12, I moved this value up to 400 because I was experimenting. Often, you will find that trying out a few different value settings will give you a better feel for how an effect can be adjusted.)

> **Note:** The Properties Sheet and the Entity Editor are the same thing. This tool lists the properties for all the entities added to the level. You can simply select the entity whose properties you want to see.

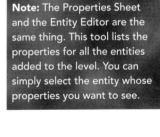

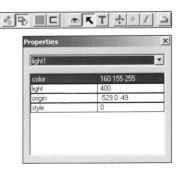

Figure 12.12

Properties for the Light entity.

4. Back in Select Mode, clone the light using the technique you used to clone the brush (see Chapter 10). Hold Shift and then press and hold the left mouse button and drag. Do this from the top view and place several lights—one in the center of each column. They should be about halfway up the columns and a few units away (see Figures 12.13 and 12.14).

Figure 12.13
The first lights placed in your castle level.

Figure 12.14
The same lights that you saw in Figure 12.13, as they appear in the compiled game. Notice how nicely these wall lights illuminate the wooden beams on the ceiling and light up the upper portions of the walls.

Now it's time to compile and test the map. To perform this process, take the following steps:

1. Choose Tools|Compile to open the Compile Manager dialog box (see Figure 12.15). Go down to the Default Light Level (RGB) option, and set it to 45,45,45. An easy way to set this default is to click in the window and delete all the digits there (128, 128,128) and then type 45,45,45.

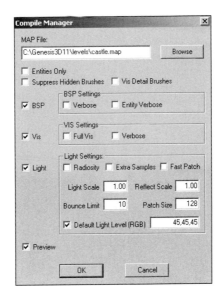

Figure 12.15
The Compile Manager dialog box; notice the lighting options.

2. Make sure that the Preview option is checked, and choose OK. Then click on Yes when prompted.

Using Dynamic Lights

To add to the castle level a dynamic light that resembles a flame, you can take the following steps:

1. Place a dynamic light, just as you would a regular light entity, from your top view, and center it.

2. Move the dynamic light right in the center of the cross on the wall. (You placed this cross in Chapter 10, the one on the wall in the back of the castle hall.) From the side view, position this light 16 to 32 texels away from the surface of the cross. You can set your Grid and turn Grid Snap on and off to help you get the position correct.

3. After you have placed the dynamic light, open the Entity Editor for it, and set the options you want according to the parameters given previously in the chapter. But you should set the Radius Function to "azaazzaazzaaaaaaaaaazzzaazazazazazazzazaaaaaaaaa" and the color to a reddish-orange.

4. Now compile and run your map. The dynamic light (the flame light) should now appear to flicker, like a failing light in front of the cross.

Using a Spotlight

As I stated previously, a spotlight is a unidirectional lighting effect; it shines in only one direction and at only one angle. You can control the circle (or Arc) of the light, the distance it shines, and the color. For an example of the spotlight in use, see Figure 12.16.

Figure 12.16

The spotlight in use in a game level. Notice how the cone of light fades off to the right because of the way the spotlight was aimed.

Using Fog Lights

As I mentioned previously, fog lights are used to simulate the haziness of fog. Fog lights are expensive to render, so use them sparingly. Fog in Genesis3D, just like fog in the real world, cannot be seen (unless it's as thick as pea soup) when you are in the center of it. In real fog, although you can always see what's close around you, it gets progressively harder to see what's farther away, deeper into the fog.

To add a fog light in front of the cross, follow these steps:

1. Put a fog light in front of the cross. Then select it and open the Entity Editor.

2. Match the color of the fog to the color of the dynamic light we put in earlier. Set the radius to about 300.

Using the Corona Light Entity

The Corona is the effect that produces a glow that you may have seen on a street light at night. You will use it here in your courtyard to give the magical torches a cool medieval effect. In the real world, however, the corona you see around the sun, for example, is a set of one or more colored rings that sometimes appear close to the sun or moon when they are viewed through a thin cloud composed of water droplets (atmosphere) or ice crystals. The corona is caused by the diffraction of light around the edges of the droplets or crystals. A corona can also be caused by a heavy pollen count in the air (this happens most often in summer and spring). Whatever their origin, in the real world, coronas are caused by something in the atmosphere, such as mist, pollen, smog, smoke, ice, or magic. For example, I always see coronas after swimming in a pool with my eyes open and then looking at point-light sources.

1. Create the Corona entity as you would create any other light entity.

2. Place your new entity slightly above one of the Light entities that you created earlier (halfway up the walls). Copy the Corona entity, and place one of these entity copies over each light.

3. You can compile your map with the default Corona setting. To see the Corona effect, see Figure 12.17.

> **Note:** You might want to brush up on your basic physics, biology, and other real-world sciences because they come into play often when you are building worlds—both "real" or imagined.

Figure 12.17
The Corona effect in your castle level.

Moving On

As you have seen, lighting is powerful and can make a huge difference in the look and feel of a level. In this chapter, you learned how to make the most of Genesis3D's powerful lighting tools. If you are more interested in lighting techniques for your levels, you can find excellent books in the photographic section of your local bookstore. These books can teach you all you ever wanted to know and more about lighting, from the basics to professional techniques.

The tools that Genesis3D gives you are powerful, but after you examine Reality Factory in the next chapter, you will realize that you can have even more tools at your disposal.

Chapter 13

The Reality Factory

After all that you learned to do with Genesis3D, you can do even more with the Reality Factory. You can add special effects, events, and lots of atmosphere to make a more detailed, whether realistic or fantastic, game.

Introduction to Reality Factory

Now that you have mastered the basics of map building with Genesis3D, you can use Reality Factory to build more into your levels and to make a complex game. You'll be able to add effects as well as other functionalities. Reality Factory, on the outside, looks like Genesis, but a lot has happened behind the scenes. Many entities have been added or enhanced. This chapter will go through some of them and explore the entities, and the effects you can create with them. You will also look at some of the other things Reality Factory has given to the designer to control.

Reality Factory is largely the effort of Rabid Games, but many other individuals have helped to improve the core Genesis3D technology. With Reality Factory, you can take the basics you learned about building a level and create more elaborate game levels. Particularly of interest to designers are the expanded entities that give you far more control over special effects, atmosphere, audio, and even artificial intelligence (AI). And best of all, you won't need a couple of programmers just to prototype your game idea. In Figures 13.1 and 13.2, you can see some of the entities in effects such as the flame and particle emitters.

Currently, Ralph Deane, Terry Morgan, and Mike Wuetherick are in charge of the organization and development of Reality Factory. The original developer, Ed Averill, has bowed out of the development and moved on to other things. For full information about Reality Factory, use your Web browser to go to **www.genesis3d.com/~rfactory/**.

Figure 13.1
Two flames, side by side.

Figure 13.2

These are particle emitters that can be used for various effects.

Although programmers are obviously still important to game development, Reality Factory is a set of rapid prototyping tools that gives artists and designers the freedom to experiment and create. Reality Factory is set up to be completely driven by entities and configuration files—these are files that can be edited and changed by designers as opposed to having programmers open up the source code, revise it, and then recompile it.

Rabid Games has also decided (in the spirit of the original Genesis3D team) to make Reality Factory an Open Source application.

The Tools That Come with Reality Factory

Reality Factory ships with a lot of tools to make game development as easy as possible. These tools include programs that pack up all your files, allow you to edit ini files and list the resources needed by a level, a tool to find files, and a font-making tool. Here, we will take a brief look at most of these tools.

> **Note:** An ini or *initialization* file is simply a text file where certain parameters of an application are read from so that you, the user, can change these settings without having to be a programmer.

rfEdit

Reality Factory comes with two editors. We will be using rfEdit because it closely resembles the Genesis World Editor that you already looked at, and it will be the easiest for you to use.

IniEditor

Reality Factory, like many applications, places a lot of its settings into an ini file that is read when the program starts. This allows you to edit the ini file and change elements, such as video driver and resolution, without recompiling the program. Although you can perform this editing with a text editor, it's very

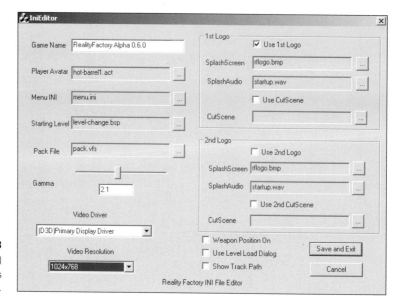

Figure 13.3
The IniEditor Interface, a tool
that makes the editing of ini files
less like programming.

easy to make mistakes and cause a program crash. The IniEditor allows you to browse and choose the correct settings and then save the ini file in the correct form. Figure 13.3 shows the IniEditor interface.

The following are entries that can be changed in the ini file:

- *Game Name*—The name that will appear at the top of the window in windowed mode.

- *Player Avatar*—The actor that will be used as the player in the game.

- *Menu INI*—The ini file containing the information for the menu structure. We look at this later in this chapter.

- *Starting Level*—The BSP file used for starting the level.

- *Pack File*—The VFS file that contains the game resources.

- *Gamma*—The initial video-gamma setting.

- *Video Driver*—The video driver to use.

- *Video Resolution*—The screen resolution to use.

- *Weapon Position On*—If checked, then weapon positioning via the NumPad is active.

- *Use Level Load Dialog*—If checked, then activate the level load dialog at startup.

You are also allowed to determine what logos, sounds, and animations play at the start of the game.

The video drivers and resolutions shown are only those that are compatible with your video card. Reality Factory will operate with any choice you make. When weapon positioning is active, you are able to move the view weapon in first-person view using the NumPad keys. See the Weapons entity section for more details. When the UseLevel Load Dialog is active, you will be able to choose the starting level at runtime via a File Open dialog. This choice will override the starting level from the ini file.

FileFind

When you are packaging up a level or group of levels, you must know which resources each level requires, and you need to include them with the level. The

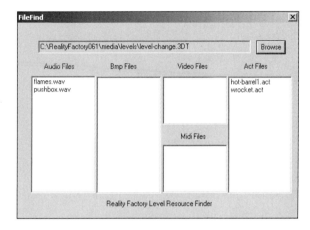

Figure 13.4
The FileFind Interface.

FileFind tool will analyze a chosen level and list all resources required. Use the Browse button to choose the desired level, and the resources for that level will be listed. See Figure 13.4 for the simple File Find Interface.

VFS Explorer

VFS is a file-packing utility, which we will not examine in this book. Feel free, however, to read and experiment with it.

TTF2Font

Reality Factory uses *bitmapped fonts* (or images of letters) to display text in the menu and during gameplay, and this tool allows you to create images of fonts from the Windows installed fonts. It comes with seven fonts; various Courier font sizes in black and white. To add custom fonts that you can use in the menu or in certain entities, you must first create the necessary bitmaps and data files by using the TTF2Font program (see Figure 13.5). Run the program and select the font type, size, and color. The height of the font in pixels is shown so you can get the size correct. Then export the font to the media\bitmaps\fonts directory. Later, you will see how to edit your menu.ini and add a line to the list of fonts.

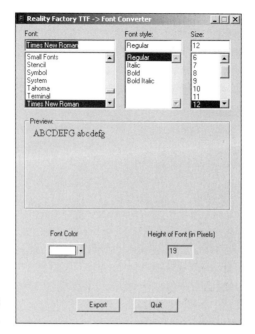

Figure 13.5
The TTF2Font interface.

What You Need to Run Reality Factory

As with any software application, there are minimum hardware requirements to running Reality Factory, and there are both good and better hardware configurations. Reality Factory will run efficiently on a faster computer with more RAM than it will on a slower computer with less RAM. Here are the levels of hardware configurations:

- *Minimum system requirements*—AMD K6-2/400 or similar performance-central processor such as the Intel PII 200 or greater; 64MB of RAM, 50MB of hard disk space for the game; a SoundBlaster Live or other PCI audio card; and an NVidia TNT-class 3D accelerator (either PCI or AGP).

- *Recommended system for better performance*—Intel Celeron 433MHz or similar performance CPU such as the Intel PII 400 or greater; 64MB of RAM; 100MB of hard disk space (for levels and content, mainly); a SoundBlaster Live or other PCI audio card; and an AGP NVidia TNT2-class 3D accelerator.

- *Preferred system for optimum performance*—Intel Celeron 500MHz or better; 128MB of RAM; 100MB of hard disk space on a UDMA/33 hard disk; SoundBlaster Live; and an AGP Voodoo3-based 3D accelerator.

Installing and Troubleshooting Reality Factory

Start by installing Reality Factory and troubleshooting a test level. When you start running increasingly more complex levels, you will most likely run into some problems. Every time Reality Factory runs, it generates a log file called realityfactory.log. This file contains information on what content was loaded, what graphics driver was selected, and any run-time error messages that Reality

Note: Although Genesis3D provides software-rendering capabilities, note that Rabid Games doesn't support it. Reality Factory needs a 3D hardware accelerator.

Note: Voodoo2 3D-only cards are not recommended and are not supported. Reality Factory may work with a Voodoo2 card, if you do a little tweaking of the initialization file, but it becomes problematic if you manage to crash Reality Factory—you will not be able see any of the error messages that may pop up. Reality Factory, however, will work with a Voodoo2 chained to another 3D card.

Factory generates. When you start having problems with your level, check the log file first. Simply install the file from the companion CD-ROM and run the application to test it. To help with testing, there is a sample level included.

If you have any problems, and after you've checked the log file, ask yourself the following questions:

- *Do you have a PlayerStart and a PlayerSetup entity on the level?* You *must* have both, not just one or the other.

- *Is all your content (BMP files, WAV files, and so on) in the correct folders, as defined in the RealityFactory.ini file?* It's always a good idea to verify that you've placed all the right files in the correct folders.

- *Do you have the TXL files in their correct place?*

- *Are you trying to use the software renderer?* Reality Factory doesn't yet support this feature.

- *Are you using the Glide driver on a Direct3D system?* Always fall back to Direct3D.

- *Are you crashing in full-screen mode?* If so, you can switch to Window-ed mode for debugging.

Reality Factory Entity Overview

With Reality Factory, and like Genesis, there are two major components that you use to build your game world: world geometry and entities. World geometry consists of all the textured brushes, or geometry, and entities are what allow the geometry to move, sounds to play, and effects to operate. In Reality Factory, some entities are new and others expanded.

Reality Factory offers several categories of entities, including the following:

- *Environmental setup*—Entities for setting up the game world and player environments.

- *Audio effects*—Control over the various soundtrack and audio effects.

- *World model helpers*—Doors, triggers, platforms, and so on.

- *Props*—Non-moving items used to add realism to the world.

- *Paths and AI support*—Pathpoints, path followers, and NPC (non-player character) AI.

- *Special effects*—Atmospheric, electrical, lighting, teleport, and particle effects.

Before Moving On...

Before looking at the entities in detail, look at some areas in which you must learn to control Reality Factory so that you, as a game developer, can make it do what you want. These things are basically controlling the art and the layout of the menus and interfaces.

Note: All the entities we will be discussing have *attributes*. Some are required, while some will be optional. When required, the attribute will be marked "REQUIRED". Entity attributes that are not marked as required are optional and may be left blank.

Note: A non-player character (NPC) is a game character that is controlled by artificial intelligence, rather than by the player.

Note: Most entities have names associated with them. These names need to be unique per level because they will be used in path following and scripting. It's okay to use the same name in different levels.

Bitmaps Using Alpha Masks

Many effect entities in Reality Factory require graphics made by using a bitmap and an *alpha mask* bitmap. A bitmap with an alpha mask bitmap are simply two bitmaps that are the same size. The first bitmap, the main bitmap, is the actual graphic you want to use. The second bitmap, called the alpha bitmap, is used to determine the transparency of each pixel in the main bitmap. Each pixel in the alpha bitmap affects the corresponding pixel in the main bitmap. Figure 13.6 shows a bitmap, an alpha mask, and both the bitmaps together to make portions of the image transparent.

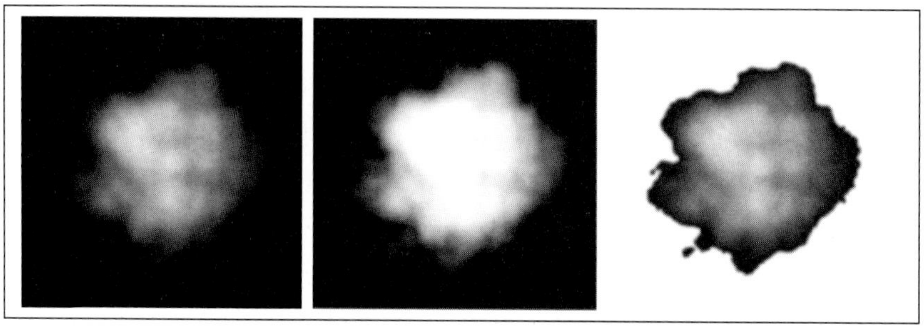

Figure 13.6
A bitmap (left), an alpha mask (center), and both the bitmaps together (right) to make portions of an image transparent.

The colors used in the alpha bitmap must be a shade of gray. The closer to black, the more transparent the alpha map, and the more of the main bitmap that will show. These settings run the gamut, with black (0,0,0) being totally transparent, while a value of white (255,255,255) makes the corresponding pixel on the main image solid. A color value of (128,128,128) will make the pixel 50 percent transparent.

Some examples of graphics made by using an alpha mask are the effects in the game, such as flames and particles, and the graphics used to make the menu titles. The area in the Alpha mask that is black will be totally transparent while the white areas will be solid. This allows us to just have the letters show over a background. Figure 13.7 shows an example of the letters of a menu and their alpha map, and then the letters over the background.

Figure 13.7
The letters of the menu and their alpha map, and then the letters over the background.

Heads Up Display

The Heads Up Display (or HUD) is configured by using an ini file that is specified in the PlayerSetup entity (which is discussed later in this chapter) as the **HUDInfoFile** entry. The default Reality Factory **HUDInfoFile** is named HUD.ini, although you can change this to any file name you want. The **HUDInfoFile** is laid out similar to a standard Windows ini file with sections containing information about each element of the HUD. This ini file is a text file and can be edited with any text editor, such as NotePad.

Each section in the HUD.ini file starts with a name enclosed in square brackets, such as [compass] or [mana]. All lines after this, up to the start of the next section, define information about that HUD element. This information varies, depending on the type of element being defined. Two modifiable built-in HUD elements in Reality Factory are a compass and the player position, (see Figure 13.8). You will look at these first.

Figure 13.8
The two built-in HUD elements are the compass (left) and player position (upper right), which you can modify.

Compass

This section of the HUD.INI starts with the bracketed word [compass]. In the ini file, the default compass section looks like Listing 13.1.

Listing 13.1   The Compass section of Reality Factory's HUD.INI file.

```
[compass]
frame = compassfrm.bmp
framealpha = a_compassfrm.bmp
indicator = compass.bmp
indicatoralpha = a_compass.bmp
```

```
framex = 0
framey = center
indicatoroffsetx = 13
indicatoroffsety = 7
```

The lines starting with **frame** and **framealpha** define the bitmap and alpha map used as the frame part of the compass. If these lines are missing, no frame will be shown. The lines **indicator** and **indicatoralpha** define the bitmap and alpha map used as the compass indicator. If these lines are missing, no indicator is shown. The compass indicator must be a specific size and layout and, if you want to change the look, you must follow the size and layout of compass.bmp. Figure 13.9 shows the parts of the compass, from the top down.

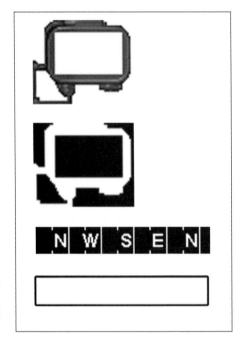

Figure 13.9

The compass parts **frame**, **framealpha**, **indicator**, and **indicatoralpha**.

The **framex** and **framey** lines define where the identifier is placed on screen. If **framex** is greater than 0, the x location of the bitmap is that number of pixels from the left side of the screen. If **framey** is greater than 0, the y location is that number of pixels from the top of the screen. If **framex** is less than 0, the x location is that many pixels from the right side of the screen. If **framey** is less than 0, the y location is that many pixels from the bottom of the screen. The (x,y) location defines the upper-left corner of the identifier bitmap in these cases. If **framex** equals center, then the center of the identifier bitmap is placed at the center of the screen width. If **framey** is equal to center, then the center of the identifier bitmap is placed at the center of the screen height.

The "**indicatoroffsetx**" and "**indicatoroffsety**" lines define the x and y offset of the indicator from (**framex, framey**). This defines the screen location of the indicator bitmap's upper-left corner, relative to the frame's location.

Player Position

The player position element requires its section to start with [position]. Instead of using an indicator bitmap, the position element displays numeric text to show the (x,y,z) location of the player. A sample section would look like the code shown in Listing 13.2.

Listing 13.2   The Player Position section of Reality Factory's HUD.INI file.

```
[position]
frame = position.bmp
framealpha = a_position.bmp
framex = -150
framey = 0
indicatoroffsetx = 15
indicatoroffsety = 5
font = 8
width = 4
```

Here, **frame** and **framealpha** define the bitmap and alpha map used as the frame (or identifier) part of the position element. If these lines are missing then no frame will be shown.

The **framex** and **framey** lines define where the identifier is placed on the screen. If, for example, **framex** is greater than 0, the x location of the bitmap is that number of pixels from the left side of the screen. If **framey** is greater than 0, the y location is that number of pixels from the top of the screen. If **framex** is less than 0, the x location is that number of pixels from the right side of the screen. If **framey** is less than 0, the y location is that number of pixels from the bottom of the screen. In these cases, the (x,y) location defines the upper-left corner of the identifier bitmap. If **framex** equals center, the center of the identifier bitmap is placed at the center of the screen width. If **framey** is equal to center, the center of the identifier bitmap is placed at the center of the screen height.

The **indicatoroffsetx** and **indicatoroffsety** lines define the x and y offset of the text from (**framex**, **framey**). This defines the screen location of the indicator text's upper-left corner, relative to the frame's location.

The **font** line defines the size and color of the font used to display the numeric text. See the "Defining Fonts" section for information on this value.

The **width** line defines the number of characters shown for each of the x, y, and z values. The default is 4. Each value is displayed with 1 space between it and the next value.

Attributes

To display an attribute as a HUD element, place its name inside square brackets to start a section. There are three different types of attribute display that can be used: vertical, horizontal, and numeric.

Vertical Display

Listing 13.3 shows the vertical display section of the HUD element.

Listing 13.3 The Vertical Display section of Reality Factory's HUD.INI file.

```
[mana]
type = vertical
frame = rHUD.bmp
framealpha = a_rHUD.bmp
indicator = hbar.bmp
indicatoralpha = a_hbar.bmp
framex = -100
framey = 0
indicatoroffsetx = 10
indicatoroffsety = 50
indicatorheight = 32
```

The attribute being displayed is "mana" (amount of magic in some games). This must be defined in the **AttributeInfoFile** in the **PlayerSetup** entity. The line type defines which display type is to be used—in this case, vertical.

The **frame** and **framealpha** lines define the bitmap and alpha map used as the frame (or identifier) part of the attribute element. If these lines are missing, no frame will be shown on screen.

The **indicator** and **indicatoralpha** lines define the bitmap and alpha map used as the attribute indicator. If these lines are missing, no indicator is shown.

The **framex** and **framey** lines define where the identifier is placed on screen. If **framex** is greater than 0, the x location of the bitmap is that number of pixels from the left side of the screen. If **framey** is greater than 0, the y location is that number of pixels from the top of the screen. If **framex** is less than 0, the x location is that number of pixels from the right side of the screen. If **framey** is less than 0, the y location is that number of pixels from the bottom of the screen. In these cases, the (x,y) location defines the upper-left corner of the identifier bitmap. If **framex** equals center, then the center of the identifier bitmap is placed at the center of the screen width. If **framey** is equal to center, then the center of the identifier bitmap is placed at the center of the screen height.

The **indicatoroffsetx** and **indicatoroffsety** lines define the x and y offset of the indicator from (**framex**, **framey**). This set defines the screen location of the indicator bitmap's upper-left corner, relative to the frame's location.

The **indicatorheight** line defines the number of pixels from the top of the indicator bitmap that will be used as the indicator graphic. This is because bitmap sizes must be even and a combination of powers of 2. Therefore, the indicator graphic may not be the entire height of the bitmap.

Horizontal Display

Listing 13.4 shows the horizontal display section of the HUD element.

Listing 13.4   The Horizontal Display section of Reality Factory's HUD.INI file.

```
[dart]
type = horizontal
frame = rockHUD.bmp
framealpha = a_dartHUD.bmp
indicator = sindic.bmp
indicatoralpha = a_sindic.bmp
framex = -64
framey = 96
indicatoroffsetx = 4
indicatoroffsety = 33
indicatorwidth = 27
```

The attribute being displayed is "dart." This attribute must be defined in the **AttributeInfoFile** in the **PlayerSetup** entity. The line type defines which display type is to be used, in this case horizontal.

The **frame** and **framealpha** lines define the bitmap and alpha map used as the frame (or identifier) part of the attribute element. If these lines are missing, then no frame will be shown.

The **indicator** and **indicatoralpha** lines define the bitmap and alpha map used as the attribute indicator. If these lines are missing, then no indicator is shown.

The **framex** and **framey** lines define where the identifier is placed on screen. If **framex** is greater than 0, the x location of the bitmap is that number of pixels from the left side of the screen. If **framey** is greater than 0 then the y location is that number of pixels from the top of the screen. If **framex** is less than 0 then the x location is that number of pixels from the right side of the screen. If **framey** is less than 0 then the y location is that number of pixels from the bottom of the screen. The (x,y) location defines the upper-left corner of the identifier bitmap in these cases. If **framex** equals center, then the center of the identifier bitmap is placed at the center of the screen width. If **framey** is equal to center, then the center of the identifier bitmap is placed at the center of the screen height.

The **indicatoroffsetx** and **indicatoroffsety** lines define the x and y offset of the indicator from (**framex**, **framey**). This defines the screen location of the indicator bitmap's upper-left corner, relative to the frame's location.

The **indicatorwidth** line defines the number of pixels from the right of the indicator bitmap that will be used as the indicator graphic. This is due to the fact that bitmap sizes must be even and a combination of powers of 2. Therefore, the indicator graphic may not be the entire width of the bitmap.

Numeric Display

Listing 13.5 shows the numeric display section of the HUD element.

Listing 13.5 The Numeric Display section of Reality Factory's HUD.INI file.

```
[health]
type = numeric
frame = rHUD.bmp
framealpha = a_rHUD.bmp
framex = -100
framey = 0
indicatoroffsetx = 36
indicatoroffsety = 38
font = 9
width = 3
```

The attribute being displayed is health. This attribute must be defined in the **AttributeInfoFile** in the **PlayerSetup** entity. The line type defines which display type is to be used, in this case numeric.

The **frame** and **framealpha** lines define the bitmap and alpha map used as the frame (or identifier) part of the attribute element. If these lines are missing, then no frame will be shown. The lines **indicator** and **indicatoralpha** define the bitmap and alpha map used as the attribute indicator. If these lines are missing, then no indicator is shown.

The **framex** and **framey** lines define where the identifier is placed on the screen. If **framex** is greater than 0, then the x location of the bitmap is that number of pixels from the left side of the screen. If **framey** is greater than 0, then the y location is that number of pixels from the top of the screen. If **framex** is less than 0, then the x location is that number of pixels from the right side of the screen. If **framey** is less than 0, then the y location is that number of pixels from the bottom of the screen. In these cases, the (x,y) location defines the upper-left corner of the identifier bitmap. If **framex** equals center, then the center of the identifier bitmap is placed at the center of the screen width. If **framey** is equal to center, then the center of the identifier bitmap is placed at the center of the screen height.

The **indicatoroffsetx** and **indicatoroffsety** lines define the x and y offset of the text from (**framex**, **framey**). This defines the screen location of the indicator text's upper-left corner, relative to the frame's location.

The **font** defines the size and color of the font used to display the numeric text. See "Defining Fonts" for information on this value.

The **width** defines the number of characters shown for the attribute value. The default is 3.

HUD Element Activation

The default setting for all HUD elements is active, which means they will be displayed when the HUD is displayed. To stop an element from being displayed, add the line "active = false" to the definition section. It will then be necessary for the program to activate the element so it can be displayed. At the moment, only weapons activate and deactivate their ammunition HUD elements. Therefore, it's necessary to add the "active = false" line to the HUD elements of all ammunition. When you switch to a weapon, it will deactivate all other ammunition HUD elements and activate its ammunition display.

Weapon and Projectile Definition

Weapons and projectiles are used over many levels and from game to game, and it is time-consuming to have to use an entity in each level to define them. Instead, we will use a weapon.ini file to predefine all weapons and projectiles. This allows us to define these objects only once, instead of in each level.

Each weapon/projectile definition is headed by the name of the weapon/projectile, enclosed in square brackets, such as [rocket] or [GrenadeLauncher]. This name will be used by other entities to reference this weapon or projectile. Following the name, up to the next weapon/projectile name or end of the file, is the information needed to define the weapon/projectile. The important line here is the one starting with type = . This defines whether the definition is for a weapon or a projectile.

Projectile

This is defined by type = projectile. The following variables must have data assigned to them to define a projectile. If a variable does not have data assigned to it in the definition block it will be set to 0 or **NULL**.

- **actor**—Name of the actor file used for the projectile.
- **rotation**—The rotation values, in degrees, required to align the actor correctly.
- **scale**—The amount that the actor is to be scaled, with 1 being 100 percent.
- **animation**—The name of the animation used by the actor, if any.
- **gravity**—TRUE if projectile is subject to gravity, FALSE if not.
- **bounce**—TRUE if projectile bounces off objects, FALSE if it explodes on contact.
- **speed**—Velocity that projectile moves, in texels per second.
- **lifetime**—Number of seconds before projectile explodes.
- **boundingbox**—Size of the bounding box cube used to determine collision.

- **explosion**—Name of the predefined explosion to use when the projectile explodes.

- **damage**—Amount of damage done by projectile impact.

- **explosionradius**—Radius of projectile explosion.

- **explosiondamage**—Amount of damage done by explosion.

- **decal**—Number of decal (or damage mark) to use at impact point.

- **movesound**—Name of the sound file played while projectile is moving.

- **impactsound**—Name of sound file played at projectile impact.

- **bouncesound**—Name of sound file played when projectile bounces off an object.

- **effect0**—Name of predefined effect attached to projectile.

- **effectbone0**—Name of bone to attach effect to; if not defined then the root bone is used.

- **effect1**—Name of predefined effect attached to projectile.

- **effectbone1**—Name of bone to attach effect to; if not defined then the root bone is used.

- **effect2**—Name of predefined effect attached to projectile.

- **effectbone2**—Name of bone to attach effect to; if not defined then the root bone is used.

- **effect3**—Name of predefined effect attached to projectile.

- **effectbone3**—Name of bone to attach effect to; if not defined then the root bone is used.

- **effect4**—Name of predefined effect attached to projectile.

- **effectbone4**—Name of bone to attach effect to; if not defined then the root bone is used.

The **boundingbox** variable is used to assign a fixed bounding box to a projectile, rather than use the actual actor's bounding box. This allows a much smaller bounding box to be used for collision testing on the projectile, which can lead to a more realistic flight. All the effects that can be attached to the projectile must be predefined and will move with the projectile as it moves. See "Playing in the Street Level" for more details on constructing these effects.

Weapon
This is defined by type = weapon. The following variables must have data assigned to them to define a weapon:

- **slot**—Which of 10 weapon slots this weapon is bound to.

- **firerate**—Number of seconds until weapon can attack again.

- **category**—Either projectile or melee, to chose which weapon type is used.

- **projectile**—The name of the projectile to fire (Projectile weapon only).

- **attribute**—Attribute that the weapon damages.

- **ammunition**—Name of the ammunition required by the weapon.

- **ammopershot**—Amount of ammunition used each attack.

- **damage**—Amount of damage done by each hit of a melee weapon (Melee weapon only).

- **attacksound**—Sound file played when weapon is used.

- **hitsound**—Sound file played when melee weapons hits something (Melee weapon only).

- **emptysound**—Sound file played if using weapon with no ammunition.

- **viewactor**—Name of actor file to use as 1st-person weapon actor.

- **viewfillcolor**—Color applied to the 1st-person weapon actor.

- **viewambientcolor**—Color used when applying lighting to the 1st-person weapon actor.

- **viewrotation**—Rotation, in degrees, in the X, Y, and Z axes needed to position 1st person weapon actor.

- **viewoffset**—Offset in X, Y, and Z directions needed to position 1st-person weapon actor.

- **viewscale**—Amount to scale the 1st-person weapon actor, with 1 equaling 100 percent.

- **viewlaunchoffset**—Offset in the X, Y, and Z directions from screen center to the projectile launch point (Projectile weapon only).

- **viewlaunchbone**—Name of bone in viewactor to launch projectile from (Projectile weapon only).

- **viewanimationspeed**—Amount to scale the speed of the 1st-person weapon animations, with 1 equaling 100 percent.

- **viewarmanim**—Name of the 1st-person weapon actor arming animation.

- **viewidleanim**—Name of the 1st-person weapon actor idle animation.

- **viewattackanim**—Name of the 1st-person weapon actor attack animation.

- **viewaltattackanim**—Name of the 1st-person weapon actor alternate attack animation (Melee weapon only).

- **viewhitanim**—Name of the 1st-person weapon actor attack and hit animation (Melee weapon only).

- **viewalthitanim**—Name of the 1st-person weapon actor alternate attack and hit animation (Melee weapon only).

- **viewwalkanim**—Name of the 1st-person weapon actor walking animation.

- **muzzleflash**—Name of the predefined explosion to use as a muzzle flash (Projectile weapon only).

- **crosshair**—Name of the bitmap file used as the weapon's crosshair (Projectile weapon only).

- **crosshairalpha**—Name of the alpha map file used to define transparency in the crosshair (Projectile weapon only).

- **crosshairfixed**—If TRUE the crosshair remains in the center of the screen, if false then it moves in/out (Projectile weapon only).

The **slot** variable assigns a weapon slot to the weapon. There are 10 slots available, corresponding to Weapon 0 through Weapon 9, which are selected by (default) keys 1 through 9 and 0. Certain variables are only required if the weapon is a projectile weapon and are marked by (Projectile weapon only). Other variables are only required if the weapon is a melee weapon and are marked by (Melee weapon only). The variables **viewfillcolor** and **viewambientcolor** are used to color and brighten the weapon actor—**viewfillcolor** changes the overall color of the actor while **viewambientcolor** changes the overall brightness.

The variables **viewrotation**, **viewoffset**, and **viewscale** are used to position the 1st-person weapon actor correctly on the screen. If you are using a converted Half-Life weapon model then set these variables to the following to roughly position them.

- **viewrotation** = −7.1 86.9 29.7

- **viewoffset** = 0 −1.5 −0.2

- **viewscale** = 0.23

If you are using a 3DStudio Max-made model, try these values for the rough positioning:

- **viewrotation** = −7.1 86.9 0

- **viewoffset** = 0 −1.5 −0.2

- **viewscale** = 0.23

To fine-tune the positioning, the following steps are required:

1. Use the IniEditor to turn on Weapon Positioning, and then run Reality Factory.

2. At the menu, go to Options|Debug and turn on the Debug Info box.

3. Run the level containing your new weapons and pick up the desired weapon.

4. Press NumLock to activate the numeric keypad. In some cases, this may have to be done prior to running the game, as some keyboards don't allow NumLock activation while Reality Factory is running.

The numeric keypad can now be used to position the weapon. The values for rotation, offset, and scale will be shown on the screen and can be copied down after the weapon is in the proper place and used to replace the rough values in the weapon.ini file.

The key pairs used to increase and decrease the values are as follows:

- *7 and 8*—Change X offset (side to side).
- *4 and 5*—Change Y offset (up and down).
- *1 and 2*—Change Z offset (in and out).
- *7 and 8*—With 0 held down, Change X rotation.
- *4 and 5*—With 0 held down, Change Y rotation.
- *1 and 2*—With 0 held down, Change Z rotation.
- *9 and 6*—Change actor scale.

The variable **viewlaunchoffset** is used to change the point at which the projectile launches. The default point is right in the center of the screen, with the projectile aimed right at where the crosshairs appear. If your view weapon is not positioned to this point then **viewlaunchoffset** must be changed. Regardless of the launch point, the projectile will be aimed right at the crosshairs in the center of the screen. Changing the X value will move the launch point side to side, with negative values moving it to the right. Changing the Y value will move the point up and down, with negative values moving it down. The Z value is a little different than the other two values. The launch point is always moved out from the center, on a line to the impact point, far enough to clear the player's bounding box. Therefore, a Z value of 0 will have the launch point forward enough to clear the player's bounding box, regardless of what values you have for X and Y. The Z value only has to be increased enough that the projectile's bounding box does not intersect the player's box. The initial starting location of the projectile is at the actor's center point, so you have to set Z to be large enough to have the projectile bounding box (set by **boundingbox** in the projectile definition) clear the player's box. This must be adjusted by trial and error, with the most likely intersection points coming when shooting upward at extreme angles.

Acquiring a Weapon in a Level

Weapons, in common with all other objects the player can pick up, are acquired by use of the Attribute entity. Weapons are considered attributes, and they must be defined in the AttributeInfo file before you can use them. See "Giving the Player Attributes" for more details. The name of the attribute is the name that you gave the weapon when defining it, such as **RocketLauncher** or **Sword**. Set the low value to 0, the high to 1, and the initial value to 0, if you want the player to have to pick it up, or 1 if you wish him to start the level with it. Use the Attribute entity to place weapon pickups in the level, with the attribute name being the weapon name and the amount being 1. The actor that you use for the Attribute entity can be anything you wish but for the already defined weapons there are supplied actors that can be used. These are:

- **Sword**—wsword.act
- **Bat**—wbat.act
- **RocketLauncher**—wrocket.act
- **GrenadeLauncher**—wgrenade.act
- **Chaingun**—wchain.act
- **Dartgun**—wmgun.act

Modifying the Menu

When you make your own game by using Reality Factory, you will want to create a custom menu layout to go along with it. The menu layout and graphics are all defined in an ini file that is named, in the default installation, menu.ini. You can call your ini file anything you want, and you can use the IniEditor to make it the default file. This ini file is a text file that can be created and edited with any text editor, such as Windows NotePad.

Defining the Graphics

The first thing you have to do when making a new menu layout is to define all the graphics you will use in the menu. This defining process includes the backgrounds, titles, buttons, boxes, and fonts. All graphics for the menu go in the media\bitmaps\menu directory. See Figure 13.10 for the menu system as it is now in Reality Factory. You can change and move all these elements.

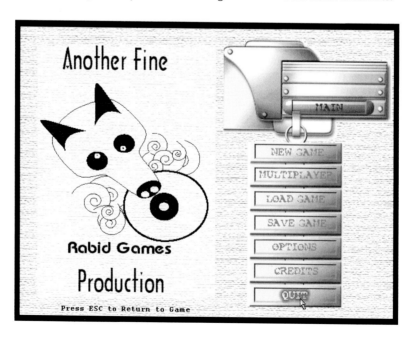

Figure 13.10
The menu system as it is in Reality Factory; you can redo all these assets and rearrange them.

Backgrounds

Backgrounds are the graphics that are placed behind all the buttons and text. A background image must be 640×480 pixels in size and have no transparent areas (i.e., it doesn't use color 256). All menus are based on a 640×480 screen size and—if a larger screen size is used—are centered on the screen. You can define a maximum of 15 background graphics, which allows a different background for each menu (if you desire it). Each background graphic has a background number assigned to it from 0 through 14. You later reference these backgrounds by the numbers.

To add a background graphic to the menu, add a line, based on the following syntax, in the form:

```
background=background# bitmapname
```

Here, *background#* must be a number from 0 to 14, and *bitmapname* is the name of the graphic bitmap. The following code lines show an example of this naming process:

```
background=0 background.bmp
background=3 rf.bmp
```

> **Note:** Backgrounds are the only graphics used in the menu that do not use an alpha mask for transparency, so only one bitmap is required.

> **Note:** It's important that no extra spaces be included in the lines in the code you work with. There should be no space between the equals sign (=) and the *background#*, and only one space between the *background#* and the *bitmapname*.

Titles

Title images are the bitmaps that hold the titles displayed on each menu, to identify which menu you are looking at (see Figure 13.11). Title images can be any size, as long as it is a multiple of 2. Title images require an alpha mask to define the transparent areas of the graphic. Therefore, they require a bitmap and an alpha bitmap.

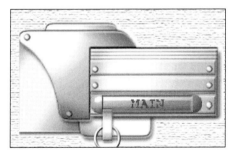

Figure 13.11
The Title Image on the menu.

You can define a maximum of 15 title images, one for each menu. To conserve space, it is possible to place more than one title graphic on a bitmap. Actually, *all* the title graphics can be placed on one bitmap, if you want. Each title image has a title image number from 0 through 14 assigned to it. You later reference this image number when defining the actual title graphic. To add a title image to the menu, add a line, based on the following syntax, in the form:

```
titles=titleimage# bitmapname alphamapname
```

Here, *titleimage#* is a number from 0 through 14, *bitmapname* is the name of the images bitmap, and *alphamapname* is the name of the images alpha mask. For example:

```
titles=0 titles.bmp a_titles.bmp
titles=1 newtitles.bmp a_newtitles.bmp
```

Again, it's important that you include no extra spaces in the line.

Images

Images are the bitmaps that hold all the button, slider, and scroll-box graphics. Again, these can be any size, as long as they are a multiple of 2. Images also require an alpha mask to define the transparent areas of the graphic. Therefore, they require both a bitmap and an alpha bitmap. You can define a maximum of 150 images for the menu. More than one graphic can be placed on an image. Certain restrictions exist on where graphics must be placed in regard to images. For buttons, for example, the button graphic and the *button mouseover* graphic (the button image to be used when the mouse cursor is placed over the button) must be on the same image. For scroll boxes, such as the Load game box, the box and highlight bars must be on one image and all parts of the scroll arrows must be on one image. Each image has an image assigned number, from 0 through 149. You reference this number later when you are defining buttons and boxes. To add an image to the menu, add a line in the form based on the following syntax line:

```
images=image# bitmapname alphamapname
```

Here, *image#* is a number from 0 through 149, *bitmapname* is the name of the images bitmap, and *alphamapname* is the name of the images alpha mask. For example :

```
images=0 images.bmp a_images.bmp
images=2 remap.bmp a_remap.bmp
```

Again, it is important that you make sure that no extra spaces are included in the line.

Cursor

The *cursor* is the graphic used to point to portions of the menu. Again, this can be any size as long as it's a multiple of 2. The cursor also requires an alpha mask to define the transparent areas of the graphic. Therefore, it requires both a bitmap and an alpha bitmap. To define the cursor, add a line in the form based on the following syntax line:

```
cursor=bitmapname alphamapname
```

where *bitmapname* is the name of the cursor bitmap and *alphamapname* is the name of the cursor alpha mask. For example:

```
cursor=cursor.bmp a_cursor.bmp
```

Again, remove all extra spaces from the line.

Crosshair

The *crosshair* is the graphic used by weapons to show where they are pointing. This can be any size as long as it's a multiple of 2. The crosshair also requires an alpha mask to define the transparent areas of the graphic. Therefore, it requires both a bitmap and an alpha bitmap. To define the crosshair, add a line in the form based on the following syntax line:

```
crosshair=bitmapname alphamapname
```

Here, *bitmapname* is the name of the crosshair bitmap, and *alphamapname* is the name of the crosshair alpha mask. For example:

```
crosshair=crosshair.bmp a_crosshair.bmp
```

Again, it is important that you include no extra spaces in the line.

Defining Fonts

Fonts used to display text in the menu are bitmap fonts created by the TTF2Font tool. Use this tool to create the necessary bitmap and dat files, which are saved in the media\bitmaps\fonts directory. You then add them to the menu (and the game) by adding a line in the form based on the following syntax line:

```
font=FONT# fontname
```

where *FONT#* is one of FONT1 through FONT29 and *fontname* is the name of the font dat file (without the .dat extension). It's best to leave the default fonts FONT1 to FONT14 installed because they are required internally by the program. Add your new fonts beginning with FONT15.

Sounds

The menu uses sounds to indicate that a button was clicked on, a scroll arrow was clicked, or a key is to be redefined. These sounds are placed in the media\audio\menu\ directory. To define these sounds, add lines in the form based on the following syntax lines:

```
mouseclick=soundname
keyclick=soundname
slideclick=soundname
```

where *soundname* is the name of the wav file to be used. For example:

```
mouseclick=pop1.wav
keyclick=pop2.wav
slideclick=pop1.wav
```

Defining Menu Titles

With all the graphics for the menu defined, you can now define each menu title graphic. These graphics will be placed over the background for each menu to identify which you are looking at. You've already defined the title images that contain the title graphics, so now you must define the portion of the image that represents each title and where it should be placed on the background. There are currently 11 different menus that require titles, so you need to define 11 different titles. The following list shows the titles for the menus:

- Main

- Multiplayer

- Load Game

- Save Game

- Options

- Debug

- Credits

- Audio

- Video

- Control

- Advanced

To define a title graphic, add a line in the form:

```
menutitle=title#  titleimage#  screen_X screen_Y width height image_X
image_Y
```

where *title#* is the number of this title graphic, you will reference later, *titleimage#* is the number of the title image containing the title graphic, *screen_X* and *screen_Y* are the location on the background that the upper-left corner of the title graphic is to be placed, *width* and *height* are the size of the graphic, and *image_X* and *image_Y* are the upper-left corner of the graphics location on the title image.

For example:

```
menutitle=0 0 480 121 100 17 0 0
menutitle=10 0 496 123 100 17 0 195
```

Buttons

There are 25 buttons used in the Reality Factory menu. They all have a unique name assigned to them and are defined by assigning data to that name. The buttons and their names are shown in Table 13.1.

There are two different types of buttons in the menu—buttons that bring up another menu and buttons that execute a function in the program. The latter set of buttons include New Game, Load, Save, and All Done/Quit. To define one of these buttons, add a line in the form:

```
buttonname=screen_X screen_Y image# width height image_X image_Y
mouseover_X mouseover_Y
```

where *screen_X* and *screen_Y* is the location on the background that the upper-left corner of the button graphic is to be placed, *image#* is the number of the images containing the button graphics, *width* and *height* is the size of the graphic, *image_X* and *image_Y* is the upper-left corner of the button graphic

Table 13.1 Reality Factory's buttons and names.

Menu Name	Button Action	Button Name
Main	New Game	newgame
	Multiplayer	multiplayer
	Load Game	loadgame
	Save Game	savegame
	Options	options
	Credits	credits
	Quit	quitmain
MultiPlayer	Done	quitmulti
Load Game	Done	quitload
	Load	load
Save Game	Done	quitsave
	Save	save
Options	Audio	audio
	Video	video
	Control	control
	Debug	debug
	Done	quitoptions
Debug	Done	quitdebug
Credits	Done	quitcredit
Audio	Done	quitaudio
Video	Done	quitvideo
Control	Advanced	advance
	Done	quitcontrol
	Default	default
Advanced	Done	quitadvance

location on the image, and *mouseover_X* and *mouseover_Y* is the upper-left corner of the button mouseover graphic location on the image.

The mouseover graphic, if you don't recall the definition from earlier in this chapter, is the button graphic to be used when the mouse cursor is placed over the button. If you do not want to have a mouseover graphic, set *mouseover_X* and *mouseover_Y* to the same values as *image_X* and *image_Y*. The button graphic and the mouseover graphic must be on the same graphic image. For example:

```
quitmain=391 422 0 164 40 0 228 0 268
load=391 222 0 164 40 328 80 328 120
```

For buttons that bring up another menu, you must add a line in the form:

```
buttonname=screen_X screen_Y image# width height image_X image_Y
mouseover_X mouseover_Y background# title#
```

where *screen_X* and *screen_Y* is the location on the background that the upper-left corner of the button graphic is to be placed, *image#* is the number of the image containing the button graphics, *width* and *height* is the size of the graphic, *image_X* and *image_Y* is the upper-left corner of the button graphic location on the image, *mouseover_X* and *mouseover_Y* is the upper-left corner of the button mouseover graphic location on the image, *background#* is the number of the background to be used on the next menu, and *title#* is the number of the title to be placed on the next menu. For example:

```
options=391 342 0 164 40 0 148 0 188 0 1
video=391 222 0 164 40 0 604 0 644 0 3
```

Main Menu

Because the Main menu is not reached by any button, you must define the background and title separately. To do this, add a line in the form:

```
main=background# title#
```

where *background#* is the number of the background to be used on the main menu and *title#* is the number of the title to be placed on the menu. For example:

```
main=0 0
```

Text Lines

Some menus have lines of text placed on them to identify things such as sliders and checkboxes. Each line of text has a unique name assigned to it, and the location and font for this line is assigned to that name. The text names and the lines of text are listed in Table 13.2.

Table 13.2 Reality Factory's text-line buttons and names.

Menu Name	Text Name	Text Line
Main	Returntext	Press ESC to Return to Game
Debug	Debugtext	Debug Info
	Fpstext	Frame Rate
	Cliptext	No Clipping
	Bbtext	Player Bounding Box
	Sebbtext	Entity Bounding Box
Audio	Voltext	Sound Volume
	Cdtext	Play CD Music
Video	gammatext	Gamma
	detailtext	Detail Level
Advanced	crosstext	Crosshair
	reversetext	Reverse mouse
	filtertext	Mouse filter
	senstext	Mouse sensitivity

To define a line of text add a line in the form:

```
textname=screen_X screen_Y FONT#
```

where *screen_X* and *screen_Y* is the location on the background that the upper-left corner of the text line is to be placed and *FONT#* is a predefined font in the range FONT1 to FONT29. For example:

```
filtertext=430 312 FONT9
```

Checkboxes

Reality Factory uses checkboxes in some menus for selecting options. There are a total of nine boxes, and each has a unique name and is defined by assigning data to the name. The box names and what they are listed in Table 13.3.

Table 13.3 Reality Factory's checkbox names and actions.

Menu	Box Name	Box Action
Debug	debugbox	Enable Reality Factory debug information
	fpsbox	Enable frame rate
	clipbox	Enable clip mode
Box	bbbox	Enable drawing of player's bounding box
	sebbbox	Enable other actors' and models' bounding box
Audio	cdbox	Enable CD music
Advanced	crossbox	Enable weapon crosshair
	reversebox	Enable reverse mouse direction
	filterbox	Enable mouse filtering

Each checkbox requires three graphics, one for when it is unchecked; another for when it is unchecked and the mouse is over it, and the last when it is checked. These graphics must be all on one image. Only one set of graphics needs to be defined because it can be used for all the checkboxes, although each box can be different. To define a checkbox add a line in the form:

```
boxname=screen_X screen_Y image# width height image_X image_Y
mouseover_X mouseover_Y set_X set_Y
```

where *screen_X* and *screen_Y* is the location on the background that the upper-left corner of the box graphic is to be placed, *image#* is the number of the image that contains the box graphics, *width* and *height* is the size of the graphic, *image_X* and *image_Y* is the upper-left corner of the unchecked box graphic location on the image, *mouseover_X* and *mouseover_Y* is the upper-left corner of the unchecked box mouseover graphic location on the image, and *set_X* and *set_Y* is the upper-left corner of the checked box graphic location on the image. For example:

```
crossbox=405 250 1 19 19 38 85 19 85 0 85
```

Graphic Images

Graphic Images are graphics placed on the menu for such things as slider backgrounds and credit screens. There are five graphic images used in the various menus, and each is given a unique name, which has data assigned to it to define the image. The Graphic Image names and use are listed in Table 13.4.

To define a Graphic Image, add a line in the form:

```
graphicimagename=screen_X screen_Y image# width height image_X
image_Y
```

Here, *screen_X* and *screen_Y* is the location on the background that the upper-left corner of the graphic image is to be placed, *image#* is the number of the image that contains the graphic image, *width* and *height* is the size of the graphic, and *image_X* and *image_Y* is the upper-left corner of the graphic image location on the image. For example:

```
sensimg=395 360 1 160 9 0 24
```

Table 13.4 Reality Factory's Graphic Image names and uses.

Menu	Graphic Image Name	Usage
Credits	creditimg	Displays credit information bitmap
Audio	volimg	Volume control slider background
Video	gammaimg	Gamma slider background
	detailimg	Detail Level slider background
Advanced	sensimg	Mouse Sensitivity slider background

Sliders

Sliders are a graphic that can be moved across the screen when you click and hold on it and move the mouse. There are four sliders used in the different menus and each is given a unique name, which is assigned data to define the slider. The slider names and usage are listed in Table 13.5.

To define a slider add a line in the following form:

```
slidername=screen_X screen_Y image# width height image_X image_Y
min_X max_X
```

Here, screen_X and screen_Y is the location on the background that the upper-left corner of the slider graphic is to be placed, image# is the number of the image containing the graphic image, width and height is the size of the graphic, image_X and image_Y is the upper-left corner of the slider graphic location on the image, min_X is the distance from screen_X that the graphic stops moving in the left direction, and max_X is the distance from screen_X that the graphic stops moving in the right direction.

Here's an example of the **volslider** setup for the Audio menu:

```
volslider=401 275 1 16 7 0 40 1 136
```

Scroll Bars

Scroll bars are used to scroll the text inside the Key Remap box, the Load Game box, and the Save Game box. Scroll bars are usually connected to those boxes but are defined separately. There are three scroll bars used in the menus, and each bar has a unique name to which is assigned data to define them. The names of the scroll bars and which text box they are attached to are listed in Table 13.6.

Table 13.5   Reality Factory's slider names and uses.

Menu	Slider Name	Usage
Audio	volslider	Volume control
Video	gammaslider	Gamma adjustment
	detailslider	Detail Level adjustment
Advanced	sensslider	Mouse sensitivity

Table 13.6   Reality Factory's scroll bars and their text boxes.

Menu	Scroll Bar Name	Attached to Text Box
Load	loadbar	Load Game
Save	savebar	Save Game
Controls	remapbar	Keyboard Remap

A scroll bar consists of an up arrow and a down arrow, each of which has three different graphics. These are the normal arrow, the arrow when the mouse is over it, and the arrow when it is clicked on. All of these six graphics must be on the same image. To define a scroll bar add a line in the following form:

```
scrollbarname=screen_X screen_Y image# up_width up_height up_nor_X
up_nor_Y up_lit_X up_lit_Y up_push_X up_push_Y dwn_width dwn_height
dwn_nor_X dwn_nor_Y dwn_lit_X dwn_lit_Y dwn_push_X dwn_push_Y up_X
up_Y dwn_X dwn_Y
```

where *screen_X* and *screen_Y* is the location on the background that the upper-left corner of the scroll bar is to be placed, *image#* is the number of the image containing the graphic images, *up_width* and *up_height* is the size of the up-arrow graphic, *up_nor_X* and *up_nor_Y* is the upper-left corner of the normal up-arrow graphic location on the image, *up_lit_X* and *up_lit_Y* is the upper-left corner of the mouseover up-arrow graphic location on the image, *up_push_X* and *up_push_Y* is the upper-left corner of the clicked-on up-arrow graphic location on the image, *dwn_width* and *dwn_height* is the size of the down-arrow graphic, *dwn_nor_X* and *dwn_nor_Y* is the upper-left corner of the normal down-arrow graphic location on the image, *dwn_lit_X* and *dwn_lit_Y* is the upper-left corner of the mouseover down-arrow graphic location on the image, *dwn_push_X* and *dwn_push_Y* is the upper-left corner of the clicked-on down-arrow graphic location on the image, *up_X* and *up_Y* is the offset from *screen_X* and *screen_Y* to the upper-left corner of the up-arrow graphic location, *dwn_X* and *dwn_Y* is the offset from *screen_X* and *screen_Y* to the upper-left corner of the down-arrow graphic location. For example:

```
remapbar=355 272 2 15 15 0 164 48 180 16 180 15 15 16 164 32 180 0
180 243 6 243 132
```

Keyboard Remap Box

To remap the keys to different actions, Reality Factory has a special text box called the Remap box. It has an attached scroll bar to scroll through the lines of text. This was defined in the previous section. The remap box requires three different graphics, which must be on the same image. These graphics are the box itself, the highlight graphic shown under the text when a line is clicked on, and the remap highlight graphic that is shown under the line of text when a key is about to be remapped. To define the remap box add a line in the form:

```
remapbox=screen_X screen_Y image# width height image_X image_Y
start_X start_Y step max_lines corner_X corner_Y click_width
highlight_X highlight_Y highlight_width highlight_height entry_X
entry_Y entry_width entry_height FONT#
```

where *screen_X* and *screen_Y* is the location on the background that the upper-left corner of the remap box graphic is to be placed, *image#* is the number of the image containing the graphic images, *width* and *height* is the size of the remap box graphic, *image_X* and *image_Y* is the upper-left corner of the remap box graphic location on the image, *start_X* and *start_Y* is the offset from *screen_X* and *screen_Y* to the upper-left corner of the first line of text, *step* is the number of pixels from the top of one line to the top of the next lower line, *max_lines* is the maximum number of lines to be displayed in the remap box at any one time, *corner_X* and *corner_Y* is the offset from *screen_X* and *screen_Y* to the upper-left corner of the highlight graphic under the first line of text, *click_width* is the width of the text line, in pixels from the left, that can be clicked on to select a line, *highlight_X* and *highlight_Y* is the upper-left corner of the highlight graphic location on the image, *highlight_width* and *highlight_height* is the size of the highlight graphic, *entry_X* and *entry_Y* is the upper-left corner of the remap highlight graphic location on the image, *entry_width* and *entry_height* is the size of the remap highlight graphic, and *FONT#* is a predefined font in the range FONT1 to FONT29. For example:

```
remapbox=355 272 2 265 153 0 0 9 12 20 7 6 6 127 128 0 196 236 20 0
216 237 20 FONT9
```

Load and Save Box

Just like the remap box, a special text box is used to display the saved games. It has an attached scroll bar to scroll through the lines of text. This was defined in the previous section. There is one saved game box in the Load Game menu and one in the Save Game menu. They both show the saved games present in the system and are laid out the same. Each saved game box has a unique name, loadbox for the Load Game menu, and savebox for the Save Game menu. By assigning data to this name we can define the saved game box. This text box requires two graphics that must be on the same image. These graphics are the box itself and the highlight graphic shown under the text when a line is clicked on. To define this text box, add a line in the form:

```
savedgameboxname=screen_X screen_Y image# width height image_X
image_Y start_X start_Y step max_lines corner_X corner_Y
click_width highlight_X highlight_Y highlight_width
highlight_height FONT#
```

where *screen_X* and *screen_Y* is the location on the background that the upper-left corner of the saved game box graphic is to be placed, *image#* is the number of the image containing the graphic images, *width* and *height* is the size of the saved game box graphic, *image_X* and *image_Y* is the upper-left corner of the saved game box graphic location on the image, *start_X* and *start_Y* is the offset from *screen_X* and *screen_Y* to the upper-left corner of the first line of text, *step* is the number of pixels from the top of one line to the top of the next lower line, *max_lines* is the maximum number of lines to be displayed in the saved game box at any one time, *corner_X* and *corner_Y* is the offset from *screen_X* and *screen_Y* to the upper-left corner of the highlight graphic under the first line of text, *click_width* is the width of the text line, in pixels from the left, that can be clicked on to select a line, *highlight_X* and *highlight_Y* is the upper-left corner of the highlight graphic location on the image, *highlight_width* and *highlight_height* is the size of the highlight graphic, and *FONT#* is a predefined font in the range FONT1 to FONT29. For example:

```
savebox=355 272 2 265 153 0 0 9 12 20 7 6 6 236 0 236 236 20 FONT9
```

Playing in the Street Level

For the Reality Factory I created a level called street. Open the file "street" that was built for this section located in the Tutorials folder on the CD ROM. The level was built using the basics learned in the chapters pertaining to Genesis3D. You will see that initially, building a world in Reality Factory is much the same as building one in Genesis. We'll now look at some of the more interesting entities in Reality Factory. Many of these entities are for use by programmers and therefore we will not look at those in depth here; however, there are many effects and entities that we can use immediately as designers and level builders.

Environmental Setup

Here, you look at the environmental setup entities first because they are usually the first to be placed in a level. The environmental setup entities are used to define level-wide attributes and behaviors. There is usually only a single instance of each type of entity per level.

> **Note:** The only required entities are the PlayerStart and the PlayerSetup entities, which tells Reality Factory where on the level to place the player when the game starts.

The PlayerStart Entity

The PlayerStart entity is used to place the player at his initial starting point in the level. It also can be used to start the music for the level. Reality Factory requires this entity and if it is not present, the game will exit with an error condition. The entries for this entity are shown in the following list:

- **szEntityName**—Name of Start Point, Blank for Default
- **szCDTrack**—Track number of CD to play
- **szMIDIFile**—Name of midi file to play
- **szStreamingAudio**—Name of WAV file to play
- **bSoundtrackLoops**—TRUE if soundtrack loops to start when finished
- **Angle**—Direction player points to start level

The szEntityName is used by the ChangeLevel entity to start a level at a named PlayerStart. If it is left blank, that entity will be used as the default start point. The initial level must have a default start point in it.

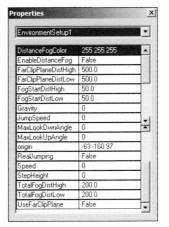

Figure 13.12
The PlayerStart Properties
dialog box.

Angle is a vector that points in the direction that you want the player to face when starting the level (see Figure 13.12).

> **Note:** Only one PlayerStart entity should be defined per level. Placing more than one PlayerStart entity in your level will cause problems.

The EnvironmentSetup Entity

The EnvironmentSetup entity (as opposed to environmental entities) defines various level-wide attributes for the current level only. Only one of these entities should be defined per level; defining more than one will cause problems (see Figure 13.13).

> **Note:** The EnvironmentSetup entity is not a required entity.

Figure 13.13
The EnvironmentSetup
dialog box.

One of the most powerful Reality Factory features is the capability to set distance fogging and the far clipping plane. Not only can fog add a great deal to the environment of your game, but distance fogging and the far clipping plane can significantly improve performance—especially on large, open-space levels.

You will see that the rest of these attributes will require some experimentation to find optimum settings for the atmosphere and feel of your level. For games, for example, that are set in a star-flight future, careful adjustment of the gravity and jump-speed parameters can provide an outer-space feel for levels in high-tech starship and/or space station environments.

The EnvironmentSetup entity has attributes discussed in the following list:

- **Gravity**—World gravity value—the default is –4.6.

- **Speed**—Player speed.

> **Balancing the Fog**
>
> Make sure that the **TotallyFoggedDistance** attribute is *less* than the **FarClipPlaneDistance** attribute. The reason is to prevent the player from seeing the level getting cut off. Also, with the fog option on, the skybox will not be visible.

- **JumpSpeed**—Player upward jump speed.

- **StepHeight**—Highest step a player automatically climbs.

- **EnableDistanceFog**—TRUE if distance fog is enabled.

- **DistanceFogColor**—Color of fog.

- **FogStartDistLow**—Min distance from camera before fog starts.

- **FogStartDistHigh**—Max distance from camera before fog starts.

- **TotalFogDistLow**—Min distance from camera before fog is solid.

- **TotalFogDistHigh**—Max distance from camera before fog is solid.

- **UseFarClipPlane**—TRUE if far clipping plane is to be used.

- **FarClipPlaneDistLow**—Min distance past which nothing will be rendered.

- **FarClipPlaneDistHigh**—Max distance past which nothing will be rendered.

- **MaxLookUpAngle**—Max angle (in degrees) player can look up.

- **MaxLookDwnAngle**—Max angle (in degrees) player can look down.

- **RealJumping**—If TRUE, use realistic jumping.

By playing with the **FogStartDistance** and **TotallyFoggedDistance** settings, you can create the "ball of light" feeling for a user, which can be scary. You can actually set your ambient light level in the level up higher and close the darkness fog around the player to make it feel like they are walking by torchlight or flashlight. (Think *X-Files* here.) Tweaking the light color can give the "ball of light" a fire or electrical feel (see Figures 13.14 through 13.17).

Figure 13.14

The screen with a nearer fog, colored white—it looks like daytime.

Figure 13.15
The screen with a fog that starts farther away. Notice that you can see more of the building on the left, and you can see the faint outline of a building straight ahead, in the distance.

Figure 13.16
The screen with black distance fog—it looks like night.

The PlayerSetup Entity

The PlayerSetup entity defines various parameters used to establish how the player appears in the game. This entity also defines the HUD (heads-up display) and any attributes the player has (see Figure 13.18).

Figure 13.17
The screen with an even farther fog distance.

Note: The **PlayerScaleFactor** and **ActorRotation** attributes are used to adjust the size and default rotation of the player avatar model. Some 3D programs output their models aligned and rotated along different (xyz) axes than those used by the Reality Factory. Careful use of the player scaling can allow you to design levels that appear larger by simply making your actor and props smaller.

Figure 13.18
The PlayerSetup dialog box.

The PlayerSetup entity attributes are discussed in the list that follows:

- **HUDInfoFile**—Name of the HUD initialization file.

- **AttributeInfoFile**—Name of the Attribute initialization file.

- **OpeningCutScene**—Name of the AVI file to play as the opening cut scene.

- **PlayerScaleFactor**—Amount to scale player by—1.0 equals 100 percent of normal size.

- **ActorScaleFactor**—Amount to scale player actor by—1.0 equals 100 percent of normal size.

- **ActorRotation**—Rotation values in degrees required to orient player correctly.

- **HeadBobbing**—TRUE if players head bobs when moving in 1st person.

- **HeadBobSpeed**—Speed of head bob in increments per move.

- **HeadBobLimit**—Maximum amount of head bob, in total units.

- **StaminaDelay**—Number of seconds for the stamina attribute to increase 1 unit.

- **UseDeathFog**—If TRUE, use fog swirl at death.

- **DeathFogColor**—Color of fog used at death.

- **DeathMessage**—Message to display at death.

- **DeathFontSize**—Font size of death message.

- **LevelViewPoint**—Player viewpoint: 0=1st person, 1=3rd person, 2=isometric.

- **LevelViewAllowed**—If TRUE, the view switching is allowed.

- **Level1stAllowed**—If TRUE, the switching to 1st person view is allowed.

- **Level3rdAllowed**—If TRUE, the switching to 3rd person view is allowed.

- **LevelIsoAllowed**—If TRUE, the switching to isometric view is allowed.

- **Level1stHeight**—If non-zero, then use as height of 1st person camera.

- **Level3rdHeight**—If non-zero, then use as height of 3rd person camera.

- **Level3rdAngle**—If non-zero, then use as angle of 3rd person camera (in degrees).

- **Level3rdDistance**—If non-zero, then use as distance from player for 3rd person camera.

- **LevelIsoHeight**—If non-zero, then use as height of isometric camera.

> **Note:** This is important! Although the player attribute system will persist for all versions of Reality Factory, the HUD system is going to change. Rabid Games is working on implementing a true 3D HUD.

- **LevelIsoAngleX**—If non-zero, then use as angle up of isometric camera.
- **LevelIsoAngleY**—If non-zero, then use as angle around of isometric camera.
- **LevelIsoDistance**—If non-zero, then use as distance from player for isometric camera.
- **Deathlevel**—Level to change to after dying.

The **LevelViewPoint** value determines what type of view is initially used. The valid entries for this are discussed in the following list:

- *0*—1st Person
- *1*—3rd Person
- *2*—Diablo Style Isometric

If **LevelViewAllowed** is TRUE, the player can switch views during game play by using the keyboard. Use **Level1stAllowed**, **Level3rdAllowed**, and **LevelIsoAllowed** to indicate to which views the player is allowed to switch.

You use the **PlayerScaleFactor** to make the player larger or smaller in relation to the level. You use the **ActorScaleFactor** to scale the player actor so that it fits the level properly. For example, the standard Reality Factory actor is 76 units high. If you want to use an actor 152 units high, you must scale it down to half size so that it matches a level made for the standard actor. The **ActorScaleFactor** in this case would be 0.5. You then can scale the whole player up or down using **PlayerScaleFactor** and still have everything fit properly. Scaling the actor and the player doesn't cause a performance hit for the level.

The **ActorRotation** values are the values, in degrees, necessary to make your player actor stand up properly. Depending on the origin of the actor, these values will vary. For example, an actor converted from a Half-Life model uses the following values:

- **X** = 0
- **Y** = 180
- **Z** = 0

For an actor made in 3DStudio Max, the values required are as follows:

- **X** = -90
- **Y** = 180
- **Z** = 0

If **Deathlevel** is not blank, it is assumed to be the name of the level (with .bsp extension) that you will be changed to upon dying.

Customizing the View

In all view types you can customize the values used to place the camera in the view. As I said previously, there are three types of views: **1st person**, **3rd person**, and **Diablo Isometric**.

In **1st-person** view (type 0), the **Level1stHeight** value is used to override the default height of the camera. The default player height is assumed to be 76 units high, and the camera height is calculated from this value. If the **Level1stHeight** value is not zero, that value will be used in calculating the camera height.

In **3rd person** view (type 1), the **Level3rdHeight** value is also used to override the default height of the camera, much in the same way as it does in 1st-person view. The **Level3rdDistance** value is also used to override the default distance (133 units) that the camera is positioned behind the player. If the **Level3rdDistance** value is not zero, that value will be used rather than the default. The default camera is rotated 5 degrees in the X direction (up/down) so that it looks slightly down toward the player. This value can be overridden if the **Level3rdAngle** value is not zero. If it is, that value (in degrees) will be used to rotate the camera up/down.

Diablo Isometric view (type 2) the **LevelIsoHeight** value is also used to override the default height of the camera, the same way as in **1st person** view. The **LevelIsoDistance** value is also used to override the default distance (266 units) that the camera is positioned behind the player. If the **LevelIsoDistance** value is not zero, that value will be used rather than the default. The default camera is rotated 45 degrees in the X direction (up/down) so it looks down toward the player. This value can be overridden if the **LevelIsoAngleX** value is non-zero. If it is, then that value, in degrees, will be used to rotate the camera up/down. The default camera is rotated 0 degrees in the Y direction (around) so it looks toward the player from behind. This value can be overridden if the **LevelIsoAngleY** value is not zero. If it is, that value (in degrees) will be used to rotate the camera around.

Giving the Player Attributes

Everything the player has or uses in a level must be defined as an attribute before it is available to the player. This includes health, stamina, and ammunition for weapons. If these items are not predefined, you can't acquire them from an Attribute entity. In the PlayerSetup entity, there is an entry called AttributeInfoFile—the name of the file that contains all the predefined player attributes. The default Reality Factory AttributeInfoFile is called player.ini, although you can change it to any file name you want.

The AttributeInfoFile is a text file that you can edit with any text editor, such as NotePad. It's laid out much like a standard Windows ini file, with each attribute having its own section. The name of the attribute is enclosed in square brackets such as [**health**] or [**light**]. Each line after the attribute name, up to the next section, contains the values used for that attribute. Every attribute requires a low value, which is the minimum amount this attribute can decrease to; a high value, which is the maximum amount of this attribute you can acquire; and the initial value, which is the amount of this attribute that the player starts the game with. These values are assigned in the form:

- **initial** =

- **low** =

- **high** =

Leading and trailing spaces are ignored. The **initial** value is used to start the player off with such things as health or a limited amount of ammunition. Some attributes are required if you want to make use of all the features built-in to Reality Factory. The player automatically receives a **health** attribute but the **high** value is only 1. This keeps the player alive if no AttributeInfoFile is specified. Therefore, a **health** attribute is required if any fighting is to take place. Also, the players can acquire a **light** from an Attribute entity (attribute name is **light**) so a **light** attribute must be predefined to use it. If you are using the default melee weapons, they require stamina in order to inflict damage—so a **stamina** attribute must also be predefined. **Stamina** will automatically increase over time (see PlayerSetup entity). All weapons require ammunition, so these attributes must be predefined before you can use them. The default player.ini file contains these predefines for the standard Reality Factory setup, although you may want to change the values.

The attributes already defined in the player.ini file are as follows:

- **Health**

- **Stamina**

- **Light**

- **Mana**

- **Rocket**

- **Bullet**

- **Dart**

- **Grenade**

- **RocketLauncher**

- **GrenadeLauncher**

- **Sword**

- **Bat**

- **ChainGun**
- **DartGun**

Attribute Entity

The Attribute entity is used to allow the player to pick up various objects during the game. These objects include health, ammunition, and even weapons. The player acquires these objects by colliding with the Attribute entity. Refer to the "Giving the Player Attributes" section earlier in this chapter for details of how to set up the player so he can use these objects. The entries for this entity's attributes are discussed in the following list:

- **szEntityName**—Name of this entity.
- **EntityName**—Name of the entity to attach this entity to.
- **BoneName**—Name of actor bone to attach to.
- **Model**—Name of the world model to attach to.
- **TriggerName**—Name of trigger entity.
- **szSoundFile**—Name of sound file to play when colliding with entity.
- **szActorName**—Name of the actor that is shown in the level.
- **ActorRotation**—Values required to rotate actor into proper position.
- **ReSpawn**—If TRUE, then entity will **respawn** after pickup.
- **Delay**—Number of seconds before **respawn** will occur.
- **Scale**—Amount to scale the entity actor, 1 equals 100 percent.
- **AttributeName**—Name of the attribute provided by this entity.
- **AttributeAmount**—Amount of attribute provided.
- **AttributeAltName**—Name of alternate attribute provided by this entity.
- **AttributeAltAmount**—Amount of alternate attribute provided.
- **Gravity**—If TRUE, then actor is subject to gravity.
- **szReSpawnSound**—Name of sound file to play when entity **respawns.**

The EnvAudioSetup Entity

The EnvAudioSetup entity is used to define the Foley sounds used when the player is moving in different environments. These sounds are played when the player moves and stop when he stops. They are looped to play continuously as the player moves. Each zone (or environment) that the player can enter has its own sound or, if none is defined, a general default sound is used. This entity allows you to define default and generic footsteps and then movement sounds while the player's character is in other assigned zones, such as sloshing through water (see Figure 13.19).

Figure 13.19

The EnvAudioSetup dialog box.

> **Note:** The sounds used should be short, looping audio effects like repeating footsteps or sloshing in water.

The EnvAudioSetup entity is discussed in the following list. The attributes for this entity are:

- **DefaultMotionSound**—Default sound to play.

- **SoundWhenInWater**—Sound to play when in water.

- **SoundWhenInLava**—Sound to play when in lava.

- **SoundWhenInToxicGas**—Sound to play when in toxic gas.

- **SoundWhenInZeroG**—Sound to play when in zero gravity.

- **SoundWhenInFrozen**—Sound to play when on frozen ground.

- **SoundWhenInSludge**—Sound to play when in sludge.

- **SoundWhenInSlowMotion**—Sound to play when in slow motion.

- **SoundWhenInFastMotion**—Sound to play when in fast motion.

- **SoundWhenUsingLadders**—Sound to play when climbing ladders.

As you can see already, Reality Factory has made a huge advancement from Genesis. The ability to add fog and a clipping plane alone allows you to do a lot more with the tools as far as level size, complexity, and atmosphere go. The EnvAudioSetup entity allows you to assign various sound files to the players as they walk over various surfaces, and that alone adds a greater degree of immersion.

Audio Effects

Sound can add a great deal to a level. The choices in Reality Factory cover environmental audio, 3D audio point sources, and soundtrack switching. Once you start adding sounds to your game, you will see how much sound adds. The ambient noises in games like Kingpin add a lot to the experience. The ambient sounds in Kingpin are actually accessible in the demo as WAV files. With these entities, you can have a crackling fire or babbling brook that the player hears when only in the vicinity of the fire or water.

There are three kinds of audio files that you can use with Reality Factory:

- MIDI files, which define a musical track to be played.

- CD audio tracks that play back a track from an audio CD (use your favorite music CD for prototyping).

- Streaming audio files. Wave files that contain a soundtrack or other sound effects loaded into the computer's memory and played back.

The AudioSource3D Entity

You will use the AudioSource3D entity to place a point in your level from which a sound appears to emanate. This entity maintains its position when the player moves around the level. So you can have the purr of an engine come from a generator and, as the player nears it, the sound grows louder. And, of course, the sound will drop off as the player walks away, mimicking the way real-world sound works. This entity can be used for running water from a sewer opening, music from a bar, or any noise source we hear in real life. This use of the entity can also serve as a player clue during game play. If all the doors you walk past are quiet, but one emits a low gurgle, what is behind that door for the player to discover?

All AudioSource3D sounds loop, or play over and over, and have an audible radius beyond which the sound is no longer heard (see Figure 13.20).

Figure 13.20
The AudioSource3D dialog box.

The AudioSource3D entity's attributes are discussed in the following list:

- **szSoundFile**—Name of the sound file to play.

- **fRadius**—Maximum distance after which sound cannot be heard.

- **szEntityName**—Name of this entity.

- **EntityName**—Name of the entity to attach this entity to.

- **BoneName**—Name of actor bone to attach to.

- **Model**—Name of the world model to attach to.

- **TriggerName**—Name of trigger entity.

The SoundtrackToggle Entity

The SoundtrackToggle entity is used to switch between soundtracks inside a level. The toggle switches back and forth between the two defined soundtracks each time the player comes within the entities' trigger ranges. You can also set a delay that will prevent the toggle from being switched repeatedly if the player chooses to run back and forth through the entity radius. The trigger range defines how close the player avatar has to get to the trigger before it switches (see Figure 13.21).

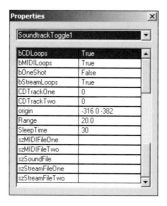

Figure 13.21

The SoundtrackToggle dialog box.

This entity can also be used to switch between two types of soundtrack—from a MIDI file to a streaming audio track, for example. The SoundtrackToggle entity can also be set to trigger only once if, for example, you want a single audio effect to play when the player passes through a certain point.

The SoundtrackToggle entity has the following attributes:

- **bCDLoops**—TRUE if the CD track should loop.

- **BMIDILoops**—TRUE if the MIDI track should loop.

- **bOneShot**—TRUE if the toggle happens only once.

- **bStreamLoops**—TRUE if the streaming audio track should loop.

- **CDTrackOne**—First CD track to switch to.

- **CDTrackTwo**—Second CD track to switch to.

- **Origin**—Origin of the entity in game space.

- **Range**—The radius of the trigger, in world units.

- **SleepTime**—Delay, in seconds, before the toggle is active after being hit.

- **szMIDIFileOne**— First MIDI track to switch to.

- **szMIDIFileTwo**—Second MIDI track to switch to.

- **szSoundFile**—Audio effect to play when the switch activates.

- **szStreamFileOne**—First streaming audio file to switch to.

- **szStreamFileTwo**—Second streaming audio file to switch to.

The StreamingAudioProxy Entity

The StreamingAudioProxy entity defines a trigger that will play a streaming audio effect. The player triggers the playback of the streaming audio effect when the player comes within range of the entity. The streaming audio can loop or not loop, as desired, and there is a delay available to prevent the trigger from being hit repeatedly (see Figure 13.22).

Figure 13.22
The StreamingAudioProxy dialog box.

The StreamingAudioProxy entity has the following attributes:

- **szStreamFile**—The name of the WAV file to play when this entity is triggered.

- **bOneShot**—TRUE if this trigger happens only once.

- **bLoops**—TRUE if this audio loops.

- **SleepTime**—Delay, in seconds, before the toggle can be triggered again after being hit.

- **Range**—Range of trigger, in world units.

This effect allows a greater degree of player interaction with the world. You can have a pay phone set to trigger a busy tone every time the player comes right up on it, for example.

> **Note:** The StreamingAudioProxy entity uses Windows to load and play the file, and bypasses the built-in sound system of Reality Factory. Therefore, the volume control in the menu doesn't affect the volume of this audio.

World Model Helpers

World model helpers are entities that provide enhancements to Genesis3D world models. These models, created in the World Editor, are pieces of world geometry that can be animated such as doors, platforms, and triggers, as you learned previously.

The Door Entity

The Door entity allows you to turn an animated world model into a door. But unlike the Genesis door entity, the Reality Factory door can be triggered in many ways. The player can hit it, shoot at it, use a trigger (a separate door trigger), or some combination of these. Doors can also be linked so that when one door opens, all the doors in the chain open. This is useful for implementing paired swinging doors or the simultaneous opening of multiple exit doors. The Genesis door did not allow for this (see Figure 13.23).

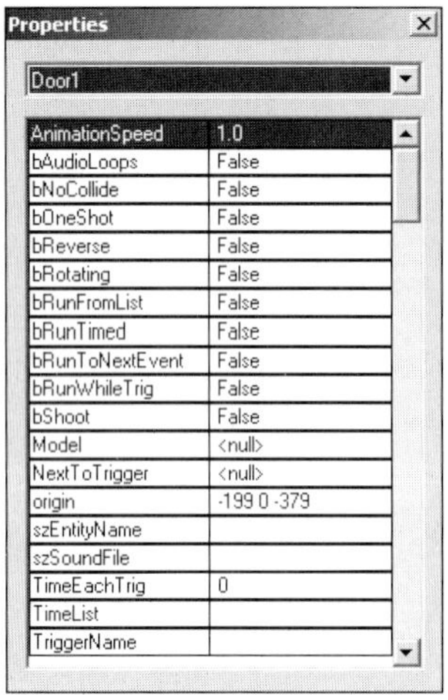

Figure 13.23
The Door dialog box.

The Door entity's attributes are as follows:

- **Model**—Model to animate when door is activated.

- **NextToTrigger**—Model of next door to trigger when this door is activated.

- **szSoundFile**—Name of sound file to play when door is activated.

- **bAudioLoops**—If TRUE, then sound file loops until opening is done; if FALSE, play only once.

- **szEntityName**—Entity name of door.

- **bOneShot**—If TRUE, door only activates once; if FALSE, door can be activated multiple times.

- **AnimationSpeed**—Speed of door model animation, with 1.0 = 100 percent of defined speed.

- **TriggerName**—Name of triggering entity.

- **bShoot**—If TRUE, the door is activated only by shooting, not by player collision.

- **bNoCollide**—If TRUE, then door does not need collision to activate but is controlled by the trigger only.

- **bReverse**—If TRUE, collision causes door to reverse direction, if animating.

- **bRotating**—If TRUE, door is a rotating (swing) model.

- **bRunWhileTrig**—If TRUE, animation only runs while trigger is on.

- **bRunTimed**—Animation runs specified time increment each time trigger goes from off to on.

- **TimeEachTrig**—Time animation will run each trigger, only valid if **bRunTimed** is TRUE.

- **bRunToNextEvent**—Animation runs until the next event time is reached each time triggered.

- **bRunFromList**—Animation runs to next time in provided list each time triggered.

- **TimcList**—List of times to run animation to each time triggered in the form (1.0 3.5 ...), only valid if **bRunFromList** is TRUE.

When animating the model for a door that can be activated more than once (**bOneShot** is false), it's important to make the animation cycle back to the starting point. If you don't do so, the second time the door is activated, the model will snap back to the starting point of its animation before continuing its sequence, and this door behavior looks very odd.

When chaining together doors using the **NextToTrigger** entry, the model pointed to by this entry must be a model used by another Door entity. Otherwise, the entry will be ignored. If this Door entity has a **NextToTrigger** entry, it, too, will be activated, and so on.

If there is an entity name in the **TriggerName** entry, the state of that entity is checked to see if the door should be activated. (See "The Trigger Entity" section later in this chapter for more details about triggered doors.)

The **bShoot** flag is used to switch the collision activation from the player actor to a Projectile actor. This allows doors to be activated only by shooting them.

The **bReverse** flag is used to make a door reverse its direction if you collide with it while it is opening.

If the **bRotating** flag is TRUE then it indicates that the door is a swinging door and certain collision detection routines are ignored. This can make it easier to pass through a door while it is opening.

If **bRunToNextEvent** is TRUE then the door will animate to the next Event time as set by the SetEvent button in the Model tab in the Level editor. The Event String can contain commands to play a sound or cause a trigger. If the Event String contains "S sound.wav" then sound.wav will be played at that Event time. If the Event String contains "T trigger1" then the Trigger entity named trigger1 will be activated the same as if it had been collided with.

The MovingPlatform Entity

The MovingPlatform entity enables you to convert an animated world model into a moving platform. If the player avatar is on the platform, the avatar will be carried along as the platform moves. This platform can be triggered in many ways: by the player hitting it, by any projectile hitting it, through a separate platform trigger, or a combination of these. MovingPlatform entities can also be linked such that when one platform moves, all platforms in the chain move. The platform can also be set to start when the level loads and to loop forever (see Figure 13.24).

Figure 13.24
The MovingPlatform dialog box.

The MovingPlatform entity's attributes are discussed in the following list:

- **Model**—Model to animate when platform is activated.

- **NextToTrigger**—Model of next platform to trigger when this platform is activated.

- **szSoundFile**—Name of sound file to play when platform is activated.

- **bAudioLoops**—If TRUE, then sound file loops until moving is done; if false, it will play only once.

- **szEntityName**—Entity name of platform.

- **bOneShot**—If TRUE, platform only activates once, if false platform can be activated multiple times.

- **AnimationSpeed**—Speed of platform model animation, with 1.0 = 100 percent of defined speed.

- **TriggerName**—Name of triggering entity.

- **bShoot**—If TRUE, the platform is activated only by shooting, not by player collision.

- **bNoCollide**—If TRUE, then platform does not need collision to activate but is controlled by the trigger only.

- **bAutoStart**—If TRUE, start model animation at level load regardless of trigger state.

- **bLooping**—If TRUE, model animation never stops after first activation.

- **bReverse**—If TRUE, then animation reverses at end.

- **bRunWhileTrig**—If TRUE, animation only runs while trigger is on.

- **bRunTimed**—Animation runs specified time increment each time trigger goes from off to on.

- **TimeEachTrig**—Time animation will run each trigger, only valid if **bRunTimed** is TRUE.

- **bRunToNextEvent**—Animation runs until the next event time is reached each time triggered.

- **bRunFromList**—Animation runs to next time in provided list each time triggered.

- **TimeList**—List of times to run animation to each time triggered in the form (1.0 3.5 ...), only valid if **bRunFromList** is TRUE.

When chaining platforms together using the **NextToTrigger** entry, the model pointed to by this entry must be a model used by another MovingPlatform entity. Otherwise, the entry will be ignored. If that MovingPlatform entity has a **NextToTrigger** entry, it, too, will be activated, and so on.

If any entity names are in the **TriggerName** entry, the state of these entities are checked to see if the platform should be activated. See "The Trigger Entity" for more details about triggered platforms.

The **bShoot** flag is used to switch the collision activation from the player actor to a Projectile actor. This allows platforms to be activated only by shooting them.

The **bAutoStart** flag is used to make a platform that will run immediately upon level load. This allows platforms to already be running when the player first sees them. In conjunction with the **bLooping** flag you can make a platform that starts immediately and runs continuously like a conveyor belt, escalator, or waterwheel.

If **bRunToNextEvent** is TRUE then the platform will animate to the next Event time as set by the SetEvent button in the Model tab in the Level editor. The Event String can contain commands to play a sound or cause a trigger. If the Event String contains "S sound.wav", then sound.wav will be played at that Event time. If the Event String contains "T trigger1", the Trigger entity named trigger1 will be activated the same as if it had been collided with.

The Trigger Entity

The DoorTrigger entity allows a Genesis3D world model to act as a trigger for a door. The door trigger itself can be animated so you can have moving switches and/or buttons (see Figure 13.25), so a trigger can be an animated model of a switch that when collided will animate and then trigger the door to open. Every trigger must have a model associated with it through the Model entry in the entity structure. If this model is animated, then the animation will start when the trigger is activated. A trigger doesn't directly control any other entity. Instead, it sets an internal flag to indicate whether it is active (on or TRUE) or inactive (off or false). Other entities read this flag to determine the state of the trigger.

Figure 13.25

The Trigger dialog box.

When a trigger is activated, it stays on for the number of seconds entered in the TimeOn field. It then stays off for the number of seconds entered in the TimeOff field before it can be reactivated. If the **bOneShot** field is TRUE, then the trigger will only activate once.

The **szSoundFile** field contains the name (if any) of the WAV file to play when the trigger is activated. The **bAudioLoops** field is used to indicate whether the sound plays once or is repeated.

If the **bShoot** field is TRUE, the trigger can only be activated by shooting it and not when the player collides with it.

Triggers can also be triggered. If there is a entity name entered in the **TriggerName** field then the state of that entity will be checked and must be on before the trigger can be activated. If the state of the TriggerName field entity is off and you attempt to activate this trigger, then its callback flag will be briefly set to on. This topic is not discussed here because it gets into Logic gates, which are beyond the scope of this book.

The Trigger entity is explained in the following list:

- **Animation Speed**—Speed of the animation 1 = 100 percent.
- **bAudioLoops**—TRUE if the audio effect loops while the model is animating.
- **bOneShot**—TRUE if this trigger operates only once.
- **bShot**—TRUE if this trigger operates by being shot.
- **Model**—The Genesis3D world model to use as the trigger.
- **szEntityName**—The name of this entity (used in scripting).
- **szSoundFile**—The name of the WAV file to play when the door trigger is activated.
- **TimeOff**—The number of seconds the trigger is off.
- **TimeOn**—The number of seconds the trigger is on.
- **TriggerName**—Name of the Trigger Entity to use.

The ChangeLevel Entity

The ChangeLevel entity allows any Genesis3D world model to be used to change levels. When the player collides with the model associated with the ChangeLevel entity, the current level is shut down, and a new level is loaded and started. A bitmap and an audio effect can be assigned to play while the new level loads (see Figure 13.26).

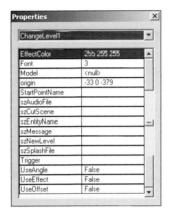

Figure 13.26
The ChangeLevel dialog box.

The ChangeLevel entity's attributes are discussed in the following list:

- **Model**—The world model used as a trigger.

- **szSplashFile**—Name of the bitmap file used as a splash screen.

- **szAudioFile**—Name of the audio file to play while the splash screen is displayed.

- **szNewLevel**—Name of the new level to switch to.

- **szCutScene**—Name of the Avi file to play before loading new level.

- **szMessage**—Message to display instead of Splash Screen.

- **Font**—Size of **szMessage** font.

- **UseOffset**—If TRUE, then offset Player at Start Position.

- **StartPointName**—Entity Name of PlayerStart to use.

- **UseEffect**—If TRUE, then use Fog Effect at level change.

- **EffectColor**—Color of Effect Fog.

- **UseAngle**—If TRUE, use the Angle direction vector for the player in the PlayerStart entity.

- **Trigger**—Name of the trigger entity.

Model can be any world model in the level. The player colliding with this model activates the level change. If the state of the Trigger entity is off, the level change will not occur on collision.

Note: The **szCutScene** attribute provides the capability to play a cut scene (or movie) between levels. Careful use of this allows you to provide additional back-story explanation as the game progresses. This is especially useful for RPGs (role-playing games to explain the events of the complex storyline between levels.

If a name is entered in the **szCutScene** entry, that Avi file is played immediately after initiating the level change. If no name is present, then the cutscene sequence is skipped.

The Splash screen is displayed, and the sound is played immediately after the cutscene and while the level is being loaded. If no bitmap name is provided, the splash screen sequence is skipped. If no Splash screen is used, the text message—if present—will be displayed in the center of the screen while the level loads.

The name of the level entered in **szNewLevel** must be that of a level's BSP file and have the .bsp extension. Otherwise, the current level will end, and you will be returned to the main menu.

When **UseOffset** is TRUE, the distance between the player's position and the ChangeLevel entity is calculated, and this distance is applied to the PlayerStart position in the next level. This allows the player to start a level in the same relative position as it exited.

If **StartPointName** is not blank, the player will start the next level at the PlayerStart entity whose name matches StartPointName. If no name match is found, then the default (unnamed) PlayerStart entity is used. If the UseAngle flag is TRUE, then point the player in that direction at level start.

A fog effect can be shown at the start of a level if **UseEffect** is set to TRUE. **EffectColor** controls the color of the fog. Nothing happens in the level while the fog is shown, and it can be used to give the player a momentary pause.

Special Effects

The special effects in Reality Factory are the best part of the package from an "eye candy" point of view. The special effects are varied and flexible. Once you understand how they each function, you will be able to simulate fire, rain, snow, and virtually anything you can conceive of for your level.

The Teleporter Entity

The Teleporter entity, in conjunction with the TeleportTarget entity, provides the typical teleportation effect used to move the player from one part of a level to another, just like *Star Trek*'s, "Beam me up, Scotty!" Teleporters have adjustable fog and audio effects to add to the variety. There is also a "teleporter effect" that can be run when the player hits the teleport; this effect plays a sound and creates visual effects, takes a few seconds to run, and can be disabled to provide "instant teleport" (see Figure 13.27).

The Teleporter entity has the following attributes:

- **bOneShot**—TRUE if the teleporter works once only.

- **bUseFogEffect**—TRUE if the fog effect around the teleporter is to be used.

> **Note:** The fog field surrounds the teleporter entity, *not* the model used. If you want the fog around the model, put the teleporter entity inside the model.

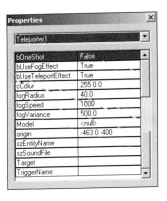

Figure 13.27
The Teleporter dialog box.

- **bUseTeleportEffect**—TRUE if the "teleporter effect" is to be run when the teleport activates.

- **cColor**—Color of the fog field surrounding the teleporter entity (not the model).

- **fogRadius**—Radius of the fog effect around the entity.

- **fogSpeed**—Speed at which the fog density around the entity changes.

- **fogVariance**—Depth of the variance in fog density, measured in world units.

- **Model**—The Genesis3D world model to be used as the teleporter.

- **szEntityName**—The name of this entity (used in scripting).

- **szSoundFile**—The name of a WAV file to play when the teleporter activates.

- **Target**—The name of the TeleportTarget entity that this teleporter uses.

- **Trigger**—The name of the Trigger to use, if any.

The TeleportTarget Entity

The TeleportTarget entity defines the target for a Teleporter entity. The TeleportTarget entity has one attribute: **Name** of *this* teleport target. The name *must* be unique.

The MorphingField Entity

The MorphingField entity defines a morphing field of fog, a cloud of fog that shrinks and grows and changes colors, with an associated 3D audio source. This is useful for adding to the atmosphere of a level (say, a red/blue morphing fog field with an electrical crackling for a dangerous reactor core). The morphing effect loops continually from start to end, then back to the start state (see Figure 13.28).

The MorphingField entity has the following attributes:

- **BoneName**—The name of the bone to attach the entity to.

- **clrEnd**—Fog color at the end of the morph.

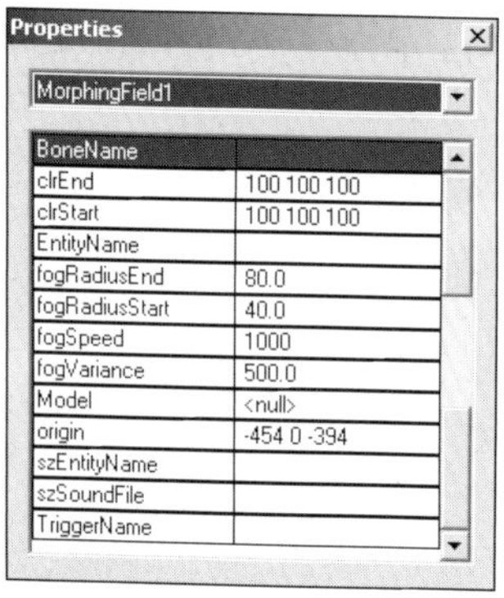

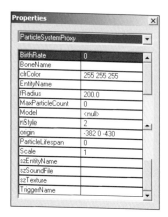

Figure 13.28
The MorphingField dialog box.

- **clrStart**—Fog color at the start of the morph.

- **EntityName**—The name of the entity to attach to.

- **fogRadiusEnd**—Radius of the fog effect at the end of the morph.

- **fogRadiusStart**—Radius of the fog effect at the start of the morph.

- **fogSpeed**—Speed at which fog density changes, in milliseconds.

- **fogVariance**—Depth of the fog density variance; measured in world units.

- **Model**—The name of the model to attach this entity to.

- **szEntityName**—The name of this entity (used in scripting).

- **szSoundFile**—The name of the WAV file to play looped as the 3D audio source.

- **Trigger**—The name of the trigger associated with this entity.

The ParticleSystemProxy Entity

The ParticleSystemProxy entity allows you to place various predefined styles of particle effects. The defaults for these styles can also be overridden to vary the look of different instances of the same style of particle effect. See Figures 13.29 and 13.30 for the particle system proxy dialog and the effect in the game.

Figure 13.29
The ParticleSystemProxy
dialog box.

Figure 13.30
The ParticleSystemProxy in the game.

There are 12 styles of particle system that you can use. Each style has a number, which you use to specify the style in the entity's **nStyle** attribute. These styles and their numbers are discussed in the following list:

- 1. *SHOCKWAVE*—Particles emitted on horizontal plane outward from center.

- 2. *FOUNTAIN*—Particles emitted with gravity and velocity, and they act like a fountain.

- 3. *RAIN*—Particles emitted a random distance on X/Z planes.

- 4. *SPHERE*—Particles emitted with varying velocity vectors outward in a sphere.

- 5. *COLUMN*—Particles emitted with velocity, no gravity in a cylindrical column.

- 6. *EXPLOSIVE ARRAY*—Particles emitted UPWARD (+Y) from emitter plane (floor).

- 7. *SPIRAL ARM*—Like the Milky Way Galaxy.

- 8. *TRAIL*—Typical particle trail, a trail of slowly falling particles by default.

- 9. *GUARDIAN*—Pseudo-columned-spiral effect.

- 10. *IMPLODING SPHERE*—An imploding sphere.

- 11. *IMPLODING SHOCKWAVE*—Imploding shockwave.

- 12. *IMPLODING SPIRAL ARM*—Collapsing galaxy.

The ParticleSystemProxy entity has the attributes shown in the following list:

- **nStyle**—Style of particle system—ranges from 1 to 12.

- **szSoundFile**—Sound file to play while particle system is active.

- **fRadius**—Maximum distance at which sound can be heard.

- **szTexture**—Name of bitmap file to use to texture particles.

- **clrColor**—Color of particles.

- **BirthRate**—Number of particles per second to create.

- **MaxParticleCount**—Maximum number of particles active at any one time.

- **ParticleLifespan**—Number of milliseconds that particle is alive.

- **szEntityName**—Name of this entity.

- **EntityName**—Name of the entity to attach this entity to.

- **BoneName**—Name of actor bone to attach to.

- **Model**—Name of the world model to attach to.

- **TriggerName**—Name of trigger entity.

- **Scale**—Scale of particle size—1.0 = 100 percent.

Note: Make sure that the bitmap you're replacing is used only where you want the video to play. The video will play on every occurrence of the texture throughout your level.

FlipBook Entity

The FlipBook entity (See Figure 13.31) is used to display a sequence of animated bitmaps. It can be placed in the level at the entity's location or used to replace a texture in the level.

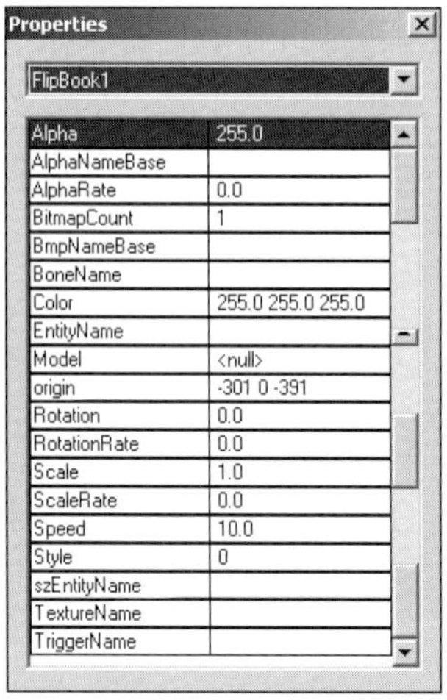

Figure 13.31
The FlipBook dialog box.

The FlipBook entity has the attributes shown in the following list:

- **szEntityName**—The name of this entity.

- **Color**—Color of texture.

- **Speed**—The number of bitmaps per second that will be displayed.
- **BitmapCount**—The total number of bitmaps in animation.
- **Style**—The animation style, range 0 to 4.
- **Scale**—The initial amount to scale the bitmaps, where 1 equals 100 percent.
- **ScaleRate**—Amount to decrease the scale per second.
- **Rotation**—Initial rotation, in degrees, of bitmaps.
- **RotationRate**—Amount to add to rotation per second.
- **Alpha**—Initial alpha of bitmaps.
- **AlphaRate**—Amount to decrease alpha per second.
- **BmpNameBase**—Base name of bitmap sequence.
- **AlphaNameBase**—Base name of alpha map sequence.
- **TextureName**—Name of texture to replace with animated bitmaps.
- **EntityName**—Name of the entity to attach this entity to.
- **BoneName**—Name of actor bone to attach to.
- **Model**—Name of the world model to attach to.
- **TriggerName**—Name of trigger entity.

The **BmpNameBase** and **AlphaNameBase** entries are the base name of a sequence of bitmaps. The first bitmap in the sequence must be <*name*>0.bmp, the second <*name*>1.bmp and so on, where <*name*> is either BmpNameBase or AlphaNameBase.

TextureName is the name of the texture (from the texture library—do not use the BMP extension) that will be replaced throughout the level with the bitmap animation sequence.

The Style of the animation is as follows:

- *0*—No animation, display first bitmap only.
- *1*—At end of animation, repeat from start (looped).
- *2*—At end of animation reverse direction of animation.
- *3*—Chose random bitmap from list. This is good for static on monitors.
- *4*—Play through only once, then stop.

The Corona Entity

The Corona entity provides that wonderful "ring around a light source" effect that you see in almost every first-person shooter made since Quake2. Used sparingly, the Corona effect can add a lot to the ambiance of a level (see Figure 13.32).

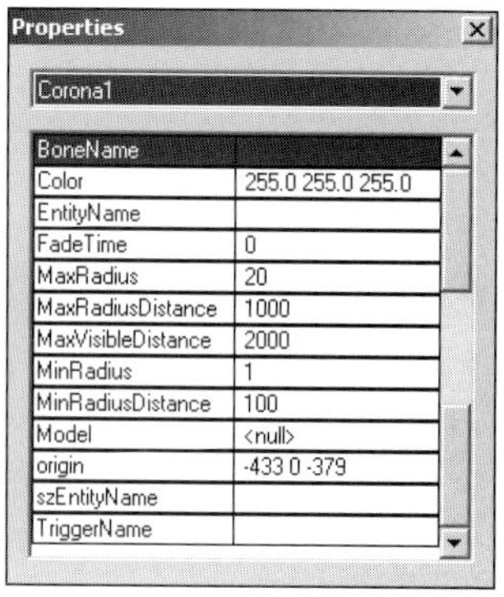

Figure 13.32
The Corona dialog box.

The Corona entity has the following attributes:

- **BoneName**—Name of bone to attach to.

- **Color**—RGB color of the corona.

- **EntityName**—The name of the entity this entity is attached to.

- **FadeTime**—Time in seconds that the fade takes to happen.

- **MaxRadius**—Maximum size (radius) corona will ever grow to (in world units).

- **MaxRadiusDistance**—Above this distance, corona stays at MaxRadius size.

- **MaxVisibleDistance**—Maximum distance corona is visible from (in world units).

- **MinRadius**—Minimum size (radius) corona will ever drop to (in world units).

- **MinRadiusDistance**—Below this distance, corona stays at MinRadius size.

- **Model**—Genesis3D world model to attach the corona to.

- **szEntityName**—The name of this entity (used in scripting).

- **TriggerName**—Name of trigger entity to use.

The DynamicLight Entity

The DynamicLight entity defines a light whose intensity changes over time, based on a pattern supplied by the level designer (see Figure 13.33).

The DynamicLight entity varies based on an attribute called the RadiusFunction. This is a string of letters, from A to Z (A being the minimum light value and Z being the maximum), that are used to determine how the intensity of the light varies. Reality Factory processes this radius function across time, varying the intensity of the light (and interpolating in-between values if desired), producing a constantly fluctuating light source.

Note: There can be a maximum of 30 DynamicLights active at any one time. If a light cannot be seen, it is considered inactive and does not count toward the total.

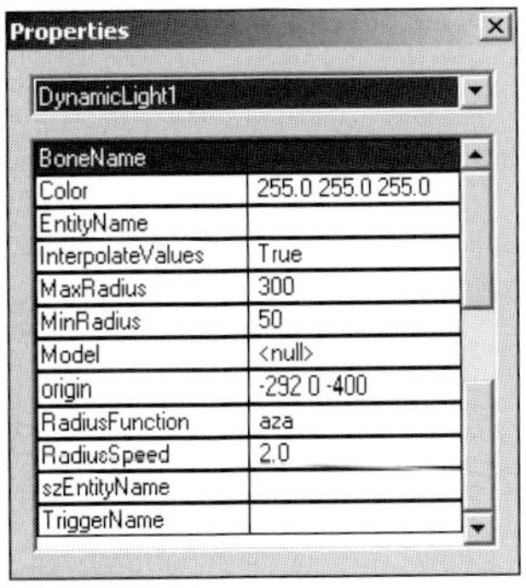

Figure 13.33
The DynamicLight dialog box.

The DynamicLight entity has the attributes shown in the following list:

- **szEntityName**—Name of this entity.

- **MinRadius**—Minimum radius of light in texels.

- **MaxRadius**—Maximum radius of light in texels.

- **InterpolateValues**—If TRUE, then interpolate RadiusFunction values.

- **RadiusFunction**—Specifies light radius over time.

- **RadiusSpeed**—Number of seconds to go through RadiusFunction values.

- **Color**—Color of light.

- **EntityName**—Name of the entity to attach this entity to.

- **BoneName**—Name of actor bone to attach to.

- **Model**—Name of the world model to attach to.

- **TriggerName**—Name of trigger entity.

Radius Function

The **RadiusFunction** is a string of letters (a to z) used to determine the radius of the light at a given time. The **RadiusSpeed** value is the number of seconds the light takes to go through all the letters in the **RadiusFunction** string, with the time being divided equally between each letter value. A letter value of "a" will set the light radius to the **MinRadius** value, while a letter value of "z" will set it to **MaxRadius**. Letter values between "a" and "z" will set the light radius to a value between **MinRadius** and **MaxRadius**, with the radius value being determined by the letter's position in the alphabet. If **InterpolateValues** is set to TRUE, the light radius will be smoothly changed from one letter value to the next during each time period. If it is set to false, the light radius will change directly from one letter value to the other at the start of each time period. When the light has cycled through the entire **RadiusFunction** string of letters, it starts again at the beginning of the string.

If, for example, **RadiusFunction** is "*azam*" and the **RadiusSpeed** is 4, then each letter value will be given 1 second of time (i.e., the light radius will be at that letter value for 1 second before changing to the next value). For the first second, the light will be at the minimum radius ("a"), for the second second, it will be at the maximum radius ("z"), the third second will be back at the minimum radius ("a"), and during the fourth second it will be halfway between the minimum and maximum radius ("m" being the middle letter of the alphabet). Then, the cycle starts again. If **InterpolateValues** is TRUE, for the first second the light radius will smoothly increase from the minimum ("a") radius to the next radius value ("z"), for the second, it will smoothly decrease to the minimum radius again, and so on. If **InterpolateValues** is false, the light radius will abruptly change size each second.

Note: Be careful to select two dominant bolt colors that are not the same (i.e., if Red is dominant, choose Green and Blue); otherwise, problems occur.

The ElectricBolt Entity

The ElectricBolt entity defines an electrical bolt source in conjunction with an ElectricBoltTerminus entity (the ElectricBoltTerminus defines the target of the electrical bolt). This effect is useful for simulating arcing electrical faults and atmospheric lightning (see Figure 13.34).

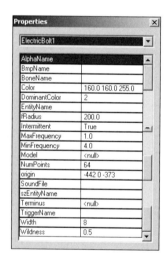

Figure 13.34
The ElectricBolt dialog box.

The ElectricBolt entity has the following attributes:

- **szEntityName**—The name of this entity (used in scripting).

- **Width**—Width, in world units, of the bolt.

- **NumPoints**—Number of control points; must be 32, 64, or 128.

- **Intermittent**—TRUE if the bolt occurs randomly, FALSE if it occurs continuously.

- **MinFrequency**—For an intermittent bolt, the minimum time in milliseconds between pulses.

- **MaxFrequency**—For an intermittent bolt, the maximum time in milliseconds between pulses.

- **Wildness**—Degree of wildness of the bolt; can range from 0 to 1 (and can be a fraction).

- **Terminus**—The ElectricBoltTerminus entity to use as the target.

- **DominantColor**—Dominant color of the bolt; 0 = Red, 1 = Green, 2 = Blue.

- **Color**—Base color of the bolt.

The ElectricBoltTerminus Entity

The ElectricBoltTerminus entity defines the target of an ElectricBolt entity. The ElectricBoltTerminus entity has one attribute: **szEntityName**. This attribute is used in scripting. See Figure 13.35 for a few electric bolt examples.

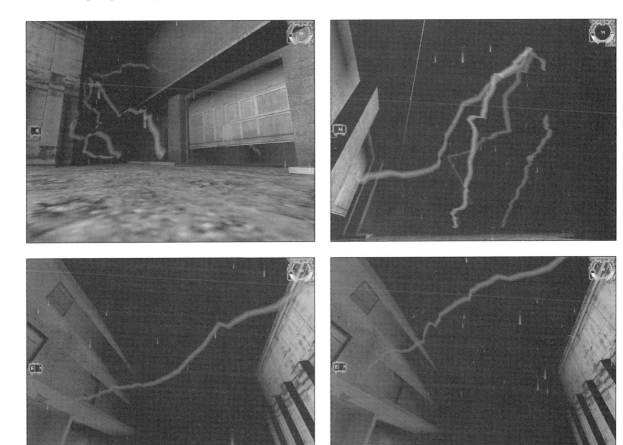

Figure 13.35

The Electric Bolt and the Electric Bolt Terminus used in various configurations.

The FloatingParticles Entity

The FloatingParticles entity produces a system of upwardly moving particles defined by a texture and an alpha bitmap. This entity can be connected to the bone of a StaticEntityProxy actor so that it will follow that particular bone's motion in the game (see Figure 13.36).

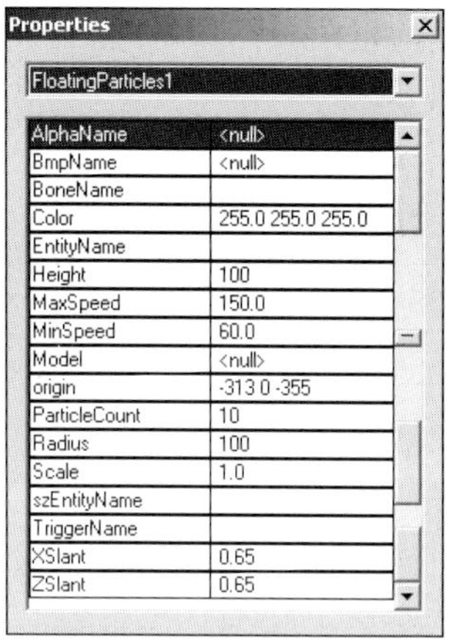

Figure 13.36
The FloatingParticles dialog box.

The FloatingParticles entity has the following attributes:

- **AlphaName**—The name of the bitmap file to use for the particle alpha texture.

- **BmpName**—The name of the bitmap file to use for the particle texture.

- **BoneName**—The bone in the StaticEntityProxy entity that the actor effect is bound to.

- **Color**—Base color of particle.

- **EntityName**—The name of the entity to attach to.

- **Height**—Maximum height each particle will travel from the base.

- **MaxSpeed**—Maximum upward speed of each particle.

- **MinSpeed**—Minimum upward speed of each particle.

- **Model**—The name of the model to attach to.

- **ParticleCount**—How many particles to use.

- **Radius**—Radius of particle cylinder.

- **Scale**—What scale to use for the particle bitmap.

- **szEntityName**—The name of this entity.

- **TriggerName**—The name of the trigger to use.

- **XSlant**—Upward slant of particle area on X axis.

- **ZSlant**—Upward slant of particle area on Z axis.

The EChaos Entity

The EChaos procedural texture entity produces a chaotic moving texture effect, replacing a texture bitmap used in the World Editor (see Figure 13.37). The effect is a rippling, crawling effect like lava. This effect doesn't replace the texture, but rather distorts it.

Figure 13.37
The EChaos dialog box.

The EChaos entity has the following attributes:

- **MaxXSway**—The total texture horizontal pixel distortion.

- **MaxYSway**—The total texture vertical pixel sway distortion.

- **XStep**—The horizontal texture scroll speed creeps in pixels.

- **YStep**—The vertical texture scroll speed.

- **AttachBmp**—The name of the texture, defined in the World Editor, to attach this effect to.

The Rain Entity

The Rain particle system entity produces a "rain of particles" effect that can be attached to a bone of a StaticEntityProxy actor. See Figures 13.38 and 13.39 for the in-game effect of rain.

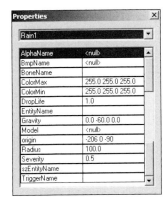

Figure 13.38
The Rain dialog box.

The Rain entity has the following attributes:

- **AlphaName**—The name of .BMP bitmap file to use as the alpha mask for the raindrops.

- **BmpName**—The name of .BMP bitmap file to use for raindrops.

- **BoneName**—The name of the bone in the StaticEntityProxy actor to attach the effect to.

- **ColorMax**—Maximum RGB color for drops.

Figure 13.39
The Rain effect in a game scene.

- **ColorMin**—Minimum RGB color for drops.

- **DropLife**—Lifespan of a single drop, in seconds.

- **Entity**—The StaticEntityProxy entity that the effect is attached to.

- **Gravity**—Velocity applied to each particle per second (in world units).

- **Model**—Model this entity is attached to.

- **Radius**—Radius of the rain coverage area (in world units).

- **Severity**—How severe the rain is, 0.0 is tame, 1.0 is insanity.

- **TriggerName**—The name of the trigger to start the rain effect.

The Spout Entity

The Spout particle emitter entity implements a fountain of particles. The fountain varies over time and is useful for many smoke and fire/plasma effects (see Figures 13.40 and 13.41).

The Spout entity has the following attributes:

- **Angles**—Direction in which particles will shoot from spout.

- **ParticleCreateRate**—Rate, in seconds, at which a new particle will be added.

- **MinScale**—Minimum scale of the particles.

- **MaxScale**—Maximum scale of the particles.

- **MinSpeed**—Minimum speed of the particles.

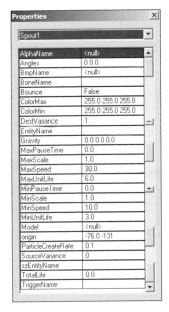

Figure 13.40
The Spout dialog box.

Figure 13.41
The Spout in a game.

- **MaxSpeed**—Maximum speed of the particles.

- **MinUnitLife**—Minimum life of each particle.

- **MaxUnitLife**—Maximum life of each particle in seconds.

- **SourceVariance**—How much to vary the source spray point.

- **DestVariance**—How much to vary the destination spray point.

- **ColorMin**—Minimum RGB color value for each particle.

- **ColorMax**—Maximum RGB color value for each particle.

- **Gravity**—Gravity vector to apply to each particle.

- **BmpName**—The name of .BMP bitmap to use as particle texture.

- **AlphaName**—The name of .BMP bitmap to use as particle alpha mask.

- **TriggerName**—The name of trigger for effect.

- **MinPauseTime**—Minimum number of seconds for randomly chosen pause time.

- **MaxPauseTime**—Maximum number of seconds for randomly chosen pause time.

- **TotalLife**—Total life for this effect; 0.0 means eternal.

- **Entity**—The name of the StaticEntityProxy entity to attach this spout to.

- **BoneName**—The name of bone in StaticEntityProxy actor to attach spout to.

The Flame Entity

The Flame entity is used to produce flame and plasma effects. This is useful for torches, fireplaces, and even steam effects. See Figure 13.42 for the dialog box and Figure 13.43 for the in-game effect.

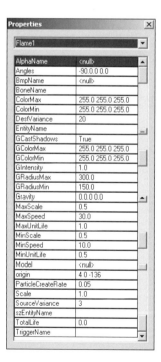

Figure 13.42

The Flame dialog box.

The Flame entity has the following attributes:

- **Angles**—Direction in which flame will shoot.

- **Scale**—Overall scale of the flame effect.

Figure 13.43
The in-game Flame effect.

- **Model**—Model flame is attached to.

- **Entity**—The StaticEntityProxy entity that the flame is attached to.

- **BoneName**—The name of the bone in the StaticEntityProxy actor to which the flame is attached.

- **ParticleCreateRate**—Create a new flame particle every this many seconds.

- **MinScale**—Minimum scale of the flame particles.

- **MaxScale**—Maximum scale of the flame particles.

- **MinSpeed**—Minimum speed of the flame particles.

- **MaxSpeed**—Maximum speed of the flame particles.

- **MinUnitLife**—Minimum life of each flame particle.

- **MaxUnitLife**—Maximum life of each flame particle.

- **SourceVariance**—How much to vary the flame source point in world units.

- **DestVariance**—How much to vary the flame destination point.

- **ColorMin**—Minimum RGB color for each flame particle.

- **ColorMax**—Maximum RGB color for each flame particle.

- **Gravity**—Gravity vector to apply to each flame particle.

- **BmpName**—The name of .BMP bitmap to use as flame texture.

- **AlphaName**—The name of .BMP bitmap to use as flame alpha mask.

- **TotalLife**—Total life for this spout, 0.0 means eternal.

- **GRadiusMin**—Minimum flame light radius (in world units).

- **GRadiusMax**—Maximum flame light radius (in world units).

- **GColorMin**—Minimum flame light RGB color.

- **GColorMax**—Maximum flame light RGB color.

- **GIntensity**—Maximum flame light intensity.

- **GDoNotClip**—TRUE if the light should be hidden if the flame isn't visible.

- **GCastShadows**—TRUE if the light can cause shadows.

Area Effects in Zones

An *area effect* in Reality Factory is not an entity, as are the other special effects; rather it is the ability to create a brush and define that brush as a *zone*. A zone, when entered by the player in the game, will exhibit behaviors as if the player entered a different environment.

For example, you can create a Genesis3D brush and set it to **empty** (no collision detection or the player can pass through it), and you can set the zone type of the brush to **water**. Furthermore, you can **texture** the brush in a water texture, make the brush **translucent**, set it to **wavy**, and in the game you will have really nice-looking water. When the players enter the zone, they will be able to move as if they are swimming. You access these zone choices through the Brush Attributes window. As noted, the only working zones are **Water** and **ZeroG**, but the other zones are in the window as the developers of Reality Factory are working to implement them. The other zones you can look forward to are shown in the following list:

- Water

- Lava

- ToxicGas

- ZeroG

- Frozen

- Sludge

- SlowMotion

- FastMotion

- Ladder

- Impenetrable

- Unclimbable

- **Two user-definable surface slots for programmers to use**

As you can see, the special effects in Reality Factory are quite varied and flexible (and continue to evolve as the program is worked on). Experimentation will continuously turn up new ways to employ these entities. With careful planning and resource management, you can even combine effects; orange floating particles and a flame look like a real outdoor fire (see Figure 13.44).

Figure 13.44
This shot includes many effects to create the right atmosphere. See if you can name them all.

The Flame entity, for example, with some colors and parameters changed can look like natural steam or, if green colored, toxic steam. A Rain entity above a surface with the Water procedural texture applied to it looks like real rain falling on water.

Creating a World in Reality Factory

Now that you are familiar with both the Genesis3D tools and Reality Factory, you are ready to build a level using some of the new aspects of RF you looked at in this chapter, a level with some cool effects and atmosphere. In the following project, you will build a deluxe city-street level.

PROJECT Creating a City-Street Level

You will use some of the basic techniques you learned in earlier chapters to place new entities. Building the city street consists mainly of the following steps:

1. Loading the "street.txl"

2. Face editing to create the world space

3. Creating the first building

4. Cloning buildings

5. Adjusting the lighting

And you will be adding some new entities, such as the following:

- EnvironmentSetup

- PlayerSetup

- AudioSource3D (flames.wav)

- Particle Systems (particle.bmp)

- Rain

- Flame

Loading the "street" Texture Library

The texture library "street.txl" is on the book's companion CD-ROM in the tutorials folder and the street subfolder. To do this project, copy it into the Levels folder of the Reality Factory program directory (\RealityFactory061\media\levels).

Remember that if you do not load the TXL file or use the wrong one with the street level, the geometry in the level of the Textured view will be covered in solid colors. After you load the TXL, all the textures will appear.

Face Editing to Create the World Space

Just like in Genesis3D, every time you start the world editor (rfEdit, in this case) you are given a new and empty world with one potential hollow cube in it. This hollow cube will define the extent of our world space. If you open the level "street.3DT" from the companion CD-ROM (Tutorials\Street), you can follow along. (You have to be in Template creation mode with a potential brush in place.)

The hollow cube I created is rather large. If you intend to make this level yourself, click on one of the view windows to activate the editor and then press Enter. You should hear the "whoosh" (again, this sound is there to make sure that you know your computer's speakers are on), and the cube will be made real in the editor. Now, you will face-edit the inside of this cube to create our world. To do so, follow these steps:

1. After you have created the world space press the Page Down key to enter face-editing mode and select the floor of the hollow cube. Go to the Texture browser and find the texture named "dirt" and apply it, using the Apply button.

2. Now select the top and four walls of the cube and activate the Face Attributes dialog box and check the Sky option (the five selected faces should turn blue).

3. Press the Page Down key again to exit face mode and go to the Sky tab in the Command Console and assign the "Stars" texture to all the faces. I usually set the rotation to "0" because I don't like seeing the stars whip around the sky, and the rotation of the stars just calls attention to the cube on which they are mapped.

Creating the First Building

This first building you can create is done in the following steps.

1. Activate Template mode by clicking on the Template Mode button in the Toolbar, or by going to the Options Panel and selecting Template, or by pressing T.

2. Select the Create Box (Or Cube) option (the first button on the left in Template mode) and create a solid cube. Position the cube roughly in the map; the bottom of the cube should be touching the floor of the world space, and the walls and roof of the building/box should fill the space, like the example shown in Figure 13.45.

3. Go to the Texture Browser and assign the "brickblk" texture to it.

> **Note:** Remember that it is easy (especially if your sound is turned off) to create multiple brushes, one on top of the other, by pressing Enter multiple times. This can lead to errors and, at the least, confusion when you edit. Be careful to avoid doing this.

> **Note:** If all the primitive icons are grayed out, that means you are not in Template mode.

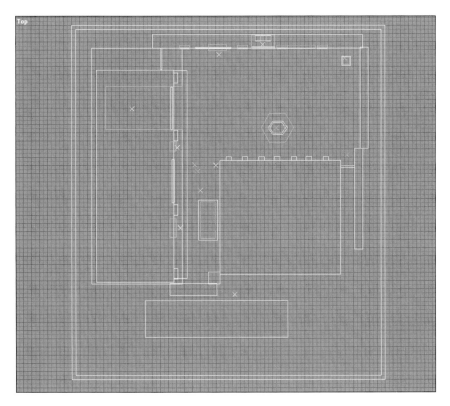

Figure 13.45
The general proportions of your first building in the world space.

Cloning to Detail and Create Buildings

As you are now the master of the one-box level, and you are ready to create more boxes to add detail to your levels. Feel free to repeat the steps in the "Creating the First Building" a few more times. By adding more buildings, you'll really begin to develop your Reality Factory muscles. Look at the street level on the companion CD-ROM, and you will see that the building you created was detailed in only a few easy steps, which I will cover in the next sections.

The Garage of Doom

Okay, I stuck a fog light in the garage in the final level to show that this location is the doom part of the garage. Adding the fog light was the easiest thing to do (it was a catchy title!), but creating the garage wasn't that much more difficult. Because the building is constructed of the same material, make sure that the "brickblk" texture is selected, and do the following.

1. Create a cut brush with the "brickblk" texture on it at the spot where you want to place the garage in the building.

2. Create a solid brush with the "door_garage" on it and place that in an almost closed position (see Figure 13.46).

Figure 13.46
The Garage of Doom, in the street level.

3. Go back to the cut brush you created for the garage bay and select it. Click on the Top view; hold down Shift, and with your left mouse button, drag the brush. This action clones the brush, and you will see the new cloned brush as it moves. Keep dragging until this new brush is well away from the original brush.

4. In the Top view, arrange the cloned brush to where you want the new building to exist.

Finishing Up the Street Level

The Street Level was built primarily to showcase Reality Factory's entities, but if you desire to create a level of this detail you can open the street map and see what I did, which was primarily the following:

1. I used many cut brushes for windows and doors. I face-edited the back face (remember to check the Texture Lock option before you align the texture) and applied the door or window texture. This procedure looks good because it sets the windows and doors back rather than just sticking the texture on a flat sheet; it adds depth.

2. I created a sidewalk that is simply a large, long box with the concrete texture that runs at the base of (and is below) the buildings.

3. Then, I made a fence over an alcove with an ice machine inside. I did this with a cut brush for the alcove and a sheet with the gate texture (turn on transparency). The ice machine is a cube with two cut brushes defining the top.

4. Finally, you want to place lights by the doors and areas of interest in your level and turn the ambient light way down to 35,35,35.

At this point, you have a fairly normal Genesis3D-like level (see Figure 13.47). The following steps, using the new Reality Factory entities, are what make the big difference in performance and atmosphere.

Clone in the Top View to Maintain Horizontal Alignment

When you use the Top view to make the clone, you can move the clone side to side but not up or down in relation to the original object. This keeps the object you are cloning at exactly the same height as the original. Remember this because it can make editing easier. If you need to keep any surface aligned with another (such as keeping floors or walls aligned across parts of a level), you may as well create them perfectly aligned.

Note: When you create an entity such as the EnvironmentalSetup Entity, for example, use names like EnvironmentalSetup1, EnvironmentalSetup2, and so on.

Figure 13.47
The street level at this point is much like a regular Genesis3D level.

EnvironmentSetup

As you have read previously, the **EnvironmentSetup** entity (as opposed to environmental entities) defines various level-wide attributes for the current level only. Only one of these entities should be defined per level; defining more than one will cause problems.

We will focus on one of the most powerful features here—the ability to set distance fogging and the far clipping plane. In Figure 13.48, you will see that fog adds a great deal of atmosphere and realism to the environment of your game.

Figure 13.48
The street level with creepy fog added.

To re-create what you see in Figure 13.48, go to the entity editor and set the values in the following list to these options:

- **EnableDistanceFog**—TRUE so fog is enabled.
- **DistanceFogColor**—Color of fog should be white.
- **FogStartDistLow**—100
- **FogStartDistHigh**—100
- **TotalFogDistLow**—500
- **TotalFogDistHigh**—500

Particle Systems

The **ParticleSystemProxy** entity allows you to place various "predefined" styles of particle effects in the world, and one of the coolest of these effects is Fountain. In this section, you will place a fountain in your street level (see Figure 13.49). Simply place the entity in the center of the area where you want the fountain and set the

Figure 13.49
The ParticleSystemProxy entity, as a fountain in the game.

parameters as listed in this section. Also, you must copy the "particle.bmp" file from this book's companion CD-ROM and place it in the BITMAP folder in the Reality Factory Folder (C:\RealityFactory061\media\bitmaps).

- **nStyle**—Set to "4", which is the fountain effect. Try copying several entities for very pretty fountains.

- **scale**—Set to "2".

- **szTexture**—Set as "particle.bmp".

Rain

To add rain to the already foggy world, simply place the Rain particle system entity in the center of the level—about 256 units above the ground. See Figure 13.50 for the in-game effect of the rain entity.

Set the following attributes in the rain entity like so:

- **DropLife**—Set this to "4" seconds.

- **Radius**—Set this to "600" so that it covers the world.

Flame

For a final touch we will add a cozy burning barrel in this otherwise bleak world. The Flame entity produces really nice flame effects. See Figure 13.51 for the in-game effect of the flame entity. Since the flame entity already is set to some usable settings you don't need to change any parameters, but the few that you may want to fool with are:

- Set the **MinScale** and **MaxScale** of the flame particles larger for a larger fire.

Figure 13.50
Rain in the game world.

Figure 13.51
The Flame entity in the game
(in the box in the corner).

- Set both the **MinUnitLife** and the **MaxUnitLife** of each flame particle higher so the flames drift upward longer, try 5 or 6 seconds.

- Change both the **SourceVariance** and the **DestVariance** to a larger value so the source and destination varies and the flame looks more natural.

- Make the **TotalLife** larger, and the flames will last longer.

AudioSource3D

Finally you can use the AudioSource3D entity to place a point in your level so that it will sound like a sound appears to emanate from that point. This entity maintains its position when the player moves around the level so that you can hear the crackle of fire from the barrel.

To do this, copy the "flame.wav" file from the companion CD-ROM and place it in the "audio" subfolder of your Reality Factory folder (which is C:\RealityFactory061\media\audio).

Place the entity into your level right next to the flame entity you placed previously and set the "szSoundFile" to "flames.wav".

As you near the barrel in the level, you will hear the sound of crackling flames grow louder. Also, of course, the sound will drop off as you walk away, mimicking the way in which sound works in the real world.

Now What?

Well, you just finished creating all the art and assets and have even done some of the planning that goes into making a game. I would hope that you come away wanting to learn more about games, game development, and computers in general. If this is the case, please look into the many fine books produced by The Coriolis Group. (No, the editors did not ask me to write this. I am a long-time fan of Coriolis books, and this has been a dream fulfilled to write for them.) Also, check out the Appendix at the end of this book to explore more resources in the area of game development that interests you.

I hope this book helps you to fulfill your dreams as a game developer.

Appendix

Game Art Resources

These game art resources are biased toward Web sites and companies that have active Web pages because, in my opinion, the Internet is the best and most up-to-date source of information for game development and related topics.

Useful Resources

Keep in mind that these resources are far from the only available resources. In fact, a mountain of information is currently available on many topics, and I would encourage you to always be on the lookout for new sources of information.

Why These Links?

I picked the links and resources in this appendix because, at the time of this writing, they contained a large list of other resources, such as *3D Links*, *The Game Development Search Engine*, and various game-news sites. The sum of online resources is vast and extensive—far too numerous for one book. The Web is ever fluid and changing, so an extensive cataloging effort would be a waste. I suggest, however, that you browse these links, bookmark the ones that you find to be the most useful, and then return to them at least once a month. You will find that the online communities are very supportive and knowledgeable. There are various forums that most of these online communities have for communicating with other artists.

The Web Site

Web sites for a company can range form a few pages like an online brochure, to a huge and constantly changing source of information. The more vibrant Web sites will offer mailing lists, forums and chat rooms—take advantage of all this!

The Mailing List

A mailing list is as it sounds, you get on a list and are emailed updates and announcements. Mailing lists function in many ways. You can get email from every individual that mails to the list address, but this can get to be a huge number of emails for an active list, so you can usually also get moderated lists, where only emails approved by the list master are sent out to the entire list, and you can also get the email list digest. This digest is one big email that contains all the emails from the list.

The Message Forum

The Message Forum is a place online where you can post messages under topics and threads. The typical forum will have many topic headings and then under those topics you can start a message thread with a post that has to do with the topic. Then people will usually respond to your post. I advise you to search the forums and get to know them before posting. Nothing is more aggravating than to have the same questions asked ten times a day because people don't bother looking at the messages to see if their question has already been answered. Most message boards also have search utilities and other tools to help you navigate them.

News Groups

News groups are similar to message forums in that you find a news group (NG) dedicated to your topic of interest, and then you can post questions and answers. Thousands of news groups exist. These groups can range from news groups about a certain product, topic, or person.

ICQ

ICQ (from the term "I Seek You") shows you when others, if they are in your list, are using ICQ are online. With ICQ, you can chat, send messages, files and URLs, or play games.

FAQs

The FAQ (Frequently Asked Question) is usually a text file that asks and answers the most frequently asked questions on a particular topic. The FAQ is the best way to come up to speed on a topic before posting questions that have been asked a million times.

Genesis3D-Related Resources

The following sections contain links to many resources on Genesis and Reality Factory. You can access them to find information, learn techniques about the applications, access tutorial files, and much more.

General Genesis Resources

This section tackles the general resources for Genesis3D. If you examine these Web sites, you can learn more about Genesis and supporting software.

The Genesis3D Home Page
www.genesis3d.com

Contains links and all the updated information you will need pertaining to Genesis3D.

Milkshape3D
www.swissquake.ch/chumbalum-soft

A low polygon count 3D package that can import and export many game model formats including the Genesis format.

WOG (World of Genesis)
www.gameznet.com/genesis

The best source for Genesis related information for newbie and professional alike.

Rabid Game—The Reality Factory
www.rabidgames.com

The tools that you encounter when you run Reality Factory are covered in Part II of this book, in Chapter 13.

University of Genesis3D
http://welcome.to/genesis3d-university

This site has a lot of tutorials and really solid Genesis3D content. This Web site is a must-visit for all Genesis users.

3D Sector
www.gen3d.de

This German and English language Web site contains news, tutorials, a forum, and a download area that contains a nice selection of game artist tools, levels, tutorial files, and more.

Genesis Games

This section contains a list of games made by using Genesis3D. If you spend a little time examining what these talents produced, you will develop a better vision of all that you can do with Genesis.

AI Wars
www.aiwars.com

First-person 3D real-time action/strategy hybrid, under development.

Henchmen
http://208.179.242.18/

This game features an outdoor area at the beginning of the game. The goal of Henchman wasn't to develop a commercial game; rather, it was intended to be a programming tutorial.

The Heir
www.ourfun.com

A 3D shooter under development.

TrilobiteShell
www.trilobiteworks.com

Trilobite is a game shell based on the Genesis3D rendering engine. A game shell is the code that organizes the capabilities of the rendering engine into a cohesive application—a game.

Cheese Frenzy
www.gametitan.com

In this Action game, the player gets the incredible perspective of a mouse who is on the hunt for his captured friend while collecting cheese bits. Avoiding enemies such as mouse traps, cats, and household dangers, the player has to scurry a boy or girl mouse through everyday household obstacles, collect cheese for points and power-up for more chances and speed boosts to exit before the timer goes off. The game play is simplistic, with the player having the option to concentrate on the score or finishing the plot. The Cheese Frenzy game contains numerous animated sequences, explaining the story before the beginning of each stage and at the end of game play. Each stage has its own levels or rooms of the house. Current stages are Suburban House, Country House, City House, Laboratory House, and Moon Base House being the grand finale with Boss Monster, Ratto. This game features a bright, stylized look that is appealing to both children and adults. The content of Cheeze Frenzy is mainly slapstick, non-gory, and child safe.

PAN—Ground Zero
http://members.home.net/g3k1d0/mainindex.html

The Prison Arena Network is multiplayer online combat fast and furious. Combining all of the classic deathmatch and traditional online variations, PAN throws the player into a life-or-death existence as an inmate in the most sadistic Prison Network ever conceived. Inmates of the Prison Arena Network are subjected to brutal hand-to-hand combat—forced to fight other inmates to survive.

SpaceBlast!
by Nitroheads
www.gfxspace.com

Space Blast is a fast and furious arcade-style multiplayer space combat game that will bring you and your friends many sleepless nights—when they finish developing it.

G-Sector
http://www.3dgamers.com/games/gsector/

The G-Sector effort is the boldest effort in freeware: a full 3D game using the Genesis 3D engine. It supports Glide and Direct3D for 3D acceleration. G-Sector is developed in-house by Freeform Interactive LLC, the owners of Ingava.com, FreeGamesWeb.com, GamesHEAD.com, and the FvF franchise.

G-Sector is a 3D action game based around hover-board combat—a hybrid between an "extreme game" and a third-person shooter. Players control the heroine Cyra as she rides her hover board through futuristic cities and arenas. Gameplay is based on using ramps and tricks to build velocity and avoid opponents' shots. Using a chase-cam and customizable mouse/keyboard interface, G-Sector should be familiar to players of the 3D shooter genre.

Features: 3D Graphics, 3rd Person View, and Extreme Hoverboard Combat Action.

Pack Rat
www.roguestudios.com

Crystal Interactive picked up the limited license to Pack Rat in August of 2000. The game is getting enhancements to the engine and the levels.

SOTA—Survivor of the Ages
www.alien-logic.com

"Survivor of the Ages" is a third-person RPG with some fighter game elements. It features a fully 3D world, populated by creatures of all virtues and kinds. SOTA also features rich textures and scenes along with original soundtracks. SOTA has some of the most advanced collision detection seen in games today. Each character has multiple damage areas distributed at key points. These points allow for precise control of the kind of damage the player wants to inflict on an enemy. There are many more fun and startling features in SOTA!

Miscellaneous Resources

In this section, you'll find the 3D game artist's mixed bag of goodies from free fonts and meshes, to textures and tutorials, and (of course) more!

Fonts 'n' Things
www.fontsnthings.com

Fonts are very useful for texture creation. On this Web site, you can find a lot of free fonts here and links to more sources of fonts.

Microsoft Typography
www.microsoft.com/typography/fontpack/default.htm

Microsoft Typography is the online resource for type users and type developers. From this page on Microsoft's Web site, you can download fonts that you can use with either Windows and Apple Macintosh computers.

1001 Freefonts
www.1001freefonts.com/fontfiles/main.htm

This site contains far more than just Windows fonts. If you have a need for Mac fonts, font tools, clipart, and so on, this is the place to surf.

Free PC Fonts
www.freepcfonts.com/index.html

This Web site contains a collection of links to other font sites. It's a nice place to start your search for "that perfect font."

3D RAPH
www.raph.com/3dartists

This Web site has lots of interviews with artists and tutorials. Also on the menu: a forum, an art gallery, a job center, and more links!

Turbo Squid
www.turbosquid.com

Turbo Squid is free, downloadable software used to buy and sell digital assets. This production tool will help digital artists find, preview, and acquire content that they need. Among Turbo Squid's uses are as follows:

- A clearinghouse where digital artists can make money selling their content

- A growing library with over 70,000 assets available for purchase or free

- An application that can run as a standalone or inside your favorite 2D and 3D programs

The 3D Studio
www.the3dstudio.com
Free pre-textured MAX models, free seamless textures, and free MAX tutorials.

Design

Of course, with a heading like "Design," you can expect some design-related material, and here are several sources and starting points for design articles and opinions, even some news Web sites for the latest in game design and game play.

Gamasutra
www.gamasutra.com

This Web site is the mother of all game-development sites. You can find articles and resources on all aspects of game development and design here.

Game Developer Search Engine
www.game-developer.com

A very full site that contains much of the information that you'll need for game development. Be sure and check out their affiliate sites.

Game Dev Net
www.gamedev.net

Another great source of development resources, this site also has an online glossary of terms.

GIG News
www.gignews.com

A source of game and game development news.

Lupine Games
www.lupinegames.com

A must-visit link site for wannabe developers. The topics are well rounded and well discussed.

The Inspiracy
www.theinspiracy.com

Noah Falstein maintains this site and has some great articles and information on this Web site.

International Game Developer Network
http://www.igdn.org/

IGDN is the International Game Developers Network, an un-incorporated membership association for the game developer community.

G.O.D. Games
www.godgames.com

These guys are Very Cool, and so is their Web site. Make sure that you read the Commandments and the Oracle.

Game News

The following Web sites have up-to-the-minute news (or, in some cases, really great archives) on many areas of game development and the industry.

Game Spy
www.gamespy.com

3D Action Planet
www.3dactionplanet.com

Looney Games
www.loonygames.com

Archives only but very useful.

Blue's News
www.bluesnews.com

Game Spot
www.gamespot.com

Adrenaline Vault
www.avault.com

Classic Gaming
www.classicgaming.com

Game-Jobs.com
www.gamejobs.com

This is the Web site for a European job recruiter who haunts the game and entertainment industry.

Happy Puppy
www.happypuppy.com

An excellent place to look around, read reviews, and see screen shots and videos that show what the cutting-edge game artists are up to.

Software and Development Engines
At these Web sites, you'll find software that you can employ to create graphics, game levels, or entire games.

Rabid Games
www.genesis3d.com/~rfactory

At this Web site, you'll find a set of tools that are an improvement on Genesis3D—featured in this book!

Genesis3D
www.genesis3d.com

The Open Source 3D engine featured in this book.

THE GIMP
www.gimp.org

A free GNU Photoshop-like application.

Photoshop
www.adobe.com

The Crystal Space Engine
http://crystal.linuxgames.com

The 3D Engines List
http://cg.cs.tu-berlin.de/~ki/engines.html

Books and Magazines

This section presents a selection of 3D-related magazines and books. There are many programming books and art books, but these are the few that are specifically dedicated to game design and development.

Books

Game Architecture and Design, Andrew Rollings and Dave Morris, The Coriolis Group; ISBN: 1576104257, Copyright 1999.

Game Developer's Marketplace, Ben Sawyer, Tor Berg, Alex Dunne, The Coriolis Group; ISBN: 1576101770, Copyright 1998.

Game Design: Secrets of the Sages, Marc Saltzman, Brady Games; ISBN: 0744000742, Copyright 2001.

Awesome Game Creation: No Programming Required, Luke Ahearn, Charles River Media; ISBN: 1886801487, Copyright 2000.

Designing 3D Games That Sell!, Luke Ahearn, Charles River Media; ISBN: 1584500433, Copyright 2001.

Magazines

Game Developer Magazine
www.gdmag.com

The premier game development magazine. An excellent resource for the latest industry news.

3D Design Magazine
www.3dgate.com/magazine

A great magazine and a great Web site.

Computer Graphics World
www.cgw.com

A great magazine and Web site. Check out their bookstore.

Conferences and Conventions

In this section, you'll find a listing of some of the more popular or applicable conferences and conventions for game developers.

Industry-Related Conferences

The Computer Game Developers Conference
www.cgdc.com

E3
www.e3expo.com

SIGGRAPH
www.siggraph.org

Modeling

3D Cafe
www.3dcafe.com

3D Links
www.3dlinks.com

Game Development Associations

This section lists the professional organizations and associations for game developers.

Computer Game Developers Association
www.cgda.org

Garage Games Dot Com
www.garagegames.com

Interactive Digital Software Association
www.idsa.com

International Game Developers Network
www.igdn.org

Index

1st-person view, 311

2D images. *See also* Images.
- aging, 7
- color balancing, 6
- color reduction, 4–5
- compression, 5
- defect removal, 6–7
- digital photos, 10–12
- filters, 4
- graphics tablets, 13
- hot spot removal, 6–7
- manipulating in Photoshop, 3–7
- online resources, 13–14
- sharpening, 8–9
- sizing images, 6, 188
- straightening images, 7
- tiling, 4
- weathering, 7

3D applications, creating 2D images, 14. *See also* Genesis3D; Reality Factory.

3D Studio Max models, 184

3DS Max exporters, 181

.3dt files, 181

3rd-person view, 311

22 Immutable Laws of Branding, 88–89

A

Acid-eaten metal logo, 99–100

Acquiring weapons, 291–292

Action recognition, interface design, 124

Actions palette, Photoshop, 153–154

Actions, Photoshop
- Actions menu, 154–155
- Actions palette, 153–154
- batch processing, 148–150
- overview, 152–153
- "rusted metal" action, 155–156

Actor Builder, 181

Actor Studio, 181

Actor Viewer, 181

Actors, 310, 311. *See also* Player parameters.

Adaptive palettes, 5

Advertising, designing logos for, 87

Aesthetic, interface design, 111, 126

Aging images
- ammo boxes, 77
- castle door, 83
- dirt, adding to complex objects, 76–77
- overview, 7
- stone textures, 101

Alpha masks, 280

Amateur designers' mistakes, 170, 171, 173

Ambient lighting, 256–257

Ammo boxes, 75–77

Amount setting, Unsharp Mask filter, 9

Angle attribute, 224

Animated bitmap sequences, 328–329

Animating models. *See also* Models.
- door animation, 251–253
- entities, 243–244
- keyframes, 242–243
- Model tab, 193
- platform animation, 251–253

teleportation effect, 324–325
turning models into doors, 317–319
windmill animation, 244–251
Apocalyptic metal logo, 99–100
Arches brush, 201–203
Arcing electrical faults, 332–333
Area brushes, 207, 236
Area effects, 340–341
Art and Science of Level Design, The, 168–169
Assets, 67–68, 162
Atmosphere of levels
changing using lighting, 257
impact on level construction, 163–164
impact on texture requirements, 65
Atmospheric dirt, 76
Attribute entity, 291–292, 313
Attribute values, player attributes, 312
AttributeInfoFile, 311
Attributes
attribute display, HUD, 283
Attribute entity, 313
brush attributes, 206–207
faces of brushes. *See* Face attributes.
horizontal attribute display, 285
numeric attribute display, 285
player attributes, 311–313
projectile attribute display, 287–288
values, player attributes, 312
vertical attribute display, 284
weapon attribute display, 288–291
Audio effects. *See also* Audio effects entities.
during player movement, 313–314
menu sounds, 295–296
Audio effects entities
AudioSource3D entity, 315, 349
SoundtrackToggle entity, 316
StreamingAudioProxy entity, 317
Audio file types, 315
AudioSource3D entity, 315, 349
Automating texture creation
batch processing, 148–150
contact sheets, 150–151
custom brushes, 151

duplicating images, 145
exporting images to Web sites, 146–148
keyboard shortcuts, 138–139, 140
multiple versions of base textures, 139, 141–144
thumbnails, 146–148, 150–151
Averill, Ed, 275

B

Background art, menu design, 129–130
Background graphics, menus, 293
Backups, default Genesis3D files, 186
Banners, 234–235
Barriers in interfaces, minimizing, 123–124
Base textures. *See also Names of specific textures.*
creating, 35–36
creating advanced textures, 69–72
depth, adding, 71–72
in level development cycle, 166
lighting, adjusting, 34–35
raw images, 59
reasons for using, 18
selecting for game worlds, 18–23
tileability, 19, 21–24
working textures, 59
Batch processing in Photoshop, 148–150
Beginning designers' mistakes, 170, 171, 173
Beta testing interface, 123
Bitmaps
alpha masks, 280
animated bitmap sequences, 328–329
bitmapped fonts, 277
Blades, windmill, 245–248
Blending images
cleaning up tiled textures, 23
color balancing, 6
Blending mode keyboard shortcuts, Photoshop, 138, 140
Bleszinski, Cliff, 168, 169
Blocky construction, 171
.bmp files, 182
Bouncing light, 224
Brush Adjustment mode, world editor, 214

Brushed metal texture, 37–39

Brushes

adding, 214

arches, 201–203

brush attributes, 206–207

cloning to create additional rooms, 226

cones, 201

cubes, 199

custom brushes, 151

cut brush, 205, 206, 226–227

cylinders, 200–201

defined, 198

faces. *See* Faces of brushes.

grouping items, 228–229

hollow brush, 204

potential brushes, 213

primitives, 198

selecting, 214

sheet brush, 205–206

solid brush, 203, 206

spheres, 199–200

stairs, 201

Template tab, Genesis3D world editor, 192

Texture Lock attribute, 220

zones, 340–341

Bryce, 14–15

Budgeting assets, 162

Building-related textures, 68

Business cards, designing logos for, 87

Buttons

interface design, 127

menu button states, 131

menu layout, 294, 297–299

C

Camera mode, world editor, 213–214

Camera placement, 311

Capabilities of Genesis3D, 182–183

Carved-from-stone logo, 100–103

Castle design project

additional rooms, creating, 226–227

banners, 234–235

first room, creating, 214–217

grates over skylights, 230

lava trenches, 231–233

lighting, 265–271

skyboxes, 229–230

texture planning, 173–177

Castle door, 81–84

ChangeLevel entity, 323–324

Character Creation screen, 132–134

Checkboxes, menu layout, 299–300

Chipped stone, 101

City-street level project

additional buildings, 344–345

audio effects, 349

environment setup, 346

first building, 343

particle effects, 346–347

world space, 342–343

Cleaning images, 6–7

Clip brushes, 206–207

Cloning brushes, 226

Cobblestones, 31–35

Collision with models, changing levels, 323–324

Color

color balancing, 6

color considerations for logos, 89–90

color reduction, 4–5

color scheme, impact on level design, 163

menu color scheme, 129

Color adjustment keyboard shortcuts, Photoshop, 138, 140

Color Burn mode, 77

Command panel, Genesis3D world editor, 191–194

Compass section, HUD INI file, 281–282

Compile Manager dialog box, 256–257

Complete textures, 60

Complex objects, building. *See also* Castle design project; City-street level project.

ammo boxes, 75–77

castle door, 81–84

fantasy shield, 96–97

fantasy sword, 92–95

problematic images, rebuilding, 78–79

signs, 78–79

spell-book cover, 103–106

Compression, 5

Computer status display, 110, 112–116

Cone brush, 201

Consistency

hidden functions, 121

interface design, 111, 118–124

in level development cycle, 167

navigation, 121–123

Console messages, Genesis3D world editor, 193

Console tab, Genesis3D world editor, 193

Constructing levels. *See* Level construction and design.

Contact Sheet II plug-in, 150–151

Control window, interface design, 124

Conventions

hidden functions, 121

interface design, 111, 118–124

navigation, 121–123

picking up game items, 119–120

Corona entity, 260, 264, 270–271, 329–330

Corporate logos, 87. *See also* Logos.

Corroding metal with Splatter filter, 81, 83

Cost considerations for logos, 90

Craquelure Filter, 80, 101

Create Arch dialog box, 201–203

Create Box dialog box, 199

Create Cone dialog box, 203

Create Cylinder dialog box, 200–201

Create Spheroid dialog box, 199–200

Create Staircase dialog box, 201

Crosshair graphic, 295

Cube brush, 199

Cursor graphic, menu layout, 294–295

Custom brushes, 151

Cut brush, 205, 206, 226–227, 236

Cylinder brush, 200–201

D

Deane, Ralph, 275

DeathMatchStart entity, 225

Decal textures, 68

Decals, creating, 205–206

Deception in level design, 170

Deep-space nebula textures, 40–42

Deep textures, 21

Default face attributes, 225

Default Genesis3D files, backing up, 186

Defect removal, 6–7

Define Brush command, 151

Demo level, 167

Depth, adding to textures, 71–72

Design Commandments, 169–170

Design considerations. *See also* Level construction and design.

logos, 87–90

Design document, in level development cycle, 166, 167

Designing levels. *See* Level construction and design.

Detail brushes, 207, 236

Development environment

impact on texture requirements, 66–67

level development cycle, 166–168

Device drivers, 185

Diablo 2, 126

Diablo Isometric view, 311

Digital images

creating textures from, 10–12

flash burn, removing, 78–79

online resources, 13

problematic images, rebuilding, 78–79

Dirt, adding to complex objects, 76–77, 106

Distance fogging, 305, 306, 346. *See also* Fog.

Distortion

chaotic moving textures, 334–335

water surfaces, 183–184

Divisions in game world, 65–67

Documentation, interface design, 112, 127–128

Door entity

Genesis3D, 244

Reality Factory, 317–319

Doors

door animation, 251–253

between rooms, 226–227

triggering, 319, 321–322

turning models into doors, 317–319

DoorTrigger entity, 321–322
Draw Scale attribute, 222
Drawing tablets, 13
Drivers, 185
Duplicating images, 145
Dynamic lighting
    Dynamic Light entity, Genesis3D, 259,
        262–263, 269–270
    dynamic RGB lighting, 183
    DynamicLight entity, Reality Factory, 330–332

E

EChaos entity, 334–335
Editing keyboard shortcuts, Photoshop, 138, 140
Editors. *See also* World editor.
    IniEditor, 275–277
    rfEdit, 275
Efficiency of use, interface design, 111, 125
Electric Bolt entity, Genesis3D, 260, 265
Electric Bolt Terminus entity, Genesis3D, 260, 265
Electrical faults, arcing, 332–333
ElectricBolt entity, Reality Factory, 332–333
ElectricBoltTerminus entity, Reality Factory, 333
Empty brushes, 206
Engines, impact on texture requirements, 66–67
Entities. *See also Names of specific entities.*
    adding, 214
    animating models, 243–244
    grouping and naming, 193
    overview, 192
    Reality Factory entities, 279
    selecting, 214
EnvAudioSetup entity, 313–314
Envelopes, designing logos for, 87
Environment, development
    impact on texture requirements, 65
    level development cycle, 166–168
Environmental setup entities
    EnvironmentSetup entity, 305–306, 346
    PlayerSetup entity, 307–310
    PlayerStart entity, 304–305
EnvironmentSetup entity, 305–306, 346
Error messages, Genesis3D installation, 185–186

Error prevention, interface design, 111, 124
Error recognition, interface design, 111, 126–127
Events, animating models, 243
EverQuest, 119–120
Existing games, using images from, 14
Exiting unwanted states, interface design, 110, 118
Extensions, file type, 181–182

F

F/x textures, 68
Face Adjustment mode, 214, 217–218, 218
Face attributes
    Angle attribute, 224
    default attributes, 225
    Draw Scale attribute, 222
    Flat attribute, 222
    Flip Horizontal attribute, 224
    Flip Vertical attribute, 224
    Full Bright attribute, 220
    Gouraud attribute, 222
    Light attribute, 222
    Light Map Scale attribute, 223
    MipMap Bias attribute, 224
    Mirror attribute, 218
    overview, 217–218
    Reflectivity Scale attribute, 224
    Sky attribute, 219
    Texture Lock attribute, 220, 222
    Texture Offset attribute, 222
    Transparency Value attribute, 224
    Transparent attribute, 224
Face Attributes dialog box, 218
Face editing, 215–217, 342–343
Faces of brushes
    defined, 206
    face editing, 215–217, 342–343
    selecting, 216
    transparency, 224
Fantasy environment, impact on level design, 163
Fantasy logo
    magic gold lettering, 98
    shield element, 92–95
    sword element, 92–95

Federal registration of logos, 91

File operations keyboard shortcuts, Photoshop, 138, 140

FileFind tool, 277

Files

audio file types, 315

default Genesis3D files, backing up, 186

file type extensions, 181–182

FileFind tool, 277

log files, 278–279

Filters, 4. *See also Names of specific filters.*

Final level, 166

First-person view genre, 62

Flame effects, 338–340, 347–348. *See also Dynamic lighting.*

Flame entity, 338–340, 347–348

Flash burns, removing, 6–7

Flat attribute, 222

Flexibility, interface design, 111, 125

Flickering lights. *See Dynamic lighting.*

Flip Horizontal attribute, 224

Flip Vertical attribute, 224

FlipBook entity, 328–329

FloatingParticles entity, 333–334

Flocking brush option, 207

Floor tiles, 73–74

Fog

distance fogging, 305, 306, 346

fog lights, 183, 260, 264, 270

morphing fog fields, 325–326

Fog Light entity, 260, 264, 270

Foley sounds, 313–314

Fonts

bitmapped, 277

installing, 98

menu layout, 295

online resources, 13, 98

Fonts & Things, 98

Fountain of particles, 336–338, 346–347

Framerate, in level design, 170

Front view, Genesis3D world editor, 191

Full Bright attribute, 220

G

Game engines, impact on texture requirements, 66–67

Game-formatted textures, 60

Game interface. *See* Interface design.

Game logos. *See also* Logos.

acid-eaten apocalyptic logos, 99–100

carved-from-stone logos, 100–103

fantasy logos, 91–98

overview, 87, 91

spell-book cover logos, 103–106

Game play points, accenting using lighting, 257–258

Game setting, impact on texture requirements, 65

Game setup, error prevention, 124

Game technology, impact on texture requirements, 66–67

Game worlds

base textures, selecting, 18–23

Default Light Level option, 256–257

world divisions, impact on texture requirements, 65–67

Games, existing, using images from, 14

Garage of Doom, 344–345

GEdit. *See* World editor.

Genesis3D

3D Studio Max models in, 184

animation effects. *See* Models.

capabilities, 182–183

components and tools, 181

features, 183–184

file type extensions, 181–182

Genesis3D 1.1, 180

installing, 184–186

Jet3D, 180

light entities, 258–265

Open Source License, 181

overview, 180–181

physics system, 184

Reality Factory, 181

render options, 184

system requirements, 182

troubleshooting installation and startup, 185–186

vertex manipulation, 171
WildTangent, Inc., 180
world editor, 189–194
Genres, impact on texture requirements, 62–64
Geometric shapes. *See also* Brushes.
    arches brush, 201–203
    cones, 201
    cubes, 199
    cylinders, 200–201
    groups, creating, 228–229
    spheres, 199–200
    stairs, 201
Geometry
    animating. *See* Models.
    grouping and naming, 193, 228–229
Gold leaf, 102
Gold lettering, 98
Gouges, 83
Gouraud attribute, 222
Graphics tablets, 13
Grates over skylights, 230
Grid Settings dialog box, world editor, 209
Grouping items, 193, 228–229
Groups tab, Genesis3D world editor, 193
GTest, 181

H

Halos, 260
Hanging banners, 234–235
Hardware requirements
    Genesis3D, 182
    Reality Factory, 278
Hazy lights, 260
Heads Up Display. *See* HUD.
Help and documentation, interface design, 112, 127–128
Heuristics, 111
Hidden functions, interface design, 121
Hidden items, 193
High value, player attributes, 312
Highlights, 71–72
Hint brushes, 207, 236
Hit Man, 119

Holes in levels, 225
Hollow brushes, 204, 207
Horizontal attribute display, HUD, 285
Horizontal tiling, 28
Hot spot removal, 6–7
HUD
    activating and deactivating elements, 287
    attribute display, 283
    compass element, 281–282
    horizontal attribute display, 285
    HUD.ini file, 281
    interface design, 113–115
    numeric attribute display, 285
    player position element, 283
    projectile attribute display, 287–288
    vertical attribute display, 284
    weapon attribute display, 288–291
HUD.ini file, 281
Hull thickness of hollow brushes, 204, 207
Human interface objects, 117

I

Icons, interface design, 116–117
Image formats, compression, 5
Image size, 4–5, 6, 188
Image sources
    3D applications, 14
    creating images in other applications, 14–15
    digital photos, 10–12
    existing games, 14
    graphics tablets, 13
    online resources, 13–14
    scanned images, 8–9
Images. *See also* 2D images; Textures.
    adding to texture libraries, 187
    alpha masks, 280
    background art, menu design, 129–130
    batch processing, 148–150
    button images, 131
    complete textures, 60
    contact sheets, 150–151
    custom brushes, 151
    deleting from texture libraries, 187

duplicating and laying out, 145
exporting to Web sites, 146–148
game-formatted textures, 60
graphics tablets, 13
importing into texture libraries, 188
manipulating in Photoshop, 3–7
menu graphics. *See* Menu layout, Reality Factory.
multiple versions of base textures, 139, 141–144
online resources, 13–14
problematic images, rebuilding, 78–79
raw images, 59
scanned images, 8–9
texture creation, 3–4
thumbnails, 146–148, 150–151
tiling, 23–28, 30–35
TPACK, 186–188
unflattened layers, 59, 139, 141–144
working textures, 59
Indicator, compass, 281–282
Indoor levels, impact on level design, 163
Ini files, editing, 275–277
IniEditor, 275–277
Initial value, player attributes, 312
Inner Glow effect, 102
Installing
fonts, 98
Genesis3D, 184–186
Reality Factory, 278–279
Instruction sets, texture planning, 177
Interface design
barriers, minimizing, 123–124
beta testing, 123
hidden functions, 121
menus. *See* Menu design.
multiple pathways, 124
navigation, 121–123
real-world conventions, 110, 116–117
system status display, 110, 112–116
usability principles, 110, 112
user control, 110, 118

J
Jet3D, 180

K
Keyboard remap box, 302–303
Keyboard shortcuts, 138–139, 140, 214
Keyframe window, Models tab, 243
Keyframes, 242–243

L
Language, in interface design, 110, 116–117
Lava brush option, 207
Lava trenches, 231–233
Law of Color, 89–90
Law of Shape, 88–89
Layers, Photoshop
keyboard shortcuts, 138, 140
unflattened layers, 59, 139, 141–144
Laying out images, 145
Leather spell-book cover logo, 103–106
Letterhead, designing logos for, 87
Lettering, 98, 100–103. *See also* Fonts.
Level construction and design
additional buildings, adding, 344–345
additional rooms, adding, 226–227
atmosphere of level, 163
bad lighting, 173
bad textures, 170
banners, 234–235
beginners' sins, 170–173
blocky construction, 171
budgeting assets, 162
deception and trickery, 170
demo level, 168
Design Commandments, 169–170
environment setup, 346
face editing, 342–343
first building, creating, 343
first room, creating, 214–217

groups, creating, 228–229

holes in levels, 225

level development cycle, 166–168

lights, magical, 231–233

location of level, 163

overview, 162

peer criticism, 169

planning levels, 164–165

player-start position, 225

prototype level, 166, 167

purpose of level, 163

Reality Factory, 341–349

reevaluating existing content, 169

research, 169

rivalries between designers, 169

skyboxes, 229–230

test level, 168

testing maps, 225

texture planning, 173–177

time period of level, 163

Level editor. *See* World editor.

Levels, changing on collision with models, 323–324

Libraries. *See* Texture libraries.

Light attribute, 222

Light entities

adding, 261–262

Corona entity, 260, 264, 270–271

Dynamic Light entity, Genesis3D, 259, 2 62–263, 269–270

DynamicLight entity, Reality Factory, 330–332

Electric Bolt entity, Genesis3D, 260, 265

Electric Bolt Terminus entity, Genesis3D, 260, 265

ElectricBolt entity, Reality Factory, 332–333

ElectricBoltTerminus entity, Reality Factory, 333

Fog Light entity, 260, 264, 270

Light entity, 259, 262, 266–269

properties, 262–265

Spotlight entity, 260, 263, 270

Light entity, 259, 262, 266–269

Light Map Scale attribute, 223, 235

Lighting. *See also* Light entities.

adjusting for textures, 34–35

amateur designers' mistakes, 173

atmosphere, changing, 257

Default Light Level option, 256–257

detail brushes, 236

dynamic lighting, 183, 259, 262–263, 269–270, 330–332

fog lights, 183, 260, 264, 270

Full Bright attribute, 220

game play points, accenting, 257–258

Gouraud attribute, 222

Light attribute, 222

Light Map Scale attribute, 223

lights, magical, 231–233

on merged layers, 105

mirrors, 183

radiosity, 236

Reflectivity Scale attribute, 224

sunlight, 257

Lightning bolts, 260, 332–333

Location of levels, 163

Log files, 278–279

Logos

acid-eaten metal logo, 99–100

in advertising, 87

audience considerations, 87

carved-from-stone logo, 100–103

color considerations, 89–90

cost considerations, 90

design guidelines, 88–90

fantasy logo, 92–99

game *vs.* corporate logos, 87

magic gold lettering, 98

marketing considerations, 88

overview, 86

shape considerations, 88–89

simplicity, 88

spell-book cover logo, 103–106

on stationery, 87

trademark protection, 90–91

Lossy and lossless compression, 5

Low value, player attributes, 312

M

Main menu, 298
Marble texture, 73–74
Marketing considerations for logos, 88
Masonry textures, 68
Menu design
    3D shooter menu, 129–134
    background art, 129–130
    button state images, 131
    Character Creation screen, 132–134
    color scheme, 129
    menu elements, 128–129
Menu layout, Reality Factory
    background graphics, 293
    button images, 294
    buttons, 297–298
    checkboxes, 299–300
    cursor graphic, 294–295
    fonts, 295
    main menu, 298
    menu sounds, 295–296
    remap box, 302–303
    saved game boxes, 303–304
    scroll-box images, 294, 301
    slider images, 294, 301
    text lines on buttons, 298–299
    title images, 293–294, 296
Menus. *See also* Interface design.
    Actions menu, 154–155
    designing. *See* Menu design.
    layout. *See* Menu layout, Reality Factory.
Messages
    console messages, Genesis3D world editor, 193
    error messages, Genesis3D installation, 185–186
Metal textures
    in 3D shooters, 68
    acid-eaten, apocalyptic metal logo, 99–100
    brushed metal texture, 37–39
    corroding with Splatter filter, 81, 83
    decorative metal caps, 103–106
    rust texture, 36–37
    "rusted metal" action, 155–156
    simulating with Render Lighting Filter, 92, 93
Metaphors, interface design, 110, 116–117
Minimalist interface design, 111, 126–127
Minimizing barriers in interfaces, 123–124
MipMap Bias attribute, 224
Mirror attribute, 218
Mirrors, Genesis3D, 183
Model Controller entity, 244, 250
Model Name drop-down list , Models tab, 241
Models
    animating. *See* Animating models.
    changing levels on collision with, 323–324
    creating, 240–241
    door animation, 251–253
    Models tab, 241–242
    motions, creating, 243
    pivot point, 242
    platform animation, 251–253
    turning into doors, 317–319
    turning into moving platforms, 319–321
    windmill animation, 244–251
Models tab, Genesis3D world editor, 193, 241–242
Mood, impact on level design, 163
Morgan, Terry, 275
MorphingField entity, 325–326
Motions, creating for models, 243
Mouseover graphic, 298
Moving Platform entity, Genesis3D, 244
Moving platforms, 251–253, 319–321
Moving textures, 334–335
MovingPlatform entity, Reality Factory, 319–321
Mud texture, 49

N

Naming conventions, texture libraries, 60–61
Navigation, interface design, 121–123
Nebula textures, 40–42
Noise filter, 77
Normal button state, 131
Numeric attribute display, HUD, 285

O

Object recognition, interface design, 124
Objects acquired by players, 313
Offsets, tiling textures, 23
One-faced brush, 205–206
One-texel rule, 235
Online image resources, 13–14
Open Source software, 180, 181
Option recognition, interface design, 124
Organic textures, 68
Orthographic view genre, 63
Outdoor levels, impact on level design, 163
Outer Glow Layer Effect, 77, 84

P

Paint, peeling, 80
Palette keyboard shortcuts, Photoshop, 138, 140
Palettes, color reduction, 4–5
Parchment texture, 50–51
Particle systems
    fountain of particles, 336–338, 346–347
    predefined particle effect styles, 326–328
    rain of particles, 335–336, 347
    upwardly moving particles, 333–334
ParticleSystemProxy entity, 326–328, 346–347
Peeling paint, 80
Peer criticism, in level design, 169
Perfectly square images, 6
Performance
    area brushes, 236
    budgeting assets, 162
    cut brush, 236
    detail brushes, 236
    framerate, in level design, 170
    hint brushes, 236
    Light Map Scale attribute, 235
    one-texel rule, 235
    perfectly square images, 6
Perspective
    correction, 7
    impact on level design, 164

Photos
    creating textures from, 10–12
    flash burn, removing, 78–79
    online resources, 13
    problematic images, rebuilding, 78–79
Photoshop
    Actions, 152–156
    aging images, 7
    base textures, creating, 35–36
    batch processing, 148–150
    color reduction, 4–5
    contact sheets, 150–151
    custom brushes, 151
    image compression, 5
    keyboard shortcuts, 138–139, 140
    layers, 59
    Picture Package command, 145
    rust texture, 36–37
    tiling textures, 23–25
    unflattened layers, 59, 139, 141–144
    Unsharp Mask filter, 8–9
    weathering images, 7
    Web Photo Gallery command, 146–148
Physics system, Genesis3D, 184
Picture Package command, 145
Pivot point, setting for models, 242
Pixel transparency, 280
Planning levels, 164–165
Plasma effects, 338–340
Platforms, moving, 251–253, 319–321
Player parameters
    appearance, 307–310
    attributes, 311–313
    camera placement, 311
    Foley sounds, 313–314
    object acquisition, 313
    start position, 225, 304–305
    view, 310, 311
Player POV, impact on texture requirements, 62–64
PlayerSetup entity, 307–311
PlayerStart entity, 304–305
Polished surfaces. *See* Mirrors, Genesis3D.

Position section, HUD INI file, 283
Positioning
    player starting point, 304–305
    weapons, 290–291
Potential brushes, 213
POV, impact on texture requirements, 62–64
Precision, in level planning, 165
Primitives, 198
Principles, usability. *See* Usability principles.
Printing, cost considerations for logos, 90
Problematic images, rebuilding, 78–79
Processing images, 148–150
Projectile attribute display, HUD, 287–288
Projects. *See* Castle design project; City-street level project.
Properties, light entities, 262–265
Prototype level, 166, 167
Purpose of levels, in level design, 163

R

Rabid Games, 274–275
Radiosity, 236
Radius function, DynamicLight entity, 263, 331
Radius setting, Unsharp Mask filter, 9
Rain entity, 335–336, 347
Random stuff, adding dirt to complex objects, 77
Real-world conventions, interface design, 110, 116–117
Realistic environment, impact on level design, 163
Reality Factory
    additional buildings, adding, 344–345
    audio effects entities, 314–317
    entities, 279. *See also Names of specific entities.*
    environmental setup entities, 304–314, 346
    FileFind tool, 277
    first building, creating, 343
    hardware requirements, 278
    HUD, 281–287
    IniEditor, 275–277
    installing, 278–279
    level construction and design, 341–349
    menus. *See* Menu layout, Reality Factory.

overview, 181, 274–275
rfEdit, 275
special effects entities, 324–340
troubleshooting, 278–279
TTF2Font tool, 277
VFS Explorer, 277
world model helpers, 317–324
Realityfactory.log file, 278–279
Recall, interface design, 111, 124
Recognition, interface design, 111, 124
Recovery from errors, interface design, 111, 126–127
Redo command, interface design, 110, 118
Reevaluating existing content, 169
Reflective surfaces. *See* Mirrors, Genesis3D.
Reflectivity Scale attribute, 224
Registering company names, 90
Registering logos, 91
Remap box, 302–303
Removing defects from images, 6–7
Render Lighting Filter, 92, 93
Render speed
    area brushes, 236
    cut brush, 236
    detail brushes, 236
    hint brushes, 236
    Light Map Scale attribute, 235
    one-texel rule, 235
Research, in level design, 169
Resources, packaging, 277
RfEdit
    additional buildings, adding, 344–345
    face editing, 342–343
    first building, creating, 343
    overview, 275
RGB dynamic lighting, 183
Ries, Al, 88
Ries, Laura, 88
Ripped-edge parchment texture, 50–51
Ripple filter, 101
Rivalries, in level design, 169
Role-playing games, Character Creation screen, 132–134

Rollover button state, 131

Rooms, creating

additional rooms, 226

banners, 234–235

doors between rooms, 226–227

first room, 214–217

grates, 230

grouping items, 228–229

lights, magical, 231–233

skyboxes, 229–230

skylights, 230

Rotating textures, 224

RPGs, Character Creation screen, 132–134

Rust texture, 36–37

"Rusted metal" action, 155–156

S

Saved game boxes, 303–304

Scaling

actors, 310

textures, 222

Scanned images, 8–9

Scripting language, interface design, 124

Scroll-box images, menu layout, 294, 301

Seams

erasing, 25, 27

horizontal and vertical tiling, 28

matching image seams to tile seams, 45

Security, logo trademark protection, 90–91

Select mode, world editor, 214

Selected button state, 131

Selection keyboard shortcuts, Photoshop, 138, 140

Setting of game, impact on texture requirements, 65

Shadows

adding depth to textures, 71–72

Light Map Scale attribute, 223

on merged layers, 105

Shape considerations for logos, 88–89

Sharpening images, 8–9

Sheet brushes, 205–206, 207

Shield element, fantasy logo, 92–95

Shimmer effect, 184

Shortcuts, interface design, 124

Side view, Genesis3D world editor, 191

Sign textures, 68

Signs, 78–79, 142–143

Simplicity

interface design, 123–125

logo design, 88

Size of buttons, interface design, 127

Size of images, 4–5, 5, 6, 188

Sketching, 165, 166

Sky attribute, 219

Sky tab, Genesis3D world editor, 193

Skyboxes

creating, 10, 229–230

grates, 230

Sky attribute, 219

Sky tab, Genesis3D world editor, 193

skylights, 230

Skylights, 230

SkyPaint, 10

Slider images, menu layout, 294, 301

Solid brush, 203, 206

Sounds

during player movement, 313–314

menu sounds, 295–296

source, specifying, 315, 349

streaming audio, 316

toggling between soundtracks, 316

SoundtrackToggle entity, 316

Source of sounds, specifying, 315, 349

Space base wall, 52–55

Special effects entities, Reality Factory

Corona entity, 329–330

DynamicLight entity, 330–332

EChaos entity, 334–335

ElectricBolt entity, 332–333

ElectricBoltTerminus entity, 333

Flame entity, 338–340, 347–348

FlipBook entity, 328–329

FloatingParticles entity, 333–334

MorphingField entity, 325–326

ParticleSystemProxy entity, 326–328, 346–347
Rain entity, 335–336, 347
Spout entity, 336–338
Teleporter entity, 324–325
TeleportTarget entity, 325
Sphere brush, 199–200
Splatter brush strokes, 102
Splatter filter, 81, 83
Spotlight entity, 260, 263, 270
Spout entity, 336–338
Square images, 6
Stairs brush, 201
Standards
hidden functions, 121
interface design, 111, 118–124
navigation, 121–123
picking up game items, 119–120
Star field textures, 39–42
Starting point, positioning player, 304–305
State registration of logos, 91
Stationery, designing logos for, 87
Status information, interface design, 110, 112–116
Stone
carved-from-stone logo, 100–103
stone texture, 46–48
Storyboarding, in level development cycle, 166
Straightening images, 7
StreamingAudioProxy entity, 317
Sunlight, faking using lighting, 257
Sword element, fantasy logo, 92–95
Symbols, interface design, 116–117
System-oriented language, interface design, 110, 116–117
System requirements
Genesis3D, 182
Reality Factory, 278
System status display, interface design, 110, 112–116

T

Tablets, graphics, 13
Technical support, interface design, 127–128

Technology, game development environment, 66–67
Teleporter entity, 324–325
TeleportTarget entity, 325
Template mode, world editor, 214
Template tab, Genesis3D world editor, 192
Terminology, interface design, 110, 116–117
Terrain textures, 68
Test level, 166, 167
Testing maps, 225
Texels, one-texel rule, 235
Texture libraries
adding textures, 187
asset lists, 67–68
castle level design, 175–177
complete textures, 60
creating, 187–188
deleting textures, 187
game-formatted textures, 60
importing textures, 188
naming conventions, 60–61
organizing, 58–61, 67–68, 178
raw images, 59
setting up for GEdit, 208, 215
subdirectory structure, 60
Textures tab, Genesis3D world editor, 192
TPACK, 186–188
.txl files, 182
working textures, 59
Texture Lock attribute, 220, 222
Texture Offset attribute, 222
Texture Packer, 181. *See also* TPACK.
Texture palettes. *See* Texture libraries.
Texture planning, 176–177
Texture requirements
determining, 61
divisions in game world, 65–67
game genres, 62–64
player POV, 62
setting and atmosphere, 65
technology and development environment, 66–67
Texture sets. *See* Texture libraries.

Textured view, Genesis3D world editor, 190–191, 213–214, 215

Textures. *See also Names of specific textures.*

    adding to texture libraries, 187

    amateur-created textures, 170

    applying to faces, 215–217

    base textures, 18–23, 35 36

    capturing from digital photos , 10–12

    complete textures, 60

    complex objects, building, 75–84

    creating, 3–4, 35–36

    creating from base textures, 69–72

    custom brushes, 151

    deleting from texture libraries, 187

    depth, adding, 71–72

    dirt, adding to objects, 76–77

    distorting chaotically, 334–335

    flipping horizontally or vertically, 224

    game-formatted textures, 60

    highlights, 71–72

    importing into texture libraries, 188

    lighting, adjusting, 34–35

    multiple versions of base textures, 139, 141–144

    online resources, 13

    replacing with animated bitmaps, 328–329

    required for games. *See* Texture requirements.

    rotating with Angle attribute, 224

    scaling with Draw Scale attribute, 222

    selecting base textures, 18–23

    shadows, 71–72

    texture libraries, organizing, 58–61, 67–68, 178

    tileability, 19, 21–24

    TPACK, 186–188

    unflattened layers, 59, 139, 141–144

    wear and tear, adding to objects, 76–77

Textures tab, Genesis3D world editor, 192

Thickness of hollow brushes, 204, 207

Third-person view genre, 62

Threshold setting, Unsharp Mask filter, 9

Thumbnails

    contact sheets, 150–151

    Web Photo Gallery, 146–148

Tiling

    horizontal tiling, 28

    lighting, adjusting, 34–35

    natural images, 30–35

    overview, 4, 23–25

    problematic images, 25–27

    seams, 25, 27, 45

    testing tiled images, 27

    tileability of textures, 19, 21–24

    vertical tiling, 28

Time period of levels, 163

Title images, menu layout, 293–294, 296

Toolbar, Genesis3D world editor, 189–190

Tools, keyboard shortcuts, Photoshop, 138, 140

Top view, world editor, 190–191

TPACK, 181, 186–188

Trademark protection for logos, 90–91

Transparency, 280

Transparency Value attribute, 224

Transparent attribute, 224

Tree textures, 68

Trespasser, 120

Trickery, in level design, 170

Trigger entity, 321–322

Triggering

    doors, 319, 321–322

    moving platforms, 321

    triggers, 322

Troubleshooting

    compiling and running levels, 225

    error recognition in interface design, 127

    help and documentation, 127–128

    installation and startup, Genesis3D, 185–186

    Reality Factory installation, 278–279

TTF2Font tool, 277

.txl files, 182, 215

U

Undo command, interface design, 110, 118

Unreal, 164

Unreal Tournament, 113–116, 117, 119

Unsharp Mask filter, 8–9

Unwanted states, exiting, 110, 118

Usability principles

    aesthetic and minimalist design, 111, 126

    consistency and standards, 111, 118–124

    error prevention, 111, 124

    error recognition and recovery, 111, 127

    flexibility and efficiency of use, 111, 125

    help and documentation, 111, 127–128

    match between system and real world, 110, 116–117

    overview, 110, 112

    recognition rather than recall, 111, 124

    user control and freedom, 110, 118

    visibility of system status, 110, 112–116

User interface. *See* Interface design.

V

Values, player attributes, 312

Vehicle-based view genre, 63

Verisimilitude, 198

Vertex manipulation, Genesis3D and, 171

Vertical tiling, 28

VFS Explorer, 277

View of game world

    camera placement, 311

    impact on texture requirements, 62–64

    player parameters, 310, 311

Views keyboard shortcuts, Photoshop, 138, 140

W

Wall thickness of hollow brushes, 204, 207

Walls, 52–55, 144

Water brush option, 207

Water surface distortion, 183

.wav files, 182

Wavy brush attribute, 207

Weapons

    acquiring, 291–292

    crosshair graphic, 295

    positioning, 290–291

    projectile attribute display, HUD, 287–288

    weapon attribute display, HUD, 288–291

Wear and tear, adding to complex objects, 76–77

Weather, impact on level design, 163

Weathering images

    ammo boxes, 77

    castle door, 83

    dirt, adding to complex objects, 76–77

    overview, 7

Web Photo Gallery command, 146–148

Wet mud texture, 49

Wet stone texture, 48

WildTangent, Inc., 180

Windmill animation, 244–251

Window brushes, 206

Wood textures, 42–46, 68, 81–84

World editor. *See also* RfEdit.

    Camera mode, 213–214

    command panel, 191–194

    Console tab, 193

    description of, 181

    editing modes, 213–214

    Front view, 191

    grid settings, 209

    Groups tab, 193

    Models tab, 193

    Select mode, 214

    Side view, 191

    Sky tab, 193

    starting, 213, 214

    Template mode, 214

    Template tab, 192

    texture libraries, setting up, 208

    Textured view, 190–191

    Textures tab, 192

    toolbar, 189–190

    Top view, 190–191

    view windows, 190–191

World model helpers

    ChangeLevel entity, 323–324

    Door entity, 317–319

    DoorTrigger entity, 321–322

    MovingPlatform entity, 319–321

Worlds
    base textures, selecting, 18–23
    Default Light Level option, 256–257
    world divisions, impact on texture
        requirements, 65–67
Wuetherick, Mike, 275

Z

Zones, 340–341

If you *like* this book, you'll *love...*

Flash™ 5 Cartoons and Games f/x & Design
by Bill Turner, James Robertson, and Richard Bazley
Media: CD-ROM

ISBN #: 1-57610-958-5
$49.99 U.S., $74.99 CAN.

Bill Turner, a top Web animator; James Robertson, expert game programmer and designer; and lead animator, Richard Bazley, cover Flash™ 5 from a cartoon and gaming aspect. Learn how to cohesively pull together and create all the necessary elements for an entertaining cartoon show. Create cartoon characters for television and music videos using storyboarding in Flash and lip-synching with Magpie Pro. Then, discover how to use those cartoon elements when scripting and programming interactive games on the Internet. The CD-ROM includes authoring files for the book's animations and games; demo versions of Flash 5, SmartSound®, and Magpie Pro; plus numerous games. The foreword for this book was written by Jon Warren Lentz, *Flash Bible* co-author, and founder of **www.Flash-Guru.com**.

3ds max® 4 In Depth
by Jon McFarland and Rob Polevoi
Media: CD-ROM

ISBN #: 1-57610-869-4
$59.99 U.S., $89.99 CAN.

3ds max™ *4 In Depth* provides you with a comprehensive reference for creating effects for films, movies, and games. This book covers the modeling and modification of structures from primitive objects, plus other parametric design tools found in the program. *3ds max 4 In Depth* contains various projects to strengthen the concepts learned, with a color studio to showcase the results.

Photoshop® 6 In Depth
by David Xenakis and Benjamin Levisay
Media: 2 CD-ROMs

ISBN #: 1-57610-788-4
$59.99 U.S., $89.99 CAN.

Takes the mystery out of the new Photoshop® functions! Readers will learn layering, channel selection, color corrections, prepress integration with other applications, and how to prepare images for the Web. The linear format in each chapter addresses individual topics, allowing readers to select according to their needs and skill levels. This book includes two CD-ROMs containing a collection of third-party software such as filters, plug-ins, stock photos, and fonts, as well as three additional chapters covering third-party filters, ImageReady, and how to prepare graphics for the Web.

Game Architecture and Design
by Andrew Rollings and Dave Morris
Media: CD-ROM

ISBN #: 1-57610-425-7
$49.99 U.S., $74.99 CAN.

This book teaches game design, architecture, and management with real-life case studies of what works and what doesn't. It takes the reader through all the necessary game creation steps—from seeing a game idea on paper to actually implementing that idea! *Game Architecture and Design* educates on the craft of design, including gameplay and game balance, team structure and software architecture, as well as more elusive creative concepts such as storytelling and style. This book advocates a rational, design-led approach to development, aiming primarily for efficiency and the ability to control change using an iterative development cycle. These theories have been applied in practice and have invariably achieved successful results. Now you can apply them to your own game development!

What's on the CD-ROM

The *3D Game Art f/x & Design*'s companion CD-ROM contains applications, files, and examples specifically selected to enhance the usefulness of this book, including:

- *The Genesis3D Game Development Studio*—A complete set of Open Source tools that let you develop 3D games. This fully functioning version is free for you to use, with no limitations.
- *The Reality Factory*—Reality Factory is an enhancement of the Genesis3D tools. This package allows you to create game worlds with special effects, custom menus, and other parameters. This fully functioning version is free for you to use, with no limitations.
- *An image library*—Over 50 high-resolution digital images for texture creation.
- *Tutorial files*—All the files and images for the tutorials and projects in this book, including the game-world files and image libraries.

System Requirements

Software

- For the applications in this book, your operating system must be Microsoft Windows 98, Windows ME, Windows 2000, or higher.

Hardware

- Reality Factory requires a 3D hardware accelerator card.
- Genesis3D can run in software-only mode, but does not perform well. A good 3D accelerator card is best, and it should support Direct3D.
- A Windows-compatible sound card.
- 64MB of RAM and 125MB of available hard-disk space is required.
- Microprocessor speed should be at least 166MHz (Pentium II 233 or higher with MMX is recommended).